THE NARRATIVE SELF
IN EARLY CHRISTIANITY

WRITINGS FROM THE GRECO-ROMAN WORLD
SUPPLEMENT SERIES

Clare K. Rothschild, General Editor

Number 15

THE NARRATIVE SELF
IN EARLY CHRISTIANITY

Essays in Honor of Judith Perkins

Edited by

Janet E. Spittler

SBL PRESS

SBL PRESS

Atlanta

Copyright © 2019 by Society of Biblical Literature

Library of Congress Cataloging-in-Publication Data

Names: Perkins, Judith, 1944– honouree. | Spittler, Janet E., 1976– editor.
Title: The narrative self in early Christianity : essays in honor of Judith Perkins / edited by Janet E. Spittler.
Description: Atlanta : SBL Press, 2019. | Series: Writings from the Greco-Roman world supplement series; Number 15 | Includes bibliographical references and index.
Identifiers: LCCN 2019026146 (print) | LCCN 2019026147 (ebook) | ISBN 9781628372519 (paperback) | ISBN 9780884143970 (hardback) | ISBN 9780884143987 (ebook)
Subjects: LCSH: Apocryphal Acts of the Apostles—Criticism, interpretation, etc. | Church history—Primitive and early church, ca. 30-600. | Perkins, Judith, 1944–
Classification: LCC BS2871 .N37 2019 (print) | LCC BS2871 (ebook) | DDC 270.1—dc23
LC record available at https://lccn.loc.gov/2019026146
LC ebook record available at https://lccn.loc.gov/2019026147

Printed on acid-free paper.

Contents

Abbreviations

Abst.	Porphyry, *De abstinentia*
Acts Andr. Mth.	Acts of Andrew and Matthias
Acts Thadd.	Acts of Thaddaeus
Acts Thom.	Acts of Thomas
Acts Thom. Skin	Acts of Thomas and His Wonderworking Skin
Acts Tim.	Acts of Timothy
ACW	Ancient Christian Writers
AION	*Annali dell'Istituto Orientale di Napoli*
AJP	*American Journal of Philology*
Alex.	Plutarch, *Alexander*
Amic.	Cicero, *De amicitia*
Anab.	Arrian, *Anabasis*
ANF	Roberts, Alexander, and James Donaldson, eds. *The Ante-Nicene Fathers*. 1885–1887. 10 vols. Repr., Peabody, MA: Hendrickson, 1994.
Ann.	Tacitus, *Annales*
ANRW	Temporini, Hildegard, and Wolfgang Haase, eds. *Aufstieg und Niedergang der römischen Welt: Geschichte und Kultur Roms im Spiegel der neueren Forschung*. Part 2, *Principat*. Berlin: de Gruyter, 1972–.
Ant.	Plutarch, *Antonius*
Apol.	Tertullian, *Apologeticus*
B.J.	Josephus, *Bellum judaicum*
Bacch.	Euripides, *Bacchae*
BETL	Bibliotheca Ephemeridum Theologicarum Lovaniensium
Bib	*Biblica*
BJRL	*Bulletin of the John Rylands Library*
BZ	*Byzantinische Zeitschrift*

BZNW	Beihefte zur Zeitschrift für die neutestamentliche Wissenschaft
CCSL	Corpus Christianorum: Series Latina
CEJL	Commentaries on Early Jewish Literature
Cel. Phryg.	Dio Chrysostom, *Celaenis Phrygiae (Or. 35)*
Chaer.	Chariton, *Chaereas and Callirhoe*
CHRC	*Church History and Religious Culture*
Chron.	Jerome, *Chronicon Eusebii a Graeco Latine redditum et continuatum*
CJ	*Classical Journal*
ClAnt	*Classical Antiquity*
CSCO	Chabot, Jean Baptiste, et al. Corpus Scriptorum Christianorum Orientalium. Paris, 1903.
CW	*Classical World*
Doctr. Add.	Doctrina Addai
Don.	Cyprian, *Donatum*
DOP	*Dumbarton Oaks Papers*
ECA	Early Christian Apocrypha
Ep.	*Epistula(e)*
Ep. 22	Jerome, *Libellus de virginitate servanda*
Ep. virg.	Athanasius, *Epistula ad virgines*
Eth. nic.	Aristotle, *Ethica nicomachea*
FCNTECW	Feminist Companion to the New Testament and Early Christian Writings
Fem. reg.	John Chrysostom, *Quod regulares feminae viris cohabitare non debeant*
Flacc.	Philo, *Flaccus*
fol(s).	folio(s)
G&H	*Gender and History*
Geog.	Strabo, *Geographica*
GiL	*Gilte Legende*
Gos. Pet.	Gospel of Peter
GRBS	*Greek, Roman, and Byzantine Studies*
Hist. Arm.	Moses of Chorene, *History of Armenia*
Hist. eccl.	*Historia ecclesiastica*
Hist. Rom.	Cassius Dio, *Historia Romana*
Hom.	Gregory Refrendarius, *Homilia*
Hom. Gen.	Origen, *Homiliae in Genesim*
HR	*History of Religions*

HSem	Horae semiticae
HTR	*Harvard Theological Review*
HTS	Harvard Theological Studies
Hug	*Hugoye: Journal of Syriac Studies*
IPriene	von Gaertringen, F. Hiller, ed. *Inschriften von Priene*. Berlin, 1906.
IBC	Interpretation: A Bible Commentary for Teaching and Preaching
Il.	Homer, *Iliad*
JAAR	*Journal of the American Academy of Religion*
JBL	*Journal of Biblical Literature*
Jdt	Judith
JECS	*Journal of Early Christian Studies*
JGRCJ	*Journal of Greco-Roman Christianity and Judaism*
JÖAI	*Jahreshefte des Österreichischen archäologischen Instituts*
JRE	*Journal of Religious Ethics*
JRS	*Journal of Roman Studies*
JSNT	*Journal for the Study of the New Testament*
JSNTSup	Journal for the Study of the New Testament Supplement Series
JSP	*Journal for the Study of the Pseudepigrapha*
JTS	*Journal of Theological Studies*
KJV	King James Version
LCL	Loeb Classical Library
LgA	*Legenda Aurea*
LSJ	Liddell, Henry George, Robert Scott, and Henry Stuart Jones. *A Greek-English Lexicon*. 9th ed. with rev. supplement. Oxford: Clarendon, 1996.
LXX	Septuagint
Marc.	Seneca, *Ad Marciam de consolatione*
MS	manuscript
NIV	New International Version
NovT	*Novum Testamentum*
NovTSup	Supplements to Novum Testament
NRSV	New Revised Standard Version
NTApoc	*New Testament Apocrypha*. 2 vols. Revised ed. Edited by Wilhelm Schneemelcher. English trans.

	ed. Robert McL. Wilson. Louisville: Westminster John Knox, 2003.
NTGL	The New Testament and Greek Literature
NTS	New Testament Studies
Num. Rab.	Numbers Rabbah
OLA	Orientalia Lovaniensia Analecta
Onom.	Pollux, Onomasticon
Pass. Perp.	Passion of Perpetua and Felicitas
Peregr. Eg.	Egeria, Peregrinatio Egeriae
PG	Migne, Jacques-Paul, ed. Patrologia Graeca [= Patrologiae Cursus Completus: Series Graeca]. 161 vols. Paris, 1857–1886.
Phaed.	Plato, Phaedo
PL	Migne, Jacques-Paul, ed. Patrologia Latina [= Patrologia Cursus Completus: Series Latina]. 217 vols. Paris, 1884–1864.
R&T	Religion and Theology
RAC	Klauser, Theodor, et al., eds. Reallexikon für Antike und Christentum. Stuttgart: Hiersemann, 1950–.
RBén	Revue Bénédictine
RGRW	Religions in the Greco-Roman World
RMCS	Routledge Monographs in Classical Studies
RSV	Revised Standard Version
Sat.	Satirae
Satyr.	Petronius, Satyricon
SBLSP	Society of Biblical Literature Seminar Papers
SCH	Studies in Church History
SEG	Supplementum epigraphicum graecum
SEL	South English Legendary
SNTSMS	Society for New Testament Studies Monograph Series
SP	Sacra Pagina
Strom.	Clement of Alexandria, Stromateis
Subintr.	John Chrysostom, Contra eos qui subintroductas habent virgines
TAPA	Transactions of the American Philological Association
TENTS	Texts and Editions for New Testament Study
TJT	Toronto Journal of Theology

TS	Text and Studies
TT	Text and Translations
v(v).	verse(s)
VC	*Vigiliae Christianae*
Vir. ill.	Jerome, *De viris illustribus*
Virg.	Ambrose, *De virginibus*
Virginit.	John Chrysostom, *De virginitate*
Vit. Apoll.	Philostratus, *Vita Apollonii*
Vit. Phil.	Diogenes Laertius, *Vitae Philosophorum*
WUNT	Wissenschaftliche Untersuchungen zum Neuen Testament
ZKG	*Zeitschrift für Kirchengeschichte*

Introduction

Janet E. Spittler

Judith Perkins, here celebrated for her contributions to the study of early Christianity, was in fact trained as a classicist. Her bachelor's degree from Mount Holyoke College is in Latin. Her graduate studies at the University of Toronto concentrated in Latin hexameter poetry. Her 1972 dissertation, "Valerius Flaccus: Synonym and Style," is a detailed study in applied stylistics of the Silver Age poet's word choice. In the thesis there is no trace of a budding interest in early Christianity, though a brief note on the signature page perhaps hints that her interests ranged beyond Latin poetry: "Second Minor Field: Mystery Religions." In 1976 she was hired to teach classics at Saint Joseph College (now the University of Saint Joseph) in West Hartford, Connecticut, where she is professor emerita of classics and humanities today.

I had known Judith for some time before I learned about this background. That she was trained in classics was not really a surprise: her philological chops are everywhere evident in her work, though I would have guessed her first scholarly love was the Greek novels or other ancient narrative—something rather closer to early Christian narrative than Silver Age Latin poetry. When I asked her when, where, and how she first got interested in early Christianity, the answer was surprisingly specific. It was 1979 in New Haven: "It all had to do with wanting to attend a NEH summer seminar, and the only one close enough to allow me to get home in time to meet my sons' day-camp bus was being offered by Wayne Meeks for classicists and New Testament scholars at Yale on the 'Social World of Early Christianity.'"

This response says so much about so many things, ranging from the degree to which academic success depends on serendipity to the importance of federal funding for research in the humanities (which peaked in the early 1980s). It speaks to matters of limitation, of opportunity, of priorities, of pragmatism, of ambition, of open-mindedness, of adventurousness. And, of course, it speaks to the realities of juggling an active research agenda and active parenthood, particularly motherhood—a feat that, to my knowledge, no one has yet perfected. But those of us—any sort of parent—doing research and writing between childcare drop-offs and pickups in 2019 surely owe a great debt to women like Judith Perkins, who somehow made it work forty years ago.

So she took the seminar, she loved it, and her publications gradually shifted from titles such as "An Aspect of Latin Comparison Construction" to "The Apocryphal Acts of Peter: An Ideological Novel." But she surely did not leave classics behind: to the contrary, one of her most significant contributions to the field of early Christianity is her insistence on bringing the two fields together. She was an early contributor to the late twentieth century's burgeoning body of scholarship on ancient Greek and Latin novelistic literature. She was an original member of the Society of Biblical Literature's Ancient Fiction and Early Christian and Jewish Narrative group, founded in 1992 as an interdisciplinary effort to bring ancient fiction to the attention of biblical scholars, and was coeditor of *Ancient Fiction and Early Christian Narrative*, the 1998 volume produced by the group. She has also been a longtime participant in the International Conference on the Ancient Novel (ICAN), in which context she, conversely, has worked to bring Christian and Jewish narratives to the attention of classicists, serving as coeditor of *The Ancient Novel and Early Christian and Jewish Narrative: Fictional Intersections*, one volume of the proceedings of ICAN IV. Very few scholars are equally at home in two distinct fields, but the scholar who can successfully bring two fields together—not just through her own work but by creating a bridge that others cross—is truly exceptional.

Her two important monographs, *The Suffering Self: Pain and Narrative Representation in the Early Christian Era* and *Roman Imperial Identities in the Early Christian Era*, both illustrate the gains that can be made when disciplinary boundaries are broken down. *The Suffering Self*, which has had an enormous impact on how scholars of early Christianity understand depictions of the body in pain, begins with an observation made while reading Apuleius and Aelius Aristides, that is, that many Greek and Latin writings of the first centuries CE take up a discursive focus on the suffering human body. This initial observation might, in the hands of a less sensitive scholar, have led to the simplistic conclusion that Christian authors had been influenced by their non-Christian Greco-Roman counterparts.

Through detailed analysis of the "particularities and specificities of the suffering body displayed in Christian narratives,"[1] however, Perkins demonstrates how Christian authors participated in and contributed to the discourse, ultimately producing a self-understanding and self-representation that allowed Christianity as an institution to thrive in the cultural context of the late first- and second-century Mediterranean world.

Her second monograph, *Roman Imperial Identities in the Early Christian Era*, expands this work on self-understanding and self-representation, examining how two specific cosmopolitan social entities (a transempire coalition of the socially elite and early Christians) constructed for themselves specific cultural identities during the consolidation of the Roman Empire. Here again, Perkins both argues for and demonstrates the value of treating Christians and non-Christians as fellow participants in a common cultural context and discourse. As she writes:

> In my discussion, I hope to destabilize [the] polarity between Christians and non-Christians, which has proved so enormously influential in structuring discussions of the early imperial period. It has allowed the interconnections between Christians and people contemporaneous with them in their social world to be obscured, with the result that historical testimony that could prove useful for understanding the social dynamics of the early imperial period has been sequestered as "Christian" rather than recognized and utilized as evidence for understanding the social and political negotiations being enacted during the period.... A basic defining characteristic of the Christians surveyed in this study, one that is too often disregarded, is that they are inhabitants of the Roman Empire. Their writings need to be recognized as productions of that empire and as being in dialogue with other writings of this period adjusting to the enlarged perspective of cosmopolitanism.[2]

Her analysis of Christian identity construction alongside that of the socially elite (including their respective self-construction vis-à-vis topics such as cosmopolitanism, death, patriarchy, and the body) reveals the specific strategies used by Christians to "intervene and interrupt" the elite imperial discourse, carving out a position for themselves to hold, a space

---

1. Judith Perkins, *The Suffering Self: Pain and Narrative Representation in the Early Christian Era* (London: Routledge, 1995), 12.

2. Judith Perkins, *Roman Imperial Identities in the Early Christian Era*, RMCS (London: Routledge, 2009), 3.

for their own institutional presence. As with all her work, the result for the reader is a better understanding of both Christianity as a distinct phenomenon *and* the broader world in which it developed.

The contributors to this Festschrift represent a very small segment of the scholars for whom Judith Perkins's work and mentorship have had a significant impact. Perhaps now is the moment to apologize to the many who would very much have liked to contribute—some of whom have worked quite closely with her over the years—but were not invited. I do indeed apologize! But a quick look at the table of contents, which includes ten women and two men, will likely suggest to the reader the context in which this Festschrift was first conceived. Judith Perkins was the first scholar, beyond my dissertation advisors, to take me and my work seriously. After my first presentation at the Annual Meeting of the Society of Biblical Literature, she approached me to talk about my work; she asked for a copy of my paper, offering to send a copy of one of her own works in progress on a similar topic; she replied to my emails with helpful bibliography and good suggestions. In short, she treated me like a full colleague, while offering the sort of help and encouragement that a graduate student and junior scholar needs. While she has spent her entire career teaching at an undergraduate institution, never training graduate students of her own, I have learned through countless conversations with others in the field that *many* people, particularly women, count her as a model and mentor. The majority of the contributors to this volume fall into that category.

The essays presented here, arranged alphabetically by author, offer the reader a small sense of the impact of Perkins's scholarship—of the various directions in which others have taken her insights. The reader will surely recognize recurring themes (e.g., representations of suffering) and texts (e.g., the apocryphal acts of the apostles), but each essay engages with these themes and texts in distinctive combinations, resisting simple categorization. Jo-Ann Brant, Virginia Burrus, Jennifer A. Glancy, and Jeannie Sellick all treat the Acts of Thomas, a text that Perkins has worked with extensively, but each from a very different angle. Brant widens the scope of comparative material, looking to Buddhist texts for insights on how best to take the seemingly extreme asceticism prescribed. Burrus takes up the depiction of animals in the text (yet another topic Perkins has treated) and widens the scope of *comparanda* in a different direction, looking to an anonymous letter from late fourth-century Spain or Gaul that, like the Acts of Thomas, muses on the nature of the ass as both distinctly animal and paradoxically human. Glancy takes up identity construction, considering the complex constructions of the self in terms of a twin or double in the Acts of Thomas. Sellick turns to the well-known bridal-chamber scene in the Acts of Thomas; taking as her starting point Perkins's assessment that the apocryphal acts "offer an opportunity to view how Christians understood and positioned themselves vis-à-vis and in dialogue with other members of a complex and highly mobile society,"[3] she asks to what degree and in what manner this episode represents and/or sheds light on the later phenomenon of spiritual marriage in late antiquity. Two further essays treat other apocryphal acts. My own contribution on the Acts of Thomas and His Wonderworking Skin offers a case study of the representation of extreme suffering in an apostle narrative. Meira Z. Kensky's essay, like Sellick's, treats the relationship between text (the Acts of Timothy) and historical phenomenon (the claiming of Ephesus as the sacred city of Timothy). Ilaria L. E. Ramelli's contribution likewise deals with the interplay of text and history, tracing the complex development of traditions surrounding the *Mandylion* image-relic (i.e., the image of Christ imprinted on a towel and sent to Abgar of Edessa). Three more essays deal with suffering in other contexts. Shelly Matthews treats the depiction of suffering in the Gospel of Luke, specifically the deeply problematic ideology of just crucifixion at play in Luke 23:41. Kate Cooper's essay turns to Prudentius's *Passio Sancti Cassiani* and its depiction of pain and violence in the Christian classroom, both in the content of instruction (the violent stories of martyrdom) and the violence mutually inflicted by teacher and student. Nicola Denzey Lewis's essay moves beyond literary representations of suffering, turning to the contemporary spectacle celebrating the torture and martyrdom of Cristina of Bolsena. The remaining two essays, by David Konstan and Dennis R. MacDonald, engage perhaps the most fundamental question raised in Perkins's work: How do narrative texts create meaning?

It has truly been a pleasure to edit this volume—not a statement one hears every day! I thank the contributors for their prompt submission of essays, for the high quality of their work, and—particularly—for their enthusiasm. I also thank Clare Rothschild, editor of this series, for her wonderful support of the project and her consummate editorial skills. But most of all, I would like to thank Judith Perkins herself for her scholarship, her mentorship, and her friendship.

---

3. Judith Perkins, "Fictional Narratives and Social Critique," in *Late Ancient Christianity: A People's History of Christianity*, ed. Virginia Burrus and Rebecca Lyman (Minneapolis: Fortress, 2005), 48.

Bibliography

Perkins, Judith. "Fictional Narratives and Social Critique." Pages 46–69 in vol. 2 of *Late Ancient Christianity: A People's History of Christianity*. Edited by Virginia Burrus and Rebecca Lyman. Minneapolis: Fortress, 2005.

———. *Roman Imperial Identities in the Early Christian Era*. RMCS. London: Routledge, 2009.

———. *The Suffering Self: Pain and Narrative Representation in the Early Christian Era*. London: Routledge, 1995.

Aversion as a Rhetorical Strategy in the
Acts of Thomas and Buddhist Tradition

Jo-Ann Brant

Armchair travelers expecting to learn something about India by reading the Acts of Thomas will no doubt be disappointed.[1] The preponderance of Greco-Roman accounts of travel to and from India delight their readers with descriptions of exotic animals, luxurious commodities, unique topography, and the extreme features of ascetic practices. The Acts of Thomas distinguishes itself from contemporary accounts by its failure to take note of anything noteworthy. The narrator seems to be protecting the reader from any allure that India might provide as though taking heed of Thomas's own protest. When, in the lottery that determines the destination of each apostle's proselytizing mission, India falls to Thomas, the apostle—ever the contrarian—responds "Anywhere but!" ostensibly because of his weak constitution (Acts Thom. 1.3, 6).[2] Thomas brings to India a call to lifelong sexual abstinence, even within the bounds of marriage, where it is treated

---

1. On July 1, 1996, with a Fulbright Fellowship in hand, Judith Perkins embarked on her passage to India to find the apostle Thomas and to teach at Stella Maris College, run by an Indian Syrian Christian order of nuns in Chennai that traces its roots to the apostle Thomas's journey to India. When Judith made her pilgrimage to Kerala, her way to the cathedral commemorating the apostle was blocked by security for a royal visit from Queen Elizabeth. Judith returned home in November with no publication to show for her efforts but the satisfaction of living among and teaching bright students and the memories of 116-degree afternoons, a society confusing to a Westerner but lively and hospitable, and spicy cuisine not yet tainted by Diet Coke. When presented with an opportunity to contribute to this Festschrift, knowing this story and given my own interest in Thomas and Indian traditions, I decided to join the quest to find Thomas in India, but like Judith I did not discover what I set out to find. Instead of Thomas in India, I began to look for India in Thomas.

2. Quotations from the Acts of Thomas are from Harold Attridge, *The Acts of*

as a wholly new concept—as though the wandering ascetics of the Hindu, Jain, and Buddhist traditions have vanished or never have been. In the fanciful world of the narrator, ideas travel from west to east and not vice versa. In the real world of the author, in which active commerce flowed along the Silk Road, it seems highly unlikely that a few ideas enshrined in the tales of Indian traditions did not slip from the stories traveling from the East into the telling of tales in the West. The following essay will situate the Acts of Thomas within the conventions of other contemporary travel narratives to India and then explore similarities to Buddhist rhetoric found within the extended arguments advocating sexual abstinence. While the evidence for Buddhist influence may be more tantalizing than convincing, understanding the role that extolling celibacy played in Buddhist societies may have something to teach modern readers about how to read the Acts of Thomas.

Legend has Thomas travel long the Malabar Coast as far as Kerala in southwest India. The Acts contains a more limited itinerary and provides little indication of routes taken. A. F. J. Klijn contends that it is impossible to prove that Thomas visited India: earlier ancient sources identify Bartholomew as the apostle to India, and what is meant by "India" is not clear.[3] The story begins in Jerusalem, where Jesus responds to Thomas's refusal to travel to India by selling him into slavery to Chaban, a merchant heading in that direction. The narrator describes a departure by boat on the following day from an unnamed port on a passage that takes the pair to Andrapolis (in Syriac Sandrok).[4] From Andrapolis they sail to the cities of India, where Thomas meets Gundafar, a ruler in need of a skilled architect. Gundafar is a name associated with several kings in a Parthian dynasty seated in the city of Taxila that ruled over the Indus Valley in the first century CE. After success in converting members of the royal household, Thomas sets out over land, visiting several cities for

---

Thomas: Translated with an Introduction and Notes by Harold W. Attridge, ECA 3 (Salem, OR: Polebridge, 2010).

3. A. F. J. Klijn, *The Acts of Thomas* (Leiden: Brill, 1962), 27. James F. McGrath, "History and Fiction in the *Acts of Thomas*: The State of the Question," *JSP* 17 (2008): 297–311, provides a more optimistic conclusion in his survey of the data.

4. The Syriac Sandrock may derive from Sandrocottus, referred to by Plutarch (*Alex.* 62) and Appian (*Syriaca* 55) as Androcottus who ruled along the banks of the Ganges in the third century BCE. George Huxley associates it with the Mesopotamian city Hatra, al Haqr, supposedly founded by Sanatriik, a name of Parthian origin, in the second century CE. See Huxley, "Geography in the *Acts of Thomas*," *GRBS* 24 (1983): 73.

which no identifying markers are provided. The narrator provides only a sweeping statement that "Judas Thomas was proclaiming the word of God throughout India" (Acts Thom. 62.1). The final episode of the story takes place in the city of King Mizdai, a name seemingly derived from Arrian's account of Alexander's journey into India (*Anab.* 3.8.6). Both Origen (*Hom. Gen.* 3) and Eusebius (*Hist. eccl.* 3.1.1) restrict the scope of Thomas's missionary activity to Parthia, but the designation of Parthia as India is not altogether misleading.

If Western authors used India to signify that the reach of their influence extended to the ends of the earth, Indian traditions seem equally eager to extend the boundaries of their territory westward. By the fourth century BCE, Taxila had become a center of Vedic learning and by the second century BCE had been heavily proselytized by Buddhism. No evidence indicates that the rulers of the Parthian Empire became Buddhists, but the majority of the population at the time of Thomas's story were. As a result, with poetic license, Taxila is given a hoary past in Indian myth.[5] According to the Rāmāyaṇa, Taxila was founded by Bharata, the younger brother of Rama, an incarnation of the god Vishnu, and according to a side story within the Mahābhārata, the great epic poem was first recited in Taxila (18.5.29). Taxila also figures in the Buddhist tradition as a center for higher studies. In Jain tradition, Ṛṣabha, the first of the Tīrthaṅkaras— spiritual teachers who revealed a fordable passage across the stream of Saṃsāra (the cycle of birth, death, and rebirth)—visits Taxila, leaving footprints that were later consecrated by his son Bahubali, the great naked standing ascetic.[6]

The contention that Thomas or the author of the Acts of Thomas never stepped foot in Indian cannot account for the lack of knowledge of India.[7] Elsewhere in early Christian literature, we find passable understanding of Brahmanic asceticism and interest in Buddhism. Bardaisan, a second-century Christian from Edessa (now Urfa in modern Turkey, the city in

---

5. O. P. Bharadwaj, *Studies in the Historical Geography of Ancient India* (Delhi: Sundeep Prakashan, 1986), 12.

6. John Marshall, *A Guide to Taxila* (Cambridge: Cambridge University Press, 2013), 9–10.

7. It is doubtful that many of the Greek and Roman authors writing about India had firsthand knowledge. Most seem to have relied on the writings of Megasthenes's *Indika* (preserved in excerpts by later authors) based on Megasthenes's assignment as Greek ambassador to the Mauryan Imperial court in Pāṭaliputra (ca. 302–298 BCE).

which the Acts of Thomas is generally believed to be written) was familiar with the Hindu practice of suttee, in which a wife was immolated alive with her deceased husband.[8] He reports having met a deputation of Buddhist monks on their way to meet with the Roman emperor, from whom he learned about Buddhist dietary practices.[9] Ephrem of Nisibis (306–373 CE) accused Mani of borrowing his understanding of reincarnation from Indian thought (*Hymn contra haereses* 3.7.3). Tertullian found it necessary to distance Christian teachings from that of Brahmins and gymnosophists/ naked ascetics (*Apol.* 42), while Clement of Alexandria praises Buddhism for its approximation of Christian monotheism (*Strom.* 1.15).

Grant Parker demonstrates in his study of Greco-Roman literature about India that its readers were familiar with and hungry for accounts of India that painted a picture of a place where everything was exotic and of excess scale.[10] Dio Chrysostom's description from the first century CE is typical:

> For in India, according to the report, there are rivers, not of water as in your land, but one of milk, one of translucent wine, another of honey, and another of olive oil.... And also these products are immeasurably superior to those we have both in flavour and in potency.... And what is more, not only is their sky clearer, but also the stars are more numerous and more brilliant. And these people live more than four hundred years, and during all that time they are beautiful and youthful and neither old age nor disease nor poverty is found among them. So wonderful and so numerous are these blessings, and yet there are people called Brachmanes who, abandoning those rivers and the people scattered along their banks, turn aside and devote themselves to private speculation and meditation, undertaking amazing physical labours without compulsion and enduring fearful tests of endurance.... And their gold is obtained from ants. These ants are larger than foxes, though in other respects similar to the ants we have. And they burrow in the earth, just as do all other ants. And that which is thrown out by their burrowing is gold, the purest of all gold and the most resplendent. (*Cel. Phryg.* 18–23 [Cohoon and Crosby])

In the accounts of Dio Chrysostom, Diodorus Siculus, Pliny, and many others, everything organic and inorganic abounds in variety, abundance,

---

8. Related by his student Philippus, *Book of the Laws of the Countries* 52–53.

9. Bardaisan, *Indica*, fragment in Porphyry, *Abst.* 4.17–18.

10. Grant Parker, *The Making of Roman India* (Cambridge: Cambridge University Press, 2008), 44.

and quality. Thomas, however, meets no elephants. Opulence belongs to heavenly palaces (Acts Thom. 22) and ambrosial fountains (25.6), and the only precious gems—Indian carnelians (108.7), beryl, and agates—adorn Thomas's robe, about which he sings in the "Hymn of the Pearl" (108–113).

The absence of Indian religious specialists in the Acts of Thomas is made all the more conspicuous by the fact that in the more famous accounts of journeys to India, curiosity about ascetic practices often drives the adventurer east. The Alexander Romance presents Alexander as a scholar who seeks out and reveres the sages of India. Alexander's advance into India begins with a show of force in which the conqueror must use wits, first to defeat the ferocious and exotic animals at the front of the Indian army and then its commander, king, and god, Poros, in single combat. He is disarmed when he marches against the Brahmins or naked philosophers who live in huts and caves. Their leader, Dandames, sends Alexander a letter:

> If you come to us in war, you will not profit from it: you will not have anything to take away from us. But if you want to take what we have, there is no need for war, only a request—not to us, but to Providence above. If you want to know who we are, the answer is: naked men who have devoted their lives to philosophy, fashioned not by ourselves, but by Providence above. War is your companion, philosophy ours. (Alexander Romance 3.5)[11]

Alexander, intrigued, responds by engaging in a philosophic dialogue that superficially resembles the Questions of Milinda (ca. 150 BCE), in which the Buddhist philosopher Nagasena instructs the Hellenistic king on the Buddhist claim that human beings are not persisting, unitary selves (along with multiple other topics) through a question-and-answer dialogue. Alexander soon abandons his military campaign in India and returns to Persia (Alexander Romance 3.17). Apollonius of Tyana embarks on a journey in the company of an Indian official, whom he meets in Taxila, that takes him to the Ganges (Philostratus, *Vit. Apoll.* 1.39–3.58). The passage across the Indus calls for a lengthy description of its breadth and surrounding topography and affords the leisure for a long discussion about elephants in which Apollonius takes great interest (*Vit. Apoll.* 2.12–19), but the

---

11. Translated by Ken Dowden in *Collected Ancient Greek Novels*, ed. B. P. Reardon (Berkeley: University of California Press, 1989), 717.

sage is equally interested in the Brahmins. The account of the Brahmins bears little resemblance to the known practices and teachings of Indian philosophers of the first century. One philosopher's statement, "We consider ourselves to be God," suggests a vague understanding of the Hindu notion that Atman (the self) and Brahman (the ineffable absolute reality) are one, but he responds to Apollonius's "Why?" not with an ontological or epistemological argument, as one would expect from a Brahmanic scholar, but with "because we are good men" (3.18). Apollonius consistently filters what he hears through Greek tradition. For example, he notes the resemblance of a song the Brahmins sing to the paean of Sophocles in honor of Asclepius (3.17). What is important here is that, however distorted or embellished, Indian philosophers are revered as ascetics.

Thomas provides no evidence that the religious practices of India are different from those encountered by the apostles who travel to Asia Minor and westward. The people of the countryside are polytheists (20.4) who make offerings to their wooden idols with libations of wine (77.3–4). Jason König situates the lack of curiosity about India in what he describes as the antinovel qualities of the Acts and concludes that the reader is invited into a confidence in "Christian cultural superiority and centrality."[12] Thomas is the object of everyone's attention, "a stranger come from a foreign land" (4.10).[13] At the wedding, he makes himself the spectacle by taking the precious oils that others apply gingerly to their faces or beards and methodically and generously applying it to the top of his head, his nostrils, ears, teeth, and chest, then placing a wreath on his head and holding a bamboo reed in his hand (5.5–9).[14] The picture painted of a man sitting silently, eating nothing, but gazing at the ground while a flute girl tries to enchant him with her music casts Thomas in the role of the ascetic guru. Indeed, every time the reader encounters anything that might excite the senses or the imagination, it turns out that the source of the exotic is Hebrew rather than Indian. The flute girl is a "Hebrew" who finds Thomas the most

---

12. Jason König, "Novelistic and Anti-novelistic Narrative in the *Acts of Thomas* and the *Acts of Andrew and Matthias*," in *Fiction on the Fringe: Novelistic Writing in the Post-classical Age*, ed. Grammatiki Karla (Leiden: Brill, 2009), 141.

13. König, "Novelistic and Anti-novelistic Narrative in the *Acts*," 139.

14. Harold W. Attridge sees this passage as a foreshadowing the baptismal anointing that takes place later in the story and as evoking the passion of Christ as described in Matt 27:28–29. See Attridge, "Intertextuality in the Acts of Thomas," *Semeia* 80 (1997): 110.

beautiful person in the room (8.5). When Thomas encounters a deadly serpent that shakes its head, rattles it tail, and speaks (31.1–2), a reader who might anticipate a story of a famed or mythological Indian *naga* is disappointed.[15] This serpent is compelled to kill a young man for violating the Lord's Day (31.9) and is the same serpent that Eve encountered in paradise (32.6). Further along the road, a foal of an ass approaches Thomas and invites him to rest by sitting on his back to ride into the city (39.1–8). The foal reveals, "I am of the lineage that attended Balaam" (40.4). Once more Thomas becomes the spectacle when the multitude parades before and behind him to see how Thomas will release the foal (40.12). Upon its release, the foal promptly dies at his feet (41.2). In the ancient Vedic horse sacrifice Ashvamedha, the death of a horse that is freed to roam signifies the boundary of a ruler's sovereignty. When the Buddha releases his horse Kanthaka after fleeing his life as heir to a kingdom in order to seek the salvation of the world, that horse also dies. In both Thomas and the Buddha's story, the immediate death of the horse signifies that the nature of their kingdom is not of this world.

Annette Yoshiko Reed represents a growing number of scholars who resist treating Christianity as part of the story of the Roman Empire.[16] In particular, she notes how Syriac Christianity, with Edessa as its center, had stronger ties to Central Asia than Europe.[17] Reed finds an affinity between the Asian tradition of wise men winning over monarchs, thereby gaining their patronage, and the concessions to Thomas's spiritual authority by members of the ruling class.[18] I find suggestions in the arguments for chastity of an affinity with Buddhist rhetorical strategies in their teaching of sexual abstinence. While I cannot prove a genetic relationship, the act of comparing does shine a light on how Thomas's extreme encratic teaching may be part of the pattern of a broader rhetorical scheme also evident in Buddhism.

The Acts of Thomas distinguishes itself from the other apocryphal acts by its preoccupation with and the length of the arguments for chastity. A quick survey of discourse about sexuality in the other apocryphal acts

---

15. Klijn, *Acts of Thomas*, 223, cites Strabo, *Geog.* 15.1.45, and Philostratus, *Vit. Apoll.* 3.6, to substantiate the claim that "for Greeks India was famous for its number of snakes."

16. Annette Yoshiko Reed, "Beyond the Land of Nod: Syriac Images of Asia and the Historiography of the West," *HR* 49 (2009): 48–87.

17. Reed, "Beyond the Land of Nod," 61.

18. Reed, "Beyond the Land of Nod," 68.

reveals a mixed bag. In the Acts of Paul, sexual abstinence signifies the virtues of purity, self-control, and renunciation of all that is worldly (3.5–6). The focus is on pleasing God, satisfying what God desires rather than what the married couple desires. The version of the Acts of Andrew found in the Epitome by Gregory of Tours saves its polemic for incest (11.12–13), adultery, and rape (23). In the Martyrdom of Peter, numerous matrons withdraw from relationships with their husbands because they fall in love with Peter's unnarrated teaching about purity (4.5). In a lacuna in the Acts of John, Drusiana once converted declines relations with her husband, Andronikos, and persuades her husband to adopt the same piety (63.4–5), but the basis for this restraint is lost. Otherwise, "bad" sex is limited to adultery (54.2) and necrophilia (70–76). The Acts of Thomas is much more philosophical and methodical in its polemic. The accent falls not so much on a concern for purity but rather on a right understanding of the nature of the human condition.

The first extended argument for sexual abstinence is provided by Jesus, who appears in the form of Thomas in the bridal chamber of the Andrapolis newlyweds just as they are preparing to consummate their marriage. Possibly recognizing the impotency of such an appeal when a young couple sits naked in bed, the narrator has Jesus present a frightening representation of the consequences of intercourse:

> Know this, that if you abandon this sordid intercourse, you'll become holy temples, pure, freed from afflictions and pains, both visible and hidden, and you'll not take on the troubles of livelihood or children, the final result of which is destruction. It's so, isn't it? If you had many children, because of them you become thieves and cheats, beating orphans and defrauding widows, and when you do such things you subject yourself to dreadful punishments. Not only that, but most children turn out to be useless, afflicted by demons, some openly, some secret: they're either epileptic, half-withered, lame, deaf, dumb, paralytic, or fools. And if they do happen to be healthy, they'll be unproductive anyway, doing useless or dreadful things. Perhaps they'll be involved in adultery, murder, theft, or fornication; you too, will be tormented by all these things. (Acts Thom. 12.2–6)

While Christian philosophers do on occasion touch on the negative consequences of childbirth, particularly labor pains, the preferred rhetorical technique is to turn attention to the beauty of virginity. Athanasius of Alexandria risks discussing the poverty and hunger of virginity for women before describing virginity as a garden that one would not want to destroy by having marital relationships:

> Be careful that no merciless stranger spoils the manifold seedlings and beautiful blossoms of the garden; that no one mars the injured vine; that no ferocious foxes from some place or other destroy the beautiful clusters of grapes; that no one disturbs the sealed fountain or muddies the bright and shining waters of virginity; that no one fills the paradise of sweet fragrance with a foul odor. (*Ep. virg.* 2.21)[19]

John Chrysostom balances the challenges of virginity—"You must walk over coals without being burned [see Prov 6:28], and walk over swords without being slashed" (*Virginit.* 27.1)—with an appeal to reason rather than emotion when he describes the attendant sorrow of loss that comes when one partner must die before the other and the dangers of childbirth, but then turns to give most of his attention to the virtues of virginity.[20]

James H. Charlesworth treats the Acts of Thomas's bridal-chamber rhetoric as evidence for misopedia, the ultimate limit of an ascetic ideology.[21] Here is an occasion when familiarity with Buddhist rhetorical techniques might save us from error. The narrative context in which the bridal couple are interrupted just at the moment when libido is driving the action calls for extreme rhetoric. Early Buddhist texts employ the same strategy when dealing with the appeal of the pleasures of the married householder, including affection toward children. Siddhartha Buddha himself names his son Rahula (fetter), because he sees the child's birth as a hindrance to his fulfilling his role as a savior. When the Buddha is approached by Visākhā grieving over the death of a grandchild, the Buddha asks how many children and grandchildren she desires, to which she responds as many as live in her village. The Buddha warns:

> Those who have a hundred dear ones have a hundred pains.... Those who have one dear one have one pain. Those who have no dear ones have

---

19. Cited and translated by Patricia Cox Miller, *Women in Early Christianity: Translations from Greek Texts* (Washington, DC: Catholic University of America Press, 2005), 119.

20. Miller, *Women in Early Christianity*, 112.

21. James H. Charlesworth, "From the Philopedia of Jesus to the Misopedia of the *Acts of Thomas*," in *By Study and Also by Faith*, ed. John M. Lundquist and Stephen David Ricks (Salt Lake City: Deseret, 1990), 56–58.

no pains. They are the sorrowless, the dispassionate, the undespairing, I say. "Sorry and mourning in the world, or suffering of every sort, happen because of one beloved, but happen not when there is none. Happy are they and sorrowless, that have no loved one in the world." (Udanā 8.8 [Ñanamoli])[22]

Suddhodana, the Buddha's father, comes to him after his son Nanda and grandson Rahula become renunciates, arguing that Nanda and Rahula should not have done so without his consent. The Buddha describes the love for a child as physical pain: "Love for our children, Lord, cuts into the outer skin; having cut into the outer skin, it cuts into the inner skin; having cut into the inner skin it cuts into the flesh; having cut into the flesh, it cuts into the sinews; having cut into the sinews, it cuts into the bones; having cut into the bones, it reaches the marrow and stays there" (Sutta-vibhaṅga 1).[23] While both traditions pull out the rhetorical stops to preach a message of sexual abstinence and the renunciation of filial obligations, behind the scenes, both depend on a lay community that supports the ascetic leaders and produces the children who become those ascetics. Gregory Schopen's study of Buddhist inscriptions found in northwest India dating from the first to the sixth centuries CE reveals a difference between the rhetorical idealism of these stories and a more fluid boundary between monastic and lay life.[24]

In the Buddhist monastic tradition, one of the preliminary strategies in taming the power of sexual desire is to swing the pendulum from the extreme of attraction to that of aversion by cultivating a sense of foulness as a remedy. One of the most famous forms of practice, designed to startle the novitiate into a state of shock and spiritual urgency, is corpse meditation, praised in the Pali Canon by the Buddha as most efficacious of means (Aṅguttara Nikāya 1.4). The Buddha explains, "Monks, when a monk lives much with the perception of the foul heaped around the mind, the mind draws back, bends back, turns from the attainment of sexual intercourses [methunadhammasamapattiya] and is not distracted thereby" (Aṅguttara

---

22. The Udanā is part of the Pali Canon, the earliest body of Buddhist literature, and appears in the Khuddaka Nikaya.

23. Ñanamoli, *Life of the Buddha*, 78.

24. Gregory Schopen, "Filial Piety and the Monk in the Practice of Indian Buddhism: A Question of 'Sinicization' Viewed from the Other Side," in *Bones, Stones, and Buddhist Monks Collected Papers on the Archaeology, Epigraphy, and Texts of Monastic Buddhism in India* (Honolulu: University of Hawaii Press, 1997), 62–64.

Nikāya 4.46–47).[25] When the monk Sadinna expresses his remorse to the Buddha after he has had intercourse with his former wife, the Buddha responds, "It were better for you that your member should enter the mouth of a hideous venomous viper ... [or] a pit of coals burning, blazing and glowing than that it should enter a woman" (Sutta-vibhaṅga 1). The rhetoric of aversion as a strategy for overcoming the pleasures set aside by the ascetic life is often seen most vividly in descriptions of food and the digestive process:

> Exquisite food and drink food hard and soft, by one opening they enter in, by nine they flow out.
> Exquisite food and drink, food hard and soft, one eats with others but hides oneself when excreting it.
> Exquisite food and drink, food hard and soft, one eats joyously but is disgusted when defecating.
> Exquisite food and drink, food hard and soft, it becomes putrid in one night's time. (Visuddhimagga)[26]

The ultimate goal of such rhetoric is not to put people off their food, but rather to help them see their relationship to food so that the desire for food does not lead to dissatisfaction.

The point of the Buddhist rhetoric of aversion is not to dwell in a state of disgust about the objects of one's desire but rather to move to a state of equanimity by which it is possible to interact with the world and all its allure without feeling the need to act on one's desires and instead view the suffering of others with compassion. As Liz Wilson explains, "As an antidote to passion, aversion is a necessary preliminary, a prerequisite for liberation."[27] She cites the Theravada monk Kāntipalo, who "suggests that meditation on the repulsiveness of the body should be seen

---

25. *Aṅguttara Nikāya*, ed. R. Morris and E. Hardy (London: Pali Text Society, 1885–1900), cited in Liz Wilson, *Charming Cadavers: Horrific Figurations of the Feminine in Indian Buddhist Hagiographic Literature* (Chicago: University of Chicago Press, 1996), 199 n. 5.

26. Translated by Caroline A. F. Rhys Davids, *Visuddhimagga* (London: Pali Text Society, 1920–1921), 345–46; cited in Wilson, *Charming Cadavers*, 45.

27. Wilson, *Charming Cadavers*, 45; see also Steve Collins, "The Body in Theravāda Buddhist Monasticism," in *Religion and the Body*, ed. Sarah Coakley (Cambridge: Cambridge University Press, 2000), 185–204, who explores the tensions between Buddhist texts that describe the repulsive nature of the body and the Buddha's teaching of the "middle way." Collins suggests that these texts are preliminary to the construction

as a 'bitter medicine' that may be discontinued once greed for bodily pleasures has been alleviated."[28] We see Thomas display such equanimity in response to the actions of a misguided youth who, having embraced Thomas's teaching that intercourse is a defiling union, swings from desire to aversion and kills his sexual partner, presumably a prostitute, before she can engage in intercourse with another. Thomas sees the youth's aversion to sex as the partner to his attraction to it: "O insane intercourse, how far into shamelessness you go! O unrestrained desire, how did you move this man to do these things?" (Acts Thom. 52.1–2). He then invites the lad to be baptized, "Come, waters from the living waters, realities from what is real and that have been sent to us; rest that has been sent from rest; salvific power that comes from the power which conquers all and subdues all things to its own will" (52.4). When Thomas looks on the fallen prostitute, he sees a lovely young woman and is moved by his compassion to resurrect her. Thomas is similarly moved by the body of a handsome young man whom a serpent kills in jealousy after watching him have intercourse with a beautiful woman (30.3; 31.6), a beautiful woman who has been raped repeatedly by a demon (42–43), and a girl in disarray from having been repeatedly cast down and stripped naked by demons (65.12; 75.2). Wilson describes how Buddhist stories of former courtesans "effectively reconfigure the male gaze" so that the female body ceases to be a sexual object and women are seen as members of the community of monks.[29] Just as Buddhist rhetoric of aversion paradoxically uses anxiety about the impurity of the body to reject social hierarchy, Thomas's attention to the miscreant progeny of a young royal couple dispels the notion of a hierarchy of those who need redemption from the human condition.

The account that the bride and groom give to the king for their failure to consummate their marriage suggests that, as in Buddhism, the rhetoric of aversion seeks to reveal that satisfaction of desire leads to suffering and that liberation comes by seeing the objects of desire as impermanent. The bride ends her explanation with the following: "I've not had intercourse with a husband who passes away—something that ends up in lewdness

---

of the individual and communal body of the monk, who represents for the laity an ideal to which they cannot aspire but can connect to through their material support.

28. Bhikku Kāntipalo, *Bag of Bones: A Miscellany on the Body* (Kandy: Buddhist Publication Society, 1980), 8.

29. Wilson, *Charming Cadavers*, 179.

and bitterness of soul—because now I've been joined to a real husband"
(14.7). The groom delivers his reasoning in a prayer of thanks to the Lord,
"who ... released me from what is temporary, and instead ... made me
worthy of things are immortal and exist forever" (15.7). The cosmology
is Christian, but the description of the right understanding of the human
condition is similar to Buddhist teachings.

The rhetoric of aversion takes another form in the story of Mygdonia,
the wife of Carish, who, driven by curiosity, comes to observe the apostle
and hear his proclamation of a new God. After addressing the people who
have been pushed aside with a promise of rest and those who have carried
the woman with the promise that the Lord will not lay difficult burdens
on them (Acts Thom. 82.7–83.7), Thomas calls them to refrain from adultery and to live a life of meekness and peacefulness, giving liberally to
those in want. Chastity is not presented as a way of winning favor but as
the prize that one receives for competing in "Christ's stadium." Chastity
is the athlete:

> Holy chastity was revealed by God: it destroys sexual immorality, over-
> turns the enemy and pleases God, for it is an unconquered athlete,
> having honor from God and esteemed by many. It is the ambassador
> of peace, proclaiming peace, if anyone acquires it, that person remains
> carefree, pleasing the Lord, expecting the time of redemption. It does
> nothing improper but affords life, rest, and joy to all who acquire it.
> (85.6–8)

As he proceeds, he shifts metaphor, and chastity becomes the temple of
Christ, a habitation in which one dwells, the resting place of God (86.5–6).
The rhetoric of attraction succeeds in motivating the woman to leap from
her carriage and throw herself to the ground, petitioning that God make
her land his habitation. Thomas is halfway there but must then employ
other means:

> This transitory world, you see, will be of no benefit to you, nor will the
> beauty of your body, nor your garments. Neither the renown of your
> rank nor the authority of this world nor the filthy intercourse with your
> husband will aid you if you're deprived of true communion. Indeed, a
> beauteous appearance is dissolved; the body ages and is transformed;
> clothes grow old; authority and power depart after being subject to judg-
> ment for what people have already done. The intercourse that produces
> children vanishes, since it has been condemned. Jesus alone remains for-
> ever, along with those who hope in him. (88.3–7)

In the chapters that follow, Mygdonia enters into a succession of arguments with her husband, Carish (who is made to appear a comic fool by
the way he suffers for the want of intercourse), many of which contain
thoughtful reflections on the nature of time. When Carish appeals to her
to resume their sexual activity by pointing to his own wealth, honor, and
beauty, she replies, "Your wealth will vanish and your beauty will disap-
pear, along with your clothes and your many works; you'll be alone with
your excesses" (117.3). When he begs her to remember the day they first
met, she reflects:

> That time had its qualities, this time has its own; that was a time of begin-
> ning, this of ending. That was a time of temporary life, this of eternal;
> that was a time of transitory joy, this of joy that abides forever.... That
> marriage stands on earth <in constant turmoil>; this one makes love of
> humanity drop down like dew.... That unveiling festival involves sums
> of money, and clothes that grow old; this involves living words that never
> end. (124.4–14; see also 130.4)

When Mygdonia invites Tertia, the wife of the king, to join her in Christian celibacy, she describes Tertia's understanding as limited by her
"time-bound state" (Acts Thom. 135.9). While sexual intercourse continues to be characterized as filthy and shameful, and Mygdonia describes
the state of Tertia's soul as "squalor" (135.10), Tertia is persuaded by the
marvelous things that she hears, and in her attempts to persuade her own
husband, she also grounds her argument in the ontology of a transitory
world (137.7). The problem with sexuality is that it is an expression of the
desire for that which is impermanent rather than eternal and, as such, is
the source ultimately of discontent rather than joy. Such observations
about impermanence are not alien to Christian writers (see Gregory of
Nyssa, *De virginitate* 4.7). What is striking about Thomas's teaching is
the ubiquity of the theme and its centrality to the speeches of those who
are converted.

Thomas's rhetorical strategy of describing the loss of beauty and libidi-
nal desire with age is also used by the Buddha in the story of Kuvalayā
(Avadānaśataka 75).[30] The Avadānaśataka, an anthology of one hundred
biographical Sanskrit legends dating to the first to fifth centuries CE that

---

30. Translations by Karen Muldoon-Hules, "Brides of the Buddha: Nuns' Stories
from the *Avadānaśataka*" (PhD diss., University of California, 2011), 107–10.

seem to have originated from northeast Afghanistan, includes ten stories of women who forswear marriage for the chaste life of a Buddhist nun. Most of these women renounce sexual intercourse with little need of persuasion because they immediately apprehend the impermanence of the world that marriage seeks to make permanent by handing down property to children. Kuvalayā, the daughter of an actor, requires more persuasion. She is "intoxicated with arrogance in her beauty, youth, and health" and to feed her vanity asks whether there is anyone in the city who rivals her beauty. The people respond that the Buddha and his followers are more beautiful. Kuvalayā prepares for battle by adorning herself and then stands in front of the Buddha singing, dancing, and showing her genitalia. The sight of her excites the monks, but the Buddha intervenes by magically transforming Kuvalaya into "a withered old woman ... gray-headed, broken-toothed, humped backed, bent with age, and twisted." Kuvalayā snaps out of her arrogance and requests, "O holy man, let the Blessed One teach the Dharma to me, so that I will be liberated with little difficulty from this stinking corpse." Kuvalayā then becomes an *arhat* (an enlightened being), "one who thought a clod of dirt the same as gold and empty space the same as the palm of her hand, indifferent to adze or sandal paste, her shell split open by knowledge, one who had attained knowledge, supernatural knowledge and special knowledge" (109). Recognizing the impermanence of the object of sexual desire leads not to despair but to equanimity. In each of these stories about women gaining enlightenment, the monks press the Buddha to explain how it is possible, to which the Buddha responds by telling a story of the women's previous incarnations, in which they give alms to the Buddha and his community.

Karen Muldoon-Hules, in her study of these stories, comes to the conclusion that they largely affirm that "marriage was the primary career path for Buddhist women" of their time, in continuity with the norms of Hindu society, with its emphasis on the responsibilities of the householder.[31] Given that their primary audience seems to be monks, getting monks to accept women as renunciates seems a logical purpose of these stories, but the stories seem also to function as inspiration to the laity to support monastic orders through generous donations.[32] If we locate the Acts of

---

31. Karen Muldoon-Hules, *Brides of the Buddha: Nuns' Stories from the Avadānaśataka* (Lanham, MD: Lexington, 2017), 165.

32. Muldoon-Hules, *Brides of the Buddha*, 15; Collins, "Body in Theravāda Buddhist Monasticism," 203.

Thomas's rhetoric of aversion to sexual relations within a similar milieu, might the purpose of the rhetoric be a call to acceptance and generosity rather than to extreme renunciation? Judith Perkins's observations about the role of talking animals in the Acts of Thomas might provide us with a cue to look at the stories of abstinence as having a social goal. Perkins argues that the talking animals "worked to challenge the contemporary social hierarchy that devalued some persons in the society as too akin to animals."[33] Perkins first points to the story of a wild ass advising Thomas that Christ wishes him to display the great deed of resurrection through his hands (Acts Thom. 78). She then draws attention to how Mygdonia, after having pushed her way through the crowd, carried by her slaves (82), and then after overhearing Thomas's meekness and holy chastity directed to those whom she has treated as beasts of burden (83–86), casts herself to the ground, grabs Thomas's fee, and compares herself to a dumb animal (87).[34] The broad picture of the result of Thomas's call to holy chastity is the creation of society structured around charitable giving rather than on a society in which wealth is preserved by elite families (26.1; 33.12; 59.1–2; 85.2; 100.10; 156.1).

Those who choose to read the broader Buddhist narratives from which my selections have been chosen will immediately be struck by some clear differences. Everyone is immediately and easily persuaded by the Buddha, whereas Thomas is not so lucky—his story ends in martyrdom. Buddhist ontology and Christian ontology are very different. Buddhist teaching is a cognitive science that examines the harmful psychological states that result from clinging onto impermanence. Christian teaching offers hope in the speculative permanence of the sacred realm. Nevertheless, Buddhism might be able to prevent Western readers from clinging onto false assumptions about the nature of the Acts of Thomas's rhetoric against sexual activity. If we see Jesus's description of the nasty children begotten through intercourse and Thomas's painting of Mygdonia's fate as a repulsive old woman as pieces of rhetoric insisting on an ethic of renunciation that finds sex repugnant, perhaps we have stopped short of reading the whole story. In doing so, we miss a story of Thomas who has overcome both lust and revulsion in order to see all who have been seen as objects to be used, abused, and possessed as the dwelling of God.

---

33. Judith Perkins, "Animal Voices," *R&T* 12 (2005): 385–96.
34. Perkins, "Animal Voices," 390.

Bibliography

Aṅguttara Nikāya. Edited by R. Morris and E. Hardy. London: Pali Text Society, 1885–1900.

Attridge, Harold. *The Acts of Thomas: Translated with an Introduction and Notes by Harold W. Attridge*. ECA 3. Salem, OR: Polebridge, 2010.

———. "Intertextuality in the Acts of Thomas." *Semeia* 80 (1997): 87–124.

Bharadwaj, O. P. *Studies in the Historical Geography of Ancient India*. Delhi: Sundeep Prakashan, 1986.

Charlesworth, James H. "From the Philopedia of Jesus to the Misopedia of the *Acts of Thomas*." Pages 46–66 in *By Study and Also by Faith*. Edited by John M. Lundquist and Stephen David Ricks. Salt Lake City: Deseret, 1990.

Collins, Steve. "The Body in Theravāda Buddhist Monasticism." Pages 185–204 in *Religion and the Body*. Edited by Sarah Coakley. Cambridge: Cambridge University Press, 2000.

Dio Chrysostom. *Discourses 31–36*. Translated by J. W. Cohoon and H. Lamar Crosby. LCL. Cambridge: Harvard University Press, 1940.

Dowden, Ken, trans. "Alexander Romance." Pages 650–728 in *Collected Ancient Greek Novels*. Edited by B. P. Reardon. Berkeley: University of California Press, 1989.

Huxley, George. "Geography in the *Acts of Thomas*." *GRBS* 24 (1983): 71–80.

Kāntipalo, Bhikku. *Bag of Bones: A Miscellany on the Body*. Kandy: Buddhist Publication Society, 1980.

Klijn, A. F. J. *The Acts of Thomas*. Leiden: Brill, 1962.

König, Jason. "Novelistic and Anti-novelistic Narrative in the *Acts of Thomas* and the *Acts of Andrew and Matthias*." Pages 121–49 in *Fiction on the Fringe: Novelistic Writing in the Post-classical Age*. Edited by Grammatiki Karla. Leiden: Brill, 2009.

Marshall, John. *A Guide to Taxila*. Cambridge: Cambridge University Press, 2013.

McGrath, James F. "History and Fiction in the *Acts of Thomas*: The State of the Question." *JSP* 17 (2008): 297–311.

Miller, Patricia Cox. *Women in Early Christianity: Translations from Greek Texts*. Washington, DC: Catholic University of America Press, 2005.

Muldoon-Hules, Karen. "Brides of the Buddha: Nuns' Stories from the Avadānaśataka." PhD diss., University of California, 2011.

————. *Brides of the Buddha: Nuns' Stories from the Avadānaśataka.* Lanham, MD: Lexington Books, 2017.

Ñanamoli, Bhikkhu. *The Life of the Buddha: According to the Pali Canon.* Kandy: Pariyatti, 2003.

Parker, Grant. *The Making of Roman India.* Cambridge: Cambridge University Press, 2008.

Perkins, Judith. "Animal Voices." *R&T* 12 (2005): 385–96.

Reed, Annette Yoshiko. "Beyond the Land of Nod: Syriac Images of Asia and the Historiography of the West." *HR* 49 (2009): 48–87. Rhys Davids, Caroline A. F. *Visuddhimagga.* London: Pali Text Society, 1920–1921.

Schopen, Gregory. "Filial Piety and the Monk in the Practice of Indian Buddhism: A Question of 'Sinicization' Viewed from the Other Side." Pages 110–26 in *Bones, Stones, and Buddhist Monks Collected Papers on the Archaeology, Epigraphy, and Texts of Monastic Buddhism in India.* Honolulu: University of Hawaii Press, 1997.

Wilson, Liz. *Charming Cadavers: Horrific Figurations of the Feminine in Indian Buddhist Hagiographic Literature.* Chicago: University of Chicago Press, 1996.

Religious Asses

Virginia Burrus

In a 2005 article titled "Animal Voices," Judith Perkins argues that the depiction of speaking animals in the apocryphal acts of the apostles offers "a message of universal inclusiveness and equal participation by all species," adding that this message "may be read to challenge the contemporary social hierarchy that devalued some persons as too akin to animals."[1] Among the animal figures that she discusses are two instances of talking asses in the Acts of Thomas: "an ass colt, who explains to Thomas that he is a descendant of Balaam's ass and the ass that bore Jesus into Jerusalem, and a wild ass."[2] Perkins passes over the ass colt quickly, while dealing with the wild ass at somewhat greater length. This is understandable. The wild ass is both independent and assertive, a fit figure for representing "the innate ability of all those people society has constructed 'as if' animals,"[3] whereas the ass colt may seem distinctly servile, practically begging the reluctant apostle Thomas to ride on his back. Moreover, the story of the ass colt ends badly, to say the least, with the sudden death of the young ass and the explicit refusal of Thomas to revive him, on the ground that he is better off dead.

More recently, Janet Spittler has proposed that the ass colt and wild ass represent two models of embodied life that are very differently valued by the author of the Acts of Thomas. "The wild ass is the ideal model for the Christian life, practicing encratism, not worrying about material needs. The domestic ass is still making poor decisions, laboring under physical burdens, thinking too much of material gains."[4] Spittler's argument offers

---

1. Judith Perkins, "Animal Voices," *R&T* 12 (2005): 392.

2. Perkins, "Animal Voices," 389.

3. Perkins, "Animal Voices," 389.

4. Janet E. Spittler, *Animals in the Apocryphal Acts of Apostles: The Wild Kingdom of Early Christian Literature*, WUNT 247 (Tübingen: Mohr Siebeck, 2008), 222.

an elegant and largely satisfying solution to the otherwise puzzling ending of the ass colt's tale.[5] The carnally oriented ass must die, giving way to the ascetic one. Yet might it *also* be possible to read this story otherwise, in such a way that the little ass with the impressive pedigree is not excluded from the promise of "universal inclusiveness and equal participation by all species" identified by Perkins?

I shall return to this question at the close of this brief essay, suggesting an affirmative answer. In the meantime, let us detour through another ancient Christian text whose author, like Thomas's ass colt, playfully claims the legacy of both Balaam's ass and Christ's. This detour will allow us to approach the story of the ass colt in the Acts of Thomas from different angles, discovering new interpretive possibilities: such, at any rate, is my wager.

———

The text I have in mind is an anonymous letter probably written in late fourth-century Spain or Gaul, addressed to a woman and possibly written by one as well; it is known by its *incipit*, "Quamlibet sciam sacerdotali."[6] The letter writer opens by flattering her addressee, acknowledging that "only choice sacrifices of words are to be offered to a priestly family"; however, the flock of her thoughts contains nothing suitable, she protests. She is like an *asina*, or she-ass, who has given birth to her first son, she states. The ass colt, an impure species unfit for sacrifice, must be redeemed with the offering of a sheep, according to the divine command of Exod 12:11 and 34:19. Thus the letter writer will "redeem the brute expression of [her] foolish mind with the simplicity of Christian innocence," as she puts it. Yet

———

5. Much more satisfying, in my opinion, than Christopher Matthews's suggestion that Num. Rab. 20.4 preserves the original rationale for the death of the ass, namely, that otherwise people might revere the talking animal too highly. See Matthews, "Articulate Animals: A Multivalent Motif in the Apocryphal Acts of the Apostles," in *The Apocryphal Acts of the Apostles: Harvard Divinity School Series*, ed. François Bovon, Ann Graham Brock, and Christopher R. Matthews (Cambridge: Harvard University Press, 1999), 224.

6. Latin text: Germain Morin, "Pages inédites de deux Pseudo-Jéromes des environs de l'an 400," *RBén* 40 (1928): 296–302. English translation: Virginia Burrus and Tracy Keefer, "Anonymous Spanish Correspondence; or the Letter of the 'She-Ass,'" in *Religions of Late Antiquity in Practice*, ed. Richard Valantasis (Princeton: Princeton University Press, 2000), 331–39.

even that is not enough, for the utterance of a foolish beast is worth still less than the offspring of an impure animal; thus, the fact that she speaks of heavenly things must be added to the ransom.[7]

Immediately she complicates matters further, however, going on to revise the terms of exchange on the authority of Lev 27:8, according to which the wish or intention to redeem an offering may substitute, in the case of the poor, for the actual redemption. Our author now begs that her addressee accept her plodding words (i.e., the offspring of the she-ass) *instead of the sheep* and not drive them from the temple of her heart. Her offering will remain the offering of a she-ass—an ass colt, that is.[8]

The rhetoric of humility is conventional in antiquity—the more artfully elaborate, the better. However, such rhetoric also intends to score a point, of course. Here, through a bit of creative exegesis, letter writing has become an act of both birthing and sacrificial offering; in the process, humility is undercut by assertiveness. The author says, in effect: my letter may be a mere baby donkey—but you should receive it as if it were a lamb fit for priestly sacrifice!

Next, our author calls for examples of the work of the she-ass. Almost by sleight of hand, the maternal ass has become exemplary. In order to develop the example, the letter writer shifts attention to a different asinine figure drawn from Scripture: the wicked prophet Balaam's ass. The scriptural reference is to Num 22:22–30. In that well-known passage, a sword-wielding angel, sent by an angry god, blocks the path of Balaam, who rides on a she-ass. Balaam cannot see the angel, but the donkey can, and thus she swerves to the side, only to have Balaam beat her until she turns back onto the path. This happens twice more, as the path grows increasingly narrow, so that first the ass scrapes Balaam's foot against a wall and then has no alternative but simply to stop, lying down before the angel. Balaam, of course, beats her again. At this point, a miracle occurs:

> Then the Lord opened the mouth of the donkey, and she said to Balaam, "What have I done to you, that you have struck me these three times?" Balaam said to the donkey, "Because you have made a fool of me! I wish I had a sword in my hand! I would kill you right now!" But the donkey said to Balaam, "Am I not your donkey, which you have ridden all your

---

7. Burrus and Keefer, "Anonymous Spanish Correspondence," 333.

8. Burrus and Keefer, "Anonymous Spanish Correspondence," 333–34.

life to this day? Have I been in the habit of treating you this way?" And
he said, "No." (vv. 28–30 NRSV)

Balaam's ass is surely one of the Bible's most famous talking animals. Strik-
ingly, however, our author discovers not a speaking but a praying ass in this
text—one who prays not with words but by falling to her knees, remem-
bering the teachings of Scripture as if they stood before her like the angel
on the path. It is not an obvious interpretation. The letter writer also makes
much of the she-ass pressing Balaam's foot against the wall—interpreting
this to signify the destruction of either "the desire to wander or the final
heel of the year, as the gentiles seem to observe it." The main purpose of the
letter, in fact, is to transform liturgical time. The author urges that the end
of the year not be observed in the frenetic motion of pagan festivities (as
exemplified in the Saturnalia and Kalends of January) but rather in with-
drawal into the stillness of solitude.[9] December, the tenth month, marks
the final phase of Mary's pregnancy: it is a time of preparation and anticipation best cultivated in ascetic retreat. As she puts it, "One who desires to
give birth to Christ ought to choose a private and quiet place."[10] Thus the
figure of the ass whose words and thoughts are her firstborn offspring is
overlaid by the figure of Mary, who gives birth to the only-begotten divine
word—another productive slip and slide between scriptural passages. The
figure of Mary (which is developed at some length) is itself superseded
by the image of the ark, enclosed and at rest amid the teeming floods,
which is in turn reconfigured as the temple of Solomon's silent fabrica-
tion.[11] Daniel's three weeks of fasting and prayer at the end of the tenth
month—December—locate the self-mastery of the "man of desires" in
time, while the prophecy of Zechariah aligns the scripturally swaddled
birth of the new age (Jesus) from the old (Joshua) with both the rebuilding
of the destroyed temple and Ezra's reinscription of the divine word.[12]

In all of this, the letter writer's task is to persuade her addressee to take
up an unfamiliar seasonal observance of solitude and quiet. She acknowledges that it may be "hard to grasp a work of unfamiliar habit" (novellae
institutionis opus).[13] The tug of habit and the lure of social intercourse

---

9. Burrus and Keefer, "Anonymous Spanish Correspondence," 334.
10. Burrus and Keefer, "Anonymous Spanish Correspondence," 334.
11. Burrus and Keefer, "Anonymous Spanish Correspondence," 335–36.
12. Burrus and Keefer, "Anonymous Spanish Correspondence," 336–37.
13. Burrus and Keefer, "Anonymous Spanish Correspondence," 336.

are strong. Yet new habits can be created, habits that are also as ancient as Noah's ark, Solomon's temple, Balaam's ass, or Mary's womb. Even the embrace of new customs becomes a way of adhering to ancient tradition: "In Maccabees ... the entire generation of fathers and priests, along with their observances, came to an end, so that we may understand that we are not to be deterred from the observance of a novel custom" (*ab observatione novellae utilitatis*), our letter writer notes.[14]

She turns in closing to reclaim the persona of the ass, sliding to yet another scriptural donkey. She has offered a baby ass in place of a sheep, but even if her addressee will not accept it—even if it cannot be redeemed— she is not worried, she asserts. "For, because Christ was born according to the flesh, an ass was also needed to serve in the passion, since 'god chooses what is the world's foolishness.'"[15] While our author here invokes the masculine *asinus*, the gospel of Matthew identifies the ass who carries Christ as an *asina* or she-ass with a colt (see Matt 21:7: ἤγαγον τὴν ὄνον καὶ πῶλον / *adduxerunt asinam et pullum*); the other gospels mention only the colt, though the Latin version of Luke refers to him as the "colt of a she-ass" (Luke 19:30: *invenietis pullum asinae*). The *asinus* of our letter may refer to the colt, then. But however we parse the gender or age of the donkey, the author's closing argument seems clear: the carnality represented by the ass has already been redeemed in the incarnation, and flesh has its own role to play in the narrative of salvation. Perhaps there are no pure and impure species after all.

Perhaps there are no good and bad asses in the Acts of Thomas either.

Like the letter writer's asinine epistle, Thomas's ass colt may be viewed as a sacrificial offering that is also a missive, a communication, a sending— at once a prayer and a call to conversion. The offering initially consists, it seems, in the colt's mute regard for Thomas: "While the apostle was standing on the road and speaking with the crowds, a she-ass's colt [πῶλος ὀνάδος] came and stood before him" (Acts Thom. 39).[16] As if accommodating human limitation, the young animal goes on to translate that stance

---

14. Burrus and Keefer, "Anonymous Spanish Correspondence," 338.
15. Burrus and Keefer, "Anonymous Spanish Correspondence," 338.
16. Greek text: Richard A. Lipsius and Max Bonnet, eds., *Acta Apostolorum Apocrypha*, vol. 2.2 (1903; repr., Darmstadt: Wissenschaftliche Buchgesellschaft, 1959),

of regard into the medium of human voice, acknowledging Thomas as one who "although being free became a slave and although bought [has] brought many into freedom" (39). The colt offers its own service freely, thus mirroring the apostle: "Get up and sit upon me and rest until you arrive at the city," he tells Thomas (39). But if the little ass has offered rest, as if in anticipation of the state of salvation, Thomas has trouble receiving the gift: he assumes that Christ is speaking through the colt, who is by nature *alogos*, without reason or speech, and initially he addresses not the colt but Christ. "O Jesus Christ…, O quiet and silence who is spoken of even by speechless animals!" (39). Nonetheless, he subsequently asks the colt: "Whose are you and to whom do you belong?" (40), as if granting him a distinct identity and agency after all.

This is when the young ass recites his pedigree: "I am of that race that served Balaam, and your lord and your teacher sat upon one belonging to me by race. And now I was sent to give you rest by sitting upon me" (40). The ass colt claims his own voice, race, and purpose: like the ass who carried Christ, he will be blessed through his service to Christ's twin, Thomas; a "portion" will be granted him that will, however, be taken back when he has served. What is that portion? We may assume, as Thomas seems to do, that it is *logos* or speech. Thomas initially refuses to ride on the colt, deferring to Christ to perfect the gift of speech in the young ass and indeed in the entire "race" of asses. But perhaps that is not what the colt means when he refers to his portion: after all, he can already talk, and the entire race of asses will not become articulate, as Thomas seems to imagine. Moreover, what is taken from him when he has served Thomas, who does finally agree to ride him, is not language but life itself. "Depart and be kept safe where you were," says Thomas, after he dismounts, and "immediately the colt fell to the ground at the apostle's feet and died" (41). When the crowd asks Thomas to revive the colt, he refuses. Thomas suggests that Christ would have prevented his death if he had wanted to; since he did not, the death must be "entirely beneficial" (41). A worthy sacrifice, then, but in what sense?

It is hard to say. It is a hard saying. Has Christ already ushered the ass colt into the resurrection? Is his death a kind of witness—that is to say, a martyrdom? And if so, a witness to what? To Thomas's greatness, which

---

99–191. English translation and commentary based on the Syriac text: A. F. J. Klijn, *The Acts of Thomas: Introduction, Text, and Commentary* (Leiden: Brill, 2003).

the colt proclaims? Alternately, to Thomas's blindness, his inability to apprehend the offering of the colt and what it might cost? Maybe the point is not so much that Christ has given the colt human speech as that the colt has found his own way to express his regard for Thomas, despite Thomas's own doubts and hesitations. He stands before Thomas, he speaks, he carries the apostle. Thomas dismounts, dismisses the colt, and the colt dies. Perhaps we are meant to understand that his mission is complete, so to speak, his own formation complete when he receives his rider. Or perhaps the colt, like the porpoises of which Scott McVay writes, is unwilling to live without the human to whom he is bonded: refusing fish from any other hand or source, these porpoises "would rather endure death by dehydration than continue to live 'unconnected.'"[17] On this reading, the ass colt dies as a witness to the faithfulness of his own enduring love.

What does "animal religion" look like? As Donovan Schaefer notes, "for many philosophers of religion, religion without language is a contradiction in terms."[18] Schaefer himself proposes, however, that religion begins not with language but with affect and the movement of bodies among other bodies—human, asinine, and so much more. Religion *is* animal religion, in other words, and animal religion is "a dance—a play between bodies and worlds."[19] Schaefer asks us to consider: "How is religion something that puts us in continuity with other animal bodies, rather than something that sets us apart? How is religion something that carries us on its back rather than something that we think, choose, or command?"[20]

On these terms, Thomas misrecognizes religion: he thinks it is about words; he marvels that the ass colt can speak. But what if religion is, instead, what carries him on its back? Then religion would be feeling and gesture— the ass colt standing and gazing, mutely offering its gift. Are we not struck by the ass colt as much in its animal distinctness as in its humanlike speech?

---

17. Scott McVay, "Prelude: 'A Siamese Connexion with a Plurality of Other Mortals,'" in *The Biophilia Hypothesis*, ed. Stephen R. Kellert and Edward O. Wilson (Washington, DC: Island Press, 1993), 8.

18. Donovan O. Schaefer, *Religious Affects: Animality, Evolution, and Power* (Durham, NC: Duke University Press, 2015), 179.

19. Schaefer, *Religious Affects*, 182.

20. Schaefer, *Religious Affects*, 3.

After all, for our letter writer, the miracle is not that Balaam's ass speaks but that she prays silently by falling to her knees when faced with one who inspires her awe. Here, then, is Perkins's "message of universal inclusiveness and equal participation by all species": religion is what happens when creatures offer themselves mutually; it is what happens when they feel awe in the face of one another. It may be most accessible precisely when human speech finally lapses into silence, when there remains only the marvel of the spontaneous yet intricately choreographed dance of creatures carrying each other, forming each other, beholding each other in their animal eyes.

Bibliography

Burrus, Virginia, and Tracy Keefer. "Anonymous Spanish Correspondence; or the Letter of the 'She-Ass.'" Pages 331–39 in *Religions of Late Antiquity in Practice*. Edited by Richard Valantasis. Princeton: Princeton University Press, 2000.

Klijn, A. F. J. *The Acts of Thomas: Introduction, Text, and Commentary*. Leiden: Brill, 2003.

Lipsius, Richard A., and Max Bonnet, eds. *Acta Apostolorum Apocrypha*. Vol. 2.2. 1903. Repr., Darmstadt: Wissenschaftliche Buchgesellschaft, 1959.

Matthews, Christopher R. "Articulate Animals: A Multivalent Motif in the Apocryphal Acts of the Apostles." Pages 205–32 in *The Apocryphal Acts of the Apostles: Harvard Divinity School Series*. Edited by François Bovon, Ann Graham Brock, and Christopher R. Matthews. Cambridge: Harvard University Press, 1999.

McVay, Scott. "Prelude: 'A Siamese Connexion with a Plurality of Other Mortals.'" Pages 3–19 in *The Biophilia Hypothesis*. Edited by Stephen R. Kellert and Edward O. Wilson. Washington, DC: Island Press, 1993.

Morin, Germain. "Pages inédites de deux Pseudo-Jéromes des environs de l'an 400." *RBén* 40 (1928): 296–302.

Perkins, Judith. "Animal Voices." *R&T* 12 (2005): 385–96.

Schaefer, Donovan O. *Religious Affects: Animality, Evolution, and Power*. Durham, NC: Duke University Press, 2015.

Spittler, Janet E. *Animals in the Apocryphal Acts of Apostles: The Wild Kingdom of Early Christian Literature*. WUNT 247. Tübingen: Mohr Siebeck, 2008.

The Master's Voice: Martyrdom and the Late Roman Schoolroom in Prudentius's *Passio Sancti Cassiani*

Kate Cooper

In his collection of poems on the martyrs, Spanish poet Prudentius tells the story of the Christian *rhetor* Cassianus, whose shrine at Forum Cornelii—modern Imola, in what is now northern Italy—he had visited while traveling to Rome. Born in Spain around 348, Prudentius rose to become a member of the imperial administration under Theodosius. He is one of the most telling witnesses to the cultural importance of the emerging cult of the martyrs in the fourth century.

Prudentius's career trajectory was not unlike that of his contemporary Augustine (b. 354): after rhetorical training in the provinces, both men had made their way to Italy in search of political office, and both had been successful in converting their gifts into visibility at court. But there, their careers had diverged. In his mid-thirties, Augustine returned to his native North Africa with the intent of retiring from public life—he eventually became a bishop—while Prudentius served out a career as a public official before retiring to a life of poetry. We will see below that the two men found contrasting ways of using their rhetorical inheritance to think about how the stories worked on the hearts and minds of the faithful.

In the *Peristephanon*, or *Crowns of the Martyrs*, Prudentius creates a poetic framework for squaring classical rhetoric with the demands of Christian belonging.[1] The passion of Cassian is in some ways the high

---

1. Michael Roberts, *Poetry and the Cult of the Martyrs: The Liber Peristephanon of Prudentius* (Ann Arbor: University of Michigan Press, 1993). See also Pierre-Yves Fux, *Les sept Passions de Prudence (Peristephanon 2.5.9.11–14): Introduction générale et commentaire* (Fribourg: Éditions Universitaires, 2003); and on Prudentius's way of engaging the reader, Catherine Conybeare, "Sanctum, lector, percense uolumen: Snakes, Readers, and the Whole Text in Prudentius' Hamartigenia," in *The Early Chris-*

point of this project of reconciliation, because Cassian himself was a teacher of rhetoric. The poet represents the predicament of a Christian teacher instructing pagan pupils as an inverted hyperbole of the relationship of social reproduction. The Christian teacher finds himself the object of the accumulated frustration of the pagan pupils during the painful process of instruction.

Prudentius's martyrdom of Cassian cultivates an ironic interest in the relationship between violence in the classroom (e.g., teachers' use of physical violence against students) and the violent content of the Christian classroom (the violent stories of the martyrs). The martyr figure was nothing less than a tool for cultivating a new subjectivity in young monks, school pupils, and Christian catechumens.

1. Talking Back

The *agon*, or contest, was central as both practice and metaphor in the ancient schoolroom. It was a central element of life of the ancient city. Just as boys competed in declamation, so they competed in the games of the palaestra. Similarly, the nexus binding the cities into the wider fabric of empire was articulated through the public games of the civic and imperial cult.[2]

The metaphor of the *agon* had taken root deeply in the Christian imagination, already from the earliest sources. Written in the sixties of the first century, Paul's first Letter to the Corinthians visualizes the Christian life as an athletic performance:

> Everyone who competes in the games goes into strict training. They do it to get a crown that will not last, but we do it to get a crown that will last forever. Therefore I do not run like someone running aimlessly; I do not fight like a boxer beating the air. No, I strike a blow to my body and make it my slave so that after I have preached to others, I myself will not be disqualified for the prize. (1 Cor 9:25–27)[3]

---

tian Book, ed. W. Klingshirn and L. Safran (Washington, DC: Catholic University of America Press, 2007), 225–40.

2. Paul Plass, *The Game of Death in Ancient Rome: Arena Sport and Political Suicide* (Madison: University of Wisconsin Press, 1995).

3. All biblical quotations in this essay follow the NIV.

The Letter to the Ephesians, probably written by one of Paul's followers a generation later, recasts Paul's own musing on struggles and sufferings into the vivid imagery of the wrestling-match, the *palē*.

> Put on the full armor [*panoplia*] of God, so that you can take your stand against the devil's schemes. For our struggle [*palē*] is not against flesh and blood, but against the rulers, against the authorities, against the powers of this dark world and against the spiritual forces of evil in the heavenly realms. Therefore put on the full armor of God, so that when the day of evil comes, you may be able to stand your ground. (Eph 6:11–13)

Again, putting on armor is used as a metaphor for living an ethical life according to Christian norms. The idea that the real enemy is not of this world, that antagonistic forces are poised behind the veil of reality to engage the Christian in mortal struggle, was one that had a long future, especially in the context of ascetic communities. On the face of it, ascetic communities are the obvious location for a literary genre celebrating the virtue of endurance. The dynamic of the *agon* carried over into the monk's interior life.[4]

Ascetic culture was itself a culture of the schoolroom, with ascetic communities increasingly the location of libraries and the scriptoria in which manuscripts were copied.[5] If martyr narrative resonated with the culture of competitive rhetorical display in the schoolroom, it also gained purchase on the imagination from its link to ascetic practice. By the end of the fourth century, the monastic "dialogue with demons" had emerged, and monks were armed with the correct response for the demons who would besiege them.[6]

In an ascetic context, martyr narratives were texts for a curriculum centered on lessons in endurance. In reading these tales of heroic endurance, whether in the arena, the brothel, or the schoolroom, young men—children, in fact—were taught fundamental lessons in suffering. The ability to endure deprivation and physical hardship, arbitrary punishment and psychological bullying: all of this was vital in breaking down earthly

---

4. David Brakke, *Demons and the Making of the Monk: Spiritual Combat in Early Christianity* (Cambridge: Harvard University Press, 2006).

5. Kim Haines-Eitzen, *Guardians of Letters: Literacy, Power, and the Transmitters of Early Christian Literature* (New York: Oxford University Press, 2000).

6. Evagrius of Pontus, *Talking Back: A Monastic Handbook for Combating Demons*, trans. David Brakke (Collegeville, MN: Cistercian Press, 2009).

attachments and in rebuilding new recruits as men who could themselves heroically embody the austere demands of their calling.

Important here is the cognitive magnetism of meditation on pain. Just as the ability to endure suffering had given the martyrs the ability to defy the Roman state, so meditation on the suffering of the martyrs played a critical role in the formation of young monks. By the sixth century, meditation on the martyrs was certainly used to offer a framework for the developmental crisis points encountered by entrants to what had become institutional monasteries.[7]

Most third-century Christians would have seen the ascetic movement as extremist,[8] and one of its documented practices was to radicalize adolescents by drawing them away from the moderate values of their parents and families—a phenomenon that has disturbing modern parallels. Christian fathers were expected to maintain religious discipline in their homes, much as their pagan counterparts were expected to do.[9] If ascetics were the first to adopt the martyrs as models for imitation, the martyrs may have been countercultural figures even within Christianity.

In the second, third, and fourth centuries, there is copious evidence to suggest that children were expected to brave the wrath of pagan or moderate Christian parents in order to express their zeal for the faith—as in the early third-century prison diary of Perpetua of Carthage.[10] But by the end of antiquity, we begin to see signs of reconciliation within the household. In the martyr narratives of the fifth and sixth century, such as the Passion of Sebastian, the initially skeptical parents are persuaded by their sons to

---

7. Kate Cooper, "Family, Dynasty, and Conversion in the Roman Gesta Martyrum," in *Zwischen Niederschrift und Wiederschrift: Frühmittelalterliche Hagiographie und Historiographie im Spannungsfeld von Kompendienüberlieferung und Editionstechnik*, ed. Maximilian Diesenberger (Vienna: Verlag der Österreichischen Akademie der Wissenschaften, 2010), 273–81.

8. James A. Francis, *Subversive Virtue: Asceticism and Authority in the Second-Century Pagan World* (University Park: Pennsylvania State University Press, 1995).

9. Kate Cooper, "Closely Watched Households: Visibility, Exposure, and Private Power in the Roman Domus," *Past and Present* 197 (2007): 3–33; Richard P. Saller, "The Hierarchical Household in Roman Society: A Study of Domestic Slavery," in *Serfdom and Slavery: Studies in Legal Bondage*, ed. M. L. Bush (London: Longman, 1996), 112–29.

10. Kate Cooper, "A Father, a Daughter, and a Procurator: Authority and Resistance in the Prison Memoir of Perpetua of Carthage," *G&H* 23 (2011): 686–703.

join the new faith; the parent is no longer required to resist the child's yearning to be reunited with God.[11]

2. "They Vent the Hatred Conceive in Silent Resentment": Cassian and His Pupils

Prudentius begins the story of Cassian with an account of his own visit to the martyr's tomb while traveling to Rome.

> stratus humi tumulo advolvebar, quem sacer ornat
>   martyr dicato Cassianus corpore.
> dum lacrimans mecum reputo mea vulnera et omnes
>   vitae labores ac dolorum acumina,
> erexi ad caelum faciem, stetit obvia contra
>   fucis colorum picta imago martyris
> plagas mille gerens, totos lacerata per artus,
>   ruptam minutis praeferens punctis cutem. (9.5–12)

> I was bowed to the ground before the tomb which the holy martyr Cassian honours with his consecrated body; and while in tears I was thinking of my sins and all my life's distresses and stinging pains, I lifted my face towards heaven, and there stood confronting me a picture of the martyr painted in colours, bearing a thousand wounds, all his parts torn, and showing his skin broken with tiny pricks.[12]

Self-examination is the starting point for learning from the martyr's example: it is only after considering his own life's "distresses and stinging pains" that the narrator is able to engage with the striking visual image of the martyr, "bearing a thousand wounds." His tormentors are not the Roman jailers of standard martyr narrative, but rather the teacher's own pupils:

> innumeri circum pueri, miserabile visu,
>   confossa parvis membra figebant stilis,
> unde pugillares soliti percurrere ceras
>   scholare murmur adnotantes scripserant. (9.12–16)

---

11. Cooper, "Family, Dynasty, and Conversion," 279. See also Kate Cooper, "Ventriloquism and the Miraculous: Conversion, Preaching, and the Martyr Exemplum in Late Antiquity," in *Signs, Wonders, and Miracles*, ed. Kate Cooper and Jeremy Gregory, SCH 41 (Woodbridge, UK: Boydell & Brewer, 2005), 22–45.

12. I have used the text and (with minor emendations) translation of H. J. Thompson, *Prudentius*, 2 vols., LCL (London: Heinemann, 1955).

Countless boys round about (a pitiful sight!) were stabbing and piercing
his body with the little styles with which they used to run over their wax
tablets, writing down the droning lesson in school.

The lesson has been turned against the teacher: the boys continue the
repetitive mechanical action of their lessons. But instead of writing on
wax, they pierce the teacher's own body with the restless motion of the
stylus.

The poem takes the form of a classical narrative description (*ekphra-
sis*). The narrator relates that he applied to the sacristan to hear the story
behind the picture and hears a recapitulation of the teacher's work.

> praefuerat studiis puerilibus et grege multo
>   saeptus magister litterarum sederat,
> verba notis brevibus conprendere cuncta peritus,
>   raptimque punctis dicta praepetibus sequi.
> aspera nonnumquam praecepta et tristia visa
>   inpube vulgus moverant ira et metu.
> doctor amarus enim discenti semper ephebo,
>   nec dulcis ulli disciplina infantiae est. (9.21–28)

He had been in charge of a school for boys and sat as a teacher of reading
and writing with a great throng round him, and he was skilled in putting
every word in short signs and following speech quickly with swift pricks
on the wax. But at times the young mob, feeling his teaching harsh and
stern, were moved with anger and fear, for the teacher is ever distasteful
to the youthful learner and childhood never takes kindly to training.

It is taken for granted that the boys will be hostile to their teacher, not
because he was a Christian and they pagan, but rather because of the pain
involved in the learning process itself. The agitation of the pupils has been
constrained by *disciplina*, but now it gains an airing:

> vincitur post terga manus spoliatus amictu,
>   adest acutis agmen armatum stilis.
> quantum quisque odii tacita conceperat ira,
>   effundit ardens felle tandem libero. (9.43–46)

So he is stripped of his garments and his hands are tied behind his back,
and all the band are there, armed with their sharp styles. All the hatred
long conceived in silent resentment they each vent now, burning with
gall that has at last found freedom.

Ironically, it is the teacher's task to goad his pupils in the work of violence—this time, because of his desire that the ordeal be completed.

"este, precor, fortes, et vincite viribus annos;
    quod defit aevo, suppleat crudelitas." (9.65–66)

"Be stout, I beg," he cries, "and outdo your years with your strength.
What you lack in age let a savage spirit make up."

The stabs of small stylus by small boys threaten to continue endlessly without achieving their aim.

The boys, in turn, taunt their teacher:

"emendes licet inspectos longo ordine versus,
    mendosa forte si quid erravit manus.
exerce imperium: ius est tibi plectere culpam,
    si quis tuorum te notavit segnius."
talia ludebant pueri per membra magistri,
    nec longa fessum poena solvebat virum. (9.79–84)

"You may examine and correct our lines in long array, in case an erring
hand has made any mistake. Use your authority; you have power to
punish a fault, if any of your pupils has written carelessly on you." Such
sport the boys had on their master's body, and yet the long-drawn suffering was not releasing him from his weariness.

The pupils' mockery of their master makes play with the power balance
between the master and his charges.

The fraught atmosphere of the schoolroom is well captured by the
poet's contemporary, Augustine of Hippo.[13] The boys were set the task
of performing speeches drawn from the emotional high points of Latin
poetry. Augustine's own prize speech captured the rage of Juno against
Aeneas, which resulted in his coming to Africa. Pedagogically, the fact that
schoolroom exercises were structured around competitions had a practical component: the practice of rhetoric was fundamentally about using
beautiful language to persuade the hearer in the context of a dispute. But

---

13. On Augustine's memoir of the schoolroom and the circumstances of his rejection of earthly ambition, see Kate Cooper, "Love and Belonging, Loss and Betrayal
in the Confessions," in *A Companion to Augustine*, ed. Mark Vessey (Oxford: Wiley-
Blackwell, 2012), 69–86.

there was also a pedagogical component to this emphasis on contest. The very structure of schoolroom competitions offered a way for the master narratives of Roman culture to gain traction in the minds of the young.

The pursuit of beautiful speech was the principal selective mechanism for upward mobility in late Roman society. Each provincial schoolroom was part of network of practice cast across the wide expanse of the empire.[14] The culture of speech and performance required of its practitioners a willingness to be constantly on view: while skill itself was a prize to be acquired and cherished, the display of prized skills must constantly be repeated.[15]

In this culture of competitive speech, the martyr's speech was a privileged form of superspeech or antispeech, the martyr a speaker whose words carried a power beyond that of mere ornament.[16] How this outstanding fact was to be represented was one of the central problems of early Christian literature.[17]

3. Visualization and the Theater of Memory

If the martyr's voice was a powerful tool for capturing the listener's attention, so, too, was the visual imagery of the martyr's suffering. Recent work on how visualization and emotive patterning give ideas greater resonance in memory can help us to understand the poet's complex strategy for harnessing the listener's imaginative faculty.[18] The politics of viewing have been the subject of extended discussion in recent decades, beginning with film critic Laura Mulvey's writing on the politics of the gaze.[19] More

---

14. Robert A. Kaster, *Guardians of Language: The Grammarian and Society in Late Antiquity* (Berkeley: University of California Press, 1988).

15. Maud W. Gleason, *Making Men: Sophists and Self-Presentation in Ancient Rome* (Princeton: Princeton University Press, 1995); Erik Gunderson, *Staging Masculinity: The Rhetoric of Performance in the Roman World* (Ann Arbor: University of Michigan Press, 2000).

16. Kate Cooper, "The Voice of the Victim: Gender, Representation, and Early Christian Martyrdom," *BJRL* 80 (1998): 147–57.

17. Cooper, "Ventriloquism and the Miraculous."

18. See Linda J. Levine and Robin S. Edelstein, "Emotion and Memory Narrowing: A Review and Goal-Relevance Approach," *Cognition & Emotion* 23 (2009): 833–75 and literature cited there.

19. Laura Mulvey, "Visual Pleasure and Narrative Cinema," *Screen* 16 (1975): 6–18. See also Mulvey, "Afterthoughts on 'Visual Pleasure and Narrative Cinema' Inspired by Duel in the Sun," in *Popular Fiction: Technology, Ideology, Production,*

recently, scholars of Roman art have placed emphasis on how decorative scenes in domestic spaces encode power relations, with the power of the patron enhanced by the exposure of those under his dominion.[20]

Harry Maier has argued that Christian writers took a distinctive approach to the power of the visual, showing an acute sensitivity to the violation of the exposed individual.[21] Virginia Burrus has shown, for example, how Ambrose of Milan harnesses the gaze of the reader through the visual magnetism of the heroine's suffering.[22]

Prudentius himself has a distinctive way of harnessing the imaginative eye of his audience.[23] Martha Malamud has shown how his *Passion of Eulalia* frames its reader as a voyeur, gaining purchase on the imagination through the progressive violation of the martyr's body.[24] Modern psychological research has shown that emotion is one of the most pow-

Reading, ed. T. Bennett (London: Routledge, 1990), 139–51; Carol Clover, *Men, Women, and Chainsaws: Gender and the Modern Horror Film* (Princeton: Princeton University Press, 1992).

20. Beth Severy-Hoven, "Master Narratives and the Wall Painting of the House of the Vettii, Pompeii," *G&H* 24 (2012): 540–80, building on the work of David Fredrick, "Beyond the Atrium to Ariadne: Erotic Painting and Visual Pleasure in the Roman House," *ClAnt* 14 (1995): 266–87; Ann Olga Koloski-Ostrow, "Violent Stages in Two Pompeian Houses: Imperial Taste, Aristocratic Response, and Messages of Male Control," in *Naked Truths: Women, Sexuality, and Gender in Classical Art and Archaeology*, ed. Ann Olga Koloski-Ostrow and Claire L. Lyons (London: Routledge, 1997), 243–66; John Pollini, "Slave-Boys for Sexual and Religious Service: Images of Pleasure and Devotion," in *Flavian Rome: Culture, Image, Text*, ed. A. Boyle and W. Dominik (Leiden: Brill, 2003), 149–66; Helen Morales, "The Torturer's Apprentice: Parrhasius and the Limits of Art," in *Art and Text in Roman Culture*, ed. Jaš Elsner (Cambridge: Cambridge University Press, 1996), 182–209; and Elsner, *Roman Eyes: Visuality and Subjectivity in Art and Text* (Princeton: Princeton University Press, 2007).

21. Harry O. Maier, "Staging the Gaze: Early Christian Apocalypses and Narrative Self-Representation," *HTR* 90 (1997): 131–54.

22. Virginia Burrus, "Reading Agnes: The Rhetoric of Gender in Ambrose and Prudentius," *JECS* 3 (1995): 25–46. See also Sandra Joshel, "The Body Female and the Body Politic: Livy's Lucretia and Verginia," in *Pornography and Representation in Greece and Rome*, ed. Amy Richlin (Oxford: Oxford University Press, 1991), 112–30; for Augustine's early fifth-century critique of the social assumptions behind this literary topos, see Dennis Trout, "Retextualizing Lucretia: Cultural Subversion in the City of God," *JECS* 2 (1994): 53–70.

23. Michael Roberts, *The Jeweled Style: Poetry and Poetics in Late Antiquity* (Ithaca, NY: Cornell University Press, 1989).

24. Martha Malamud, "Making a Virtue of Perversity: Prudentius and Classical

erful memory anchors, so this meant that the narratives could become embedded more deeply in the memory.[25]

We know from Augustine that schoolboys were taught to imagine subjectively as well as objectively, to project themselves into the figure whom they represented, creating an emotional paradox of simultaneously considering the figure as object and identifying with the figure as subject.[26] So, for example, Augustine's childhood performance of the rage of Juno, or the moments in the *Confessions* where the narrator reads his own departure from Africa through the lens of the *Aeneid*, with his own abandonment of Monica an echo of the hero's betrayal of Dido.[27]

Christian writers made a great deal out of the tension between subjective and objective engagement, encouraging readers—even female readers—to think of themselves as shadow protagonists and at the same time as viewers considering the picture from the outside.[28] This made sense pedagogically. Modern work on memory and cognition has shown that visualization serves to fix ideas in memory.[29] If visualization and emo-

---

Poetry," in *The Imperial Muse: Ramus Essays on Roman Literature of the Empire*, ed. A. J. Boyle (Victoria, Australia: Aureal, 1990), 2:274–98.

25. Levine and Edelstein, "Emotion and Memory Narrowing," 833–75.

26. Marjorie Curry Woods, "Weeping for Dido: Epilogue on a Premodern Rhetorical Exercise in the Postmodern Classroom," in *Latin Grammar and Rhetoric: From Classical Theory to Medieval Practice*, ed. Carol Dana Lanham (London: Continuum Books, 2002), 284–94. See also Woods, "Boys Will Be Women: Musings on Classroom Nostalgia and the Chaucerian Audience(s)," in *Speaking Images: Essays in Honor of V. A. Kolve*, ed. Robert F. Yeager and Charlotte C. Morse (Asheville, NC: Pegasus, 2001), 143–66; Woods, "Rape and the Pedagogical Rhetoric of Sexual Violence," in *Criticism and Dissent in the Middle Ages*, ed. Rita Copeland (Cambridge: Cambridge University Press, 1996), 56–86; Woods, "Teaching the Tropes in the Middle Ages: The Theory of Metaphoric Transference in Commentaries on the Poetria nova," in *Rhetoric and Pedagogy: Its History, Philosophy, and Practice; Essays in Honor of James J. Murphy*, ed. Winifred Bryan Horner and Michael Leff (Mahwah, NJ: Lawrence Erlbaum and Associates, 1995), 73–82.

27. Camille Bennett, "The Conversion of Vergil: The Aeneid in Augustine's Confessions," *REAug* 34 (1988): 47–69; William Werpehowski, "Weeping at the Death of Dido: Sorrow, Virtue, and Augustine's Confessions," *JRE* 19 (1991): 175–91.

28. Kate Cooper, "The Bride of Christ, the 'Male Woman,' and the Female Reader in Late Antiquity," in *Oxford Handbook of Women and Gender in Medieval Europe*, ed. Judith Bennett and Ruth Mazo Karras (New York: Oxford University Press, 2013), 529–44.

29. Levine and Edelstein, "Emotion and Memory Narrowing."

tional identification are distinct memory triggers, our writers may have reasoned that the two strategies could gain even greater purchase on the imagination if they worked alongside each other.

The charm of a heroine's fear was a stock technique of ancient authors. In the Acts of Agape, Irene, and Chione, the sneering governor condemns the heroine to labor in a brothel; her blushes are meant to frame the reader as a voyeur even as her fortitude excites admiration. Often the implicit reader's sympathy will be cultivated through a proxy within the narrative, who directs and amplifies the reaction that the reader is invited to take. Eusebius tells a story of the martyr Basilides, who stops to offer a passing kindness to a Christian maiden who has had rough treatment from a jeering crowd (Eusebius, *Hist. eccl.* 6.5); the story is also found in the *Lausiac History* of Palladius, who heard the story from Isidore of Alexandria, who in turn claimed to have heard it from St. Antony himself.[30] But sometimes the crowd itself is the proxy and takes pity on the martyr heroine. Thus the crowd in the Martyrdom of Carpus, Papylus, and Agathonike calls out to her to have pity on herself and her children, and wails all the more furiously at her execution when she is stripped for burning and her striking physical beauty is fully revealed.[31]

In principle, tales of Christian heroic suffering were meant to be far more ethically demanding in return for the visual and emotional stimulation. Augustine makes this much clear in a sermon on the feast day of St. Cyprian:

> modo legebatur passio beati Cypriani: aure audiebamus, mente spectabamus, certamen videbamus, periclitanti quodammodo timebamus, sed dei adiutorium sperabamus. Denique vultis nosse cito, quid intersit inter spectacula nostra et theatrica? Nos, quantum in nobis viget sana mens, martyres, quos spectamus, cupimus imitari.

The passion of St. Cyprian has just been read. We heard it with our ears, we watched it in our minds, we saw him struggling, we feared somehow for him in his danger, but we trusted in the help of God. Do you then want to know in brief what the difference is between our spectacles and

---

30. Discussion in Herbert Musurillo, *Acts of the Christian Martyrs* (Oxford: Clarendon, 1972), xxvii–xxviii.

31. Martyrdom of Carpus, Papylus and Agathonike 6; see Musurillo, *Acts of the Christian Martyrs*, 22–37.

theatrical spectacles? We, in as much as a sane mind flourishes in us, want to imitate the martyrs we watch.[32]

In his discussion of *Peristephanon* 9, Tobin Sieber draws a firm contrast between the classicizing Prudentius and Augustine's emphasis on the ethical:

> Tearful Prudentius, abased before the martyr's picture, is … representing himself in the authoritative physical and mental position for a Christian. Augustine … offers a very different version of reading a saint's story…. He attacks "base curiosity, empty desire of the eyes, greed for trivial spectacles" (3), which he opposes to the glorious narratives of the Church.[33]

Building on the work of Michael Roberts, Sieber reads Prudentius's emphasis on his own sensitivity to the martyr's suffering as ironic play with the rhetorical profession shared by the poet and the martyr, extending a narrative parallel between the pupils' writing on the martyr's body and the poet's own act of writing.

Here Prudentius engages in an act of ethical response worthy of Augustine: writing itself has become an act of self-transformation.[34] Or perhaps it always had been: the efforts of the *rhetor* had always pointed toward a transformative act of the imagination. In conjuring an image that could capture the marriage between logic and emotion, the *rhetor* not only moved his audience; he reinvented himself. This was not merely illusion— though it was also that. At its most powerful, the rhetorical art was a way of revealing a deeper truth. All were agreed that a rhetorical gift could draw a man out of obscurity and into a conversation with emperors and even gods.

---

32. Augustine, *Sermo Denis* 14, cited in Tobin Siebers, *The Body Aesthetic: From Fine Art to Body Modification* (Ann Arbor: University of Michigan Press, 2000), 65–66.

33. Sieber, *Body Aesthetic*, 66. Sieber's discussion of *Peristephanon* 9 is at 64–69.

34. Derek Krueger has explored the problem of writing and self-transformation for Gregory Nazianzen and others among Prudentius's Greek contemporaries in *Writing and Holiness: The Practice of Authorship in the Early Christian East* (Philadelphia: University of Pennsylvania Press, 2004).

4. Conclusion

Pain played a central role in this process of making and unmaking the self, and the martyr was its avatar.[35] The memory of suffering would emerge, at the end of antiquity, as a priceless form of cultural capital. Not only the sufferings of the martyrs but the battle of the desert fathers against the demons of temptation, sleeplessness, and even thirst would become the touchstone of moral authority for a leadership who would carry Christian ideals forward into a post-Roman future.[36]

But Cassian's fierce pupils are not so much an instance of a specifically Christian rhetoric as they are a reminder of how the literate culture of the Latin West had found a way to accommodate Christian preoccupations without abandoning its frame of reference. Here the martyr's pain is the pain of teachers who wrestle with the attention spans of bored and distracted pupils, and the ferocity of the persecutors is an outpouring of the resentment that pupils have felt toward their teachers since the beginning of time. These observations are offered with a dose of irony, but at the same time they reflect the sobering insight that everyday resentments can be instrumentalized by the powerful. Literate Christians of the late fourth century knew all too well that students can be turned against their teachers, yet theirs was an age in which increasingly it was pagan teachers, not Christians, who found themselves vulnerable to this kind of rage. In other words, within the arc of Christian apologetic, Prudentius may have wanted to encourage sympathy for colleagues who found themselves excluded by the requirements of Christian theocracy.

Bibliography

Bennett, Camille. "The Conversion of Vergil: The Aeneid in Augustine's Confessions." *REAug* 34 (1988): 47–69.

Brakke, David. *Demons and the Making of the Monk: Spiritual Combat in Early Christianity.* Cambridge: Harvard University Press, 2006.

Burrus, Virginia. "Reading Agnes: The Rhetoric of Gender in Ambrose and Prudentius." *JECS* 3 (1995): 25–46.

---

35. Maureen Tilley, "The Ascetic Body and the (Un)making of the World of the Martyr," *JAAR* 59 (1991): 467–79; Cooper, "Voice of the Victim."

36. Conrad Leyser, "The Uses of the Desert in the Sixth-Century West," *CHRC* 86 (2006): 113–34.

Clover, Carol. *Men, Women, and Chainsaws: Gender and the Modern Horror Film*. Princeton: Princeton University Press, 1992.

Conybeare, Catherine. "Sanctum, lector, percense uolumen: Snakes, Readers, and the Whole Text in Prudentius' Hamartigenia." Pages 225–40 in *The Early Christian Book*. Edited by W. Klingshirn and L. Safran. Washington, DC: Catholic University of America Press, 2007.

Cooper, Kate. "The Bride of Christ, the 'Male Woman,' and the Female Reader in Late Antiquity." Pages 529–44 in *Oxford Handbook of Women and Gender in Medieval Europe*. Edited by Judith Bennett and Ruth Mazo Karras. New York: Oxford University Press, 2013.

———. "Closely Watched Households: Visibility, Exposure, and Private Power in the Roman Domus." *Past and Present* 197 (2007): 3–33.

———. "Family, Dynasty, and Conversion in the Roman Gesta Martyrum." Pages 273–81 in *Zwischen Niederschrift und Wiederschrift: Frühmittelalterliche Hagiographie und Historiographie im Spannungsfeld von Kompendienüberlieferung und Editionstechnik*. Edited by Maximilian Diesenberger. Vienna: Verlag der Österreichischen Akademie der Wissenschaften, 2010.

———. "A Father, a Daughter, and a Procurator: Authority and Resistance in the Prison Memoir of Perpetua of Carthage." *G&H* 23 (2011): 686–703.

———. "Love and Belonging, Loss and Betrayal in the Confessions." Pages 69–86 in *A Companion to Augustine*. Edited by Mark Vessey. Oxford: Wiley-Blackwell, 2012.

———. "Ventriloquism and the Miraculous: Conversion, Preaching, and the Martyr Exemplum in Late Antiquity." Pages 22–45 in *Signs, Wonders, and Miracles*. Edited by Kate Cooper and Jeremy Gregory. SCH 41. Woodbridge, UK: Boydell & Brewer, 2005.

———. "The Voice of the Victim: Gender, Representation, and Early Christian Martyrdom." *BJRL* 80 (1998): 147–57.

Elsner, Jaš. *Roman Eyes: Visuality and Subjectivity in Art and Text*. Princeton: Princeton University Press, 2007.

Evagrius of Pontus. *Talking Back: A Monastic Handbook for Combating Demons*. Translated by David Brakke. Collegeville, MN: Cistercian Press, 2009.

Francis, James A. *Subversive Virtue: Asceticism and Authority in the Second-Century Pagan World*. University Park: Pennsylvania State University Press, 1995.

Fredrick, David. "Beyond the Atrium to Ariadne: Erotic Painting and Visual Pleasure in the Roman House." *ClAnt* 14 (1995): 266–87.

Fux, Pierre-Yves. *Les sept Passions de Prudence (Peristephanon 2.5.9.11– 14): Introduction générale et commentaire.* Fribourg: Éditions Universitaires, 2003.

Gleason, Maud W. *Making Men: Sophists and Self-Presentation in Ancient Rome.* Princeton: Princeton University Press, 1995.

Gunderson, Erik. *Staging Masculinity: The Rhetoric of Performance in the Roman World.* Ann Arbor: University of Michigan Press, 2000.

Haines-Eitzen, Kim. *Guardians of Letters: Literacy, Power, and the Transmitters of Early Christian Literature.* New York: Oxford University Press, 2000.

Joshel, Sandra. "The Body Female and the Body Politic: Livy's Lucretia and Verginia." Pages 112–30 in *Pornography and Representation in Greece and Rome.* Edited by Amy Richlin. Oxford: Oxford University Press, 1991.

Kaster, Robert A. *Guardians of Language: The Grammarian and Society in Late Antiquity.* Berkeley: University of California Press, 1988.

Koloski-Ostrow, Ann Olga. "Violent Stages in Two Pompeian Houses: Imperial Taste, Aristocratic Response, and Messages of Male Control." Pages 243–66 in *Naked Truths: Women, Sexuality, and Gender in Classical Art and Archaeology.* Edited by Koloski-Ostrow and Claire L. Lyons. London: Routledge, 1997.

Krueger, Derek. *Writing and Holiness: The Practice of Authorship in the Early Christian East.* Philadelphia: University of Pennsylvania Press, 2004.

Levine, Linda J., and Robin S. Edelstein. "Emotion and Memory Narrowing: A Review and Goal-Relevance Approach." *Cognition & Emotion* 23 (2009): 833–75.

Leyser, Conrad. "The Uses of the Desert in the Sixth-Century West." *CHRC* 86 (2006): 113–34.

Maier, Harry O. "Staging the Gaze: Early Christian Apocalypses and Narrative Self-Representation." *HTR* 90 (1997): 131–54.

Malamud, Martha. "Making a Virtue of Perversity: Prudentius and Classical Poetry." Pages 274–98 in vol. 2 of *The Imperial Muse: Ramus Essays on Roman Literature of the Empire.* Edited by A. J. Boyle. Victoria, Australia: Aureal, 1990.

Morales, Helen. "The Torturer's Apprentice: Parrhasius and the Limits of Art." Pages 182–209 in *Art and Text in Roman Culture.* Edited by Jaš Elsner. Cambridge: Cambridge University Press, 1996.

Mulvey, Laura. "Afterthoughts on 'Visual Pleasure and Narrative Cinema' Inspired by Duel in the Sun." Pages 139–51 in *Popular Fiction: Technology, Ideology, Production, Reading*. Edited by T. Bennett. London: Routledge, 1990.

———. "Visual Pleasure and Narrative Cinema." *Screen* 16 (1975): 6–18.

Musurillo, Herbert. *Acts of the Christian Martyrs*. Oxford: Clarendon, 1972.

Plass, Paul. *The Game of Death in Ancient Rome: Arena Sport and Political Suicide*. Madison: University of Wisconsin Press, 1995.

Pollini, John. "Slave-Boys for Sexual and Religious Service: Images of Pleasure and Devotion." Pages 149–66 in *Flavian Rome: Culture, Image, Text*. Edited by A. Boyle and W. Dominik. Leiden: Brill, 2003.

Roberts, Michael. *The Jeweled Style: Poetry and Poetics in Late Antiquity*. Ithaca, NY: Cornell University Press, 1989.

———. *Poetry and the Cult of the Martyrs: The Liber Peristephanon of Prudentius*. Ann Arbor: University of Michigan Press, 1993.

Saller, Richard P. "The Hierarchical Household in Roman Society: A Study of Domestic Slavery." Pages 112–29 in *Serfdom and Slavery: Studies in Legal Bondage*. Edited by M. L. Bush. London: Longman, 1996.

Severy-Hoven, Beth. "Master Narratives and the Wall Painting of the House of the Vettii, Pompeii." *G&H* 24 (2012): 540–80.

Siebers, Tobin. *The Body Aesthetic: From Fine Art to Body Modification*. Ann Arbor: University of Michigan Press, 2000.

Thompson, H. J., trans. *Prudentius*. 2 vols. LCL. London: Heinemann, 1955.

Tilley, Maureen. "The Ascetic Body and the (Un)making of the World of the Martyr." *JAAR* 59 (1991): 467–79.

Trout, Dennis. "Retextualizing Lucretia: Cultural Subversion in the City of God." *JECS* 2 (1994): 53–70.

Werpehowski, William. "Weeping at the Death of Dido: Sorrow, Virtue, and Augustine's Confessions." *JRE* 19 (1991): 175–91.

Woods, Marjorie Curry. "Boys Will Be Women: Musings on Classroom Nostalgia and the Chaucerian Audience(s)." Pages 143–66 in *Speaking Images: Essays in Honor of V. A. Kolve*. Edited by Robert F. Yeager and Charlotte C. Morse. Asheville, NC: Pegasus, 2001.

———. "Rape and the Pedagogical Rhetoric of Sexual Violence." Pages 56–86 in *Criticism and Dissent in the Middle Ages*. Edited by Rita Copeland. Cambridge: Cambridge University Press, 1996.

———. "Teaching the Tropes in the Middle Ages: The Theory of Metaphoric Transference in Commentaries on the Poetria nova." Pages 73–82 in *Rhetoric and Pedagogy: Its History, Philosophy, and Practice; Essays in Honor of James J. Murphy*. Edited by Winifred Bryan Horner and Michael Leff. Mahwah, NJ: Lawrence Erlbaum and Associates, 1995.

———. "Weeping for Dido: Epilogue on a Premodern Rhetorical Exercise in the Postmodern Classroom." Pages 284–94 in *Latin Grammar and Rhetoric: From Classical Theory to Medieval Practice*. Edited by Carol Dana Lanham. London: Continuum Books, 2002.

Sex, Suffering, Subversion, and Spectacle: The Feast of Saint Cristina of Bolsena

Nicola Denzey Lewis

I begin this tribute to Judith Perkins in Bolsena, a small Tuscan town in modern Italy. The townspeople have all gathered to celebrate their patron saint, Cristina, on the day in which Catholic martyrological calendars tell us that she entered heaven after bravely enduring a series of tortures as lengthy as they are ghastly. A great spectacle is about to begin, and Perkins—although far away and unaware that she is about to be "cited" (to use a term from another Judith: Judith Butler, this time)—will help us to think through what we are about to see.

Cristina has been venerated since the fourth century, and we recognize in Cristina's modern *passio* the broad outlines of a story familiar to those of us who work in early Christian and late antique martyrologies—a genre that, perversely, is still called Christian romance. Like her sisters within this genre, Cristina is young, beautiful, and stubborn in her Christian faith. Her pagan father, Urbanus—angered by his daughter's headstrong instinct for Christ—instigates the tortures that will end his child's life. Cristina survives being flogged, burned in a furnace, drowned, tortured on a wheel, assaulted by poisonous snakes, and finally shot through by arrows, in a narrative series of calamities that with each tour through a medieval or Renaissance redactor escalated in its sadism. Her body is mutilated; her tongue and her breasts are sliced off. Yet at the end of her story, the dead Cristina is miraculously restored, exalted, in heaven.

Perkins's work gave us new ways to think about bodily suffering, particularly in relation to narratives of martyrdom in the context of Christian self-fashioning within the Roman Empire. In the chapter titled "Suffering and Power" in her masterful *The Suffering Self: Pain and Narrative Representation in the Early Christian Era*, Perkins focuses on the tales of primarily female martyrs, particularly Perpetua and Blandina. She notes that Perpetua fulfilled the narrative trope of the "unruly woman," a woman who "refuses to bow to society's expectations."[1] Perpetua's rejection of her father's authority, in particular, subverted the Roman patriarchal system of power. But it was not merely her acts of verbal rebellion that spoke necessary truth to power in order to subvert it; Perpetua's (and Blandina's) suffering constituted a puissant self-fashioning that ultimately reoriented Roman society around different moral ideals—one forward-looking to heaven, drawn through our gaze fixed on the suffering (female) body.

It is with my own gaze fixed on Perkins's text that I come to Bolsena, to shift my attention to an annual reenactment of a young woman's suffering. Scholars of Christian martyrdom have a fondness for speaking of it as theater or spectacle.[2] While that may be provocative, what I am about to witness actually is both theater and spectacle, quite literally. The rules of engagement for theater are naturally quite different from the rules of judicial torture in a Roman amphitheater. Similarly, the late antique reader of a martyrological text responds from a different context altogether from a modern viewer of a martyrological text acted out in contemporary Italy. Many elements of both performance and text will come together here in Bolsena—the effectiveness of ancient tropes, the act(s) of suffering of Cristina herself, the story of a church made triumphant through that suffering.

I am interested not only in the poetics of Cristina's written *passio*, but also in its reception within a living, thriving community. Bolsena is unique in being the only place where an entire town comes together each year to enact a large-scale passion play devoted to a female martyr. Bolsena prepares for months to create a series of *tableaux vivants* bringing her narrative to life. Threading through the town are five high, curtained stages, one in each of the medieval *contrade* or neighborhoods. Each *contrada* selects a girl to play the role of Cristina. There are only three requirements:

---

1. Judith Perkins, *The Suffering Self: Pain and Narrative Representation in the Early Christian Era* (London: Routledge, 1995), 105.

2. See, most trenchantly, David Potter, "Martyrdom as Spectacle," in *Theater and Society in the Classical World*, ed. Ruth Scodel (Ann Arbor: University of Michigan Press, 1993), 53–88, although the use of the term in secondary literature on Christian martyrdom is endemic. See, for instance, Lucy Grig: "A victim requires a persecutor, pain requires agency: the stories told by Christians required violence, they demanded it, and they staged it." Grig, "Torture and Truth in Late Antique Martyrology," *Early Medieval Europe* 11 (2002): 324.

the girl must be between eleven and eighteen, she must have long hair, and she must be slim. To be chosen is an honor, and a girl may remain a Cristina for a number of years. Indeed, the year I witnessed the living scenes (2016), the youngest Cristina looked like a mere child—vulnerable and wide-eyed—and as curtains opened around her, there were whispered murmurs of "Guarda la bambina!" ("Look at her! She's just a child!"). The oldest Cristina—evidently somewhat of a local celebrity—was celebrating her last year in the role, and her final performance was roundly and loudly marked with shouts of "Brava!!" and wild applause.

Each *contrada* is assigned two tortures to depict—one for the evening of July 23 and one for the morning of July 24—and this changes from year to year, requiring new scenery, staging, and broad concept, all done in secret and finalized behind tightly drawn curtains.[3] But the aim is both thrilling spectacle and a certain kind of attempt at realism for Cristina's tortures; thus the scene of the martyr boiled in a cauldron involves real fire as Cristina stands stoically in an oversized basin amid dancing flames. Cristina being tormented by poisonous snakes involves real snakes, brought in from a local pet store and anxiously overseen by a snake wrangler backstage to ensure that the snakes are not harmed or overheated in the scorching July sun. There are elaborate, albeit cheap, costumes, lighting setups, and even pyrotechnics crews and cues. Each year, the townspeople aim to outdo themselves.[4]

On the evening of July 23, amid darkening skies, a celebratory Mass empties out from Cristina's modest Romanesque church. A procession of priests and altar boys threads its way out to the sound of hymns, brass band, and the crackle of firecrackers, as a medieval wooden effigy of Cristina herself, gorgeously adorned, is borne aloft on a bier, carried by the older men of Bolsena. The procession makes its way to the first stage, where at the moment she arrives, the curtains are swept back, and the effigy Cristina watches the live Cristina being tortured. In the first tableau, she is stretched on a Catherine wheel, flames licking her feet, the

---

3. Technically, there are eight tortures for ten scenes; the additional two scenes feature Cristina's baptism (at the hands of Christ and in the company of angels) and her exaltation to heaven.

4. The festival has not attracted any English-language scholarship. For an Italian study of this and other local religious festivals, see A. Achilli and Q. Galli, *Riti, feste primaverili e il Lago di Bolsena: atti del convegno tenutosi a Bolsena il 7–8 giugno 1986* (Viterbo: Cultura Subalterna, 1988).

blood from her body represented with billowing, slashed scarlet fabric. Despite nearly thirty townspeople on stage in elaborate costumes, nothing moves in the tableau save the dancing flames. Everything pauses, just for a moment, as wooden Cristina looks on human Cristina; the audience gasps and shouts, claps and sings—and then the curtain swings closed, and Cristina is carried on through the next spectacle, and the next, until she watches herself high atop the walls of the town's *castello*, the human Cristina peering down on a stage alive with writhing, shrieking demons. (The hellscape is the only tableau to feature movement and sound.) In the climax of the evening's festivities, Cristina—still high on the city wall—crushes Satan's head underfoot, at which point the tower above her erupts in a blinding white shower of cascading fireworks. The wooden Cristina turns away and enters a church, where she will spend the night before watching herself endure four more tortures the next morning, winding her way with her procession back down the hill and back into her own church. The festival concludes with a huge Mass in her honor in her packed church and an extravagant fireworks display that night over Lake Bolsena.

What to make of all this? Certainly the frank spectacle of a young woman's torture—so earnestly and vividly depicted by the Bolsenese—gives us fodder enough to think with. Many questions inevitably arise. *What* remains compelling about watching, reading, listening to, the torturing of ancient women within the frame of Catholic Christianity in the twenty-first century? What do readers, listeners, and viewers take from these accounts that remains central to their faith? What is the connection between Cristina and civic community or identity? What work does her suffering do in crafting a local Christianity? How do we think about bodies—specifically female, holy bodies—in this local, living context? Finally, what is to be said about the power of spectacle, and the very curious way in which Cristina's ancient narrative is staged in the twenty-first century? This passion play not only brings to life an ancient trope of the suffering virgin; it also interprets it—and does so through a complex set of social maneuvers that involve the gaze, the eroticization of violence, the co-optation of power reconstellated in the face of female suffering. It also reinterprets female suffering through modern Italian social values, which sometimes stand directly opposed to those of the Catholic Church. This tension is manifest in Bolsena's striking performances, such that the annual staging of her *passio* within a civic context produces a densely complex set of visual negotiations between civic and ecclesiastical power, domestic and civic power, and (finally) gendered notions of power.

But first, let us examine who Cristina ostensibly was and what happens to her legend as it passes through the hands of redactors and readers.

On Cristina

The late antique Mediterranean martyr Cristina's connection to Bolsena appears to rest on a curious coincidence, in that Bolsena was once known by the Italian name Tiro (Tyre). Thus Cristina, originally associated with the eastern Mediterranean city of Tyre in modern Lebanon, became, at some point, Cristina of Bolsena. With Cristina of Tyre's identity as Cristina of Tiro/Bolsena well entrenched by the early modern period, nineteenth-century excavations searching for her grave beneath the town's main church began in earnest. Within the town's late antique catacombs, dug into the volcanic soil, Catholic excavators rejoiced in finding Cristina's body.[5] It was quickly exhumed with great ceremony, and a proper tomb constructed for her at the mouth of the catacombs. At her annual festival, her remains are placed on display at the main altar—crumbling, brown fragments of human decay.[6]

The first literary attestation for Cristina's life derives from a papyrus fragment from Oxyrhynchus, probably dating to the fifth century.[7] A Latin *acta* (Codex Farfense 29) dating from the ninth or tenth century fills out her story.[8] There, Cristina's sole love for Jesus in the face of pagan worship around her earns her the enmity of her father, Urbanus, who orders that his daughter should be tied to a wheel with a fire ignited beneath it. Cristina's prayer for salvation results in the spectacular spread of the fire outward, burning fifteen hundred people (men?) assembled to watch her torture. After she descends unharmed from the wheel, her irate father orders her seized and brought before a tribunal.

---

5. See the account of Giovanni Battista De Rossi's and James Stevenson's discovery of Cristina's tenth-century tomb and adjacent catacomb in Carlo Carletti and Vincenzo Fiocchi Nicolai, *Die Katakombe von der Heiligen Christine in Bolsena* (Vatican City: Pontifical Commissione di Archeologia Sacra, 1989).

6. These relics come from the catacombs, but there are relics of Cristina scattered throughout Europe and beyond from the medieval relic trade. The Cathedral of Saint John the Evangelist in Cleveland supposedly owns a reliquary containing Cristina's whole skeleton, a gift from Pope Pius XI in 1928.

7. Marcello Moscani, *Cristina di Bolsena Culto e Iconographia* (Bolsena: Parroco della Basilica di Santa Cristina, 2002), 15.

8. Moscani, *Cristina di Bolsena Culto e Iconographia*, 15.

Eighth-century abbot Aldhelm of Malmesbury also recorded Cristina's story in his tractate *De virginitate*. It gives us additional details.[9] Here, Cristina's father (unnamed) is a military general in the city; further, he has his daughter well educated in the arts. Reacting to Cristina's tendency to be an "unruly woman," to use Perkins's term, he confines his daughter to a tower.[10] This Cristina ultimately dies after being struck through by two arrows, which remains her defining iconographic feature. Aldhelm's martyrology is also the earliest reference to the cutting out of Cristina's tongue.[11]

In a Greek martyrology of 1308, Cristina is identified, briefly, as a female virgin from Tyre.[12] After being tortured on the wheel, she is thrown into a lake with a stone collar around her neck. Again, Cristina's prayers are answered: her robes are transformed into purple raiment; a golden crown descends from heaven to rest on her head, and Christ himself on top of a cloud appears with his angels, baptizing Cristina and returning her safely to the shore. This narrative element of Cristina receiving baptism directly from Christ's hand remains the most stable component of her story. Her tortures, by contrast, shift from manuscript to manuscript, not increasing in number so much as betraying a textual instability that is reconciled ultimately only by the decision to consider each and every account equally true and equally significant.

Cristina's legend has not received much attention from modern scholars, but medievalist Larissa Tracy has recently outlined its elements within medieval English martyrological collections, where it enjoyed great popularity.[13] Tracy considers three recensions of Cristina's narrative: the Middle English *South English Legendary* (1270–1280); Jacobus de Voragine's thirteenth-century *Legenda Aurea*, literarily independent from the *South English Legendary* but present in nearly a thousand separate manuscripts in both French and Middle English before an English

---

9. Scott Gwara, ed., *Aldhelmi Malmesbiriensis Prosa de virginitate: Cum glosa latina atque anglosaxonica*, 2 vols., CCSL 124, 124a (Turnhout: Brepols, 2001).

10. For the "unruly woman," see Perkins, *Suffering Self*, 105 and *passim*.

11. This feature is already there in the Boesbrariense, Molsheimense, and Windbergense codices. See Hippolyte Delehaye, "Vita S. Danielis Stylitae," *Analecta Bollandiana* 32 (1913): 121–229.

12. Medea Norsa, "Martirio di Santa Cristina nel cod. Messin. 29," *Studi Italiani di Filologia Classica* 19 (1912): 316–27.

13. Larissa Tracy, *Torture and Brutality in Medieval Literature: Negotiations of National Identity* (London: Boydell & Brewer, 2012).

translation and printing by William Caxton in 1483 as *The Golden Legend*; and the *Gilte Legende* of 1438. Tracy notes that in all these recensions, Cristina consistently embodies an example of "vocal defiance and stoic opposition."[14] Tracy observes that Cristina suffers far more ordeals than her sisters in martyrdom Lucy and Agnes, speaking out against her tormenters with "eloquence and dignity."[15] Even as she is being boiled, for example, "her voice triumphs as she sings with the angels for five days."[16] Tracy notes, "For a female saint, whose role as a woman is traditionally one of silence, her speech elevates her above the society constraints of her gender but also voices opposition to the cruelty of pagan authority manifested in the repeated attempts to make her suffer."[17] She continues, "The judge Julianus commands that her tongue be cut out because it appears to be the root of her power, but significantly, that does not stop her from speaking."[18] This theme of the powerful female martyr who speaks out against her domination becomes the scarlet thread tying together English versions of Cristina's legend.

It is fascinating to compare Cristina's medieval European legends with the Bolsena plays. The medieval literary Cristina is far more of an "unruly woman" than we might suspect from watching the Bolsena Cristinas. In the medieval texts that Tracy presents, Cristina "taunts the men for failing in their strength and urges them to pray to their gods to sustain them in punishing her."[19] In the *Gilte Legende*, Cristina's father orders his daughter's flesh to be torn with hooks. Cristina feels no pain and, gathering up a chunk of her own flesh, throws it back defiantly at her father. Thus her father resorts to more and more violent efforts to force his child into submission: breaking her under a burning wheel, tossing her into the sea with a millstone around her neck, throwing her into an iron cauldron filled with burning pitch ("where she simply feels as though she '*shulde be rocked in a cradell as a childe*'"; GiL 72–73).[20] Her head shaved, Cristina is then sent to a temple of Apollo, where her very presence shatters the image of the god. Increasingly desperate to punish her, her father sends a snake

14. Tracy, *Torture and Brutality*, 32.
15. Tracy, *Torture and Brutality*, 43.
16. Tracy, *Torture and Brutality*, 44.
17. Tracy, *Torture and Brutality*, 43.
18. Tracy, *Torture and Brutality*, 43.
19. Tracy, *Torture and Brutality*, 41.
20. Tracy, *Torture and Brutality*, 41.

charmer with poisonous snakes, which turn on the charmer instead, biting him to death. Cristina's tortures, however, are not yet complete: her breasts are cut off, followed by her tongue. The Cristina of the *Gilte Legende* even takes her severed tongue and flings it at her torturer's face, "smiting [out] both his eyes" (*GiL* 90–95).

The medieval legendary Cristina, therefore, is continually locked in a power struggle with malevolent male authority figures, starting with her own father. Her tale is primarily one of particularly egregious domestic abuse filtered through a rather unconvincing—even suppressed—conflict between Christian virtue and pagan civic cruelty. Inasmuch as the drama between Cristina and her father plays out in the public forum, her torturers are hired by her father, and the (male) spectators of her sufferings are ultimately punished for their gaze—burned en masse or else literally blinded, as in the case of the torturer who cuts out her tongue.

Tracy speculates that the framing of violence in Cristina's medieval narratives away from an explicit setting of Roman, civic torture relies directly on the context in which these narratives were read in the Middle Ages, where the church in its zealous attempts to ferret out and punish heretics had become the new civic torturers to be feared in the public forum. The medieval texts all give us a particular Cristina: spunky, rebellious, learned, and above all vocal. To paraphrase Perkins (writing here of Perpetua), this "unruly woman" displays all the potentiality that Christian empowerment offered for subverting the social and political body of the Roman Empire.[21] Cristina starts, however, at the very heart of that social body: defying the *paterfamilias*, with his obsessive need to control his daughter's religious activities. With this drama as one with which her medieval readers (particularly female readers) might identify, the more dominant theme of hegemonic social power might recede into the background.

Like Perpetua, Cristina also acquires her considerable social power from her almost miraculous ability to endure protracted, even unimaginable suffering. Perkins writes, "Bruises, wounds, broken bodies, provided unassailable, palpable evidence of realized power. But Christian discourse reverses this equation and thus redefines some of the most basic signifiers in any culture—the body, pain, and death."[22] Perkins's insight

---

21. Perkins, *Suffering Self*, 113.
22. Perkins, *Suffering Self*, 115.

is spot-on and useful for understanding why the anonymous author(s) of Cristina's narrative is seemingly so obsessed with account after account of her torture; her suffering is doing great work: recalibrating the core value system of society through the medium of a young woman's suffering. In the medieval iterations of Cristina's legend, Tracy proposes that Cristina's suffering reflects "cultural anxieties about legal procedures that permitted interrogatory torture" still active in medieval Europe;[23] thus Cristina's suffering similarly establishes the naming and overturning of patriarchal, hegemonic power. Of course, by the time we get to twenty-first-century Tuscany, we are dealing with a more irenic cultural context. Is Perkins's insight still useful? I believe it is, mutatis mutandis. More complex social forces are at work in the staging of Cristina's passion play in Bolsena—because the status of Christianity as a now-dominant cultural system stands in a different relationship to secular power, but also because a theatrical performance offers additional ways to mark or even subvert cultural or ecclesiastical norms as opposed to a literary text. Thus, I would argue that the Bolsena plays do not negate Perkins's insight but enrich it. Let us start with the simpler matter of the violence done, narratively and visually, to Cristina's tender flesh, in both text and performance.

Violence, Representation, and the Female Body

First, we must contend with the issue of historical reality—or more to the point, with the issue of Cristina's existence. Despite the "discovery" of her body in the nineteenth century, she is purely legendary.[24] In fact, the opaque nature of her martyrological pedigree has long since rendered Cristina not just a second-class Christian martyr but one who was struck

---

23. Tracy, *Torture and Brutality*, 32.

24. The tomb discovered by catacomb archaeologists dates no earlier than the tenth century; while there are late antique catacombs under the church, they exhibit no signs of a martyrium or privileged burial. There are also no funerary inscriptions from these catacombs that bear Cristina's name or which name her as a martyr. It must be said that the era of the famous catacomb excavator Giovanni Battista De Rossi, who conducted the excavations, coincided with a massive coordinated attempt of Catholic "sacred archaeologists" to uncover new saints' tombs in the turbulent period of Vatican I reforms (1869–1870) and the papacy's struggle against the rise of the secular Italian state. De Rossi was instrumental in the foundation of the Collegium Cultorum Martyrum, one of ten Pontifical Academies, and dedicated to the cult of saints and martyrs.

from the most recent recension of the General Roman Calendar in 1969 due to the lack of solid historical information on her. She remains in the official *Roman Martyrology*, but with only the terse information that she was a virgin martyr and is buried in Bolsena.

Cristina's martyrological account is not based on historical fact, then, but stems from a "series of master genealogies of martyrdom," as Lucy Grig aptly terms them.[25] These accounts were highly formulaic, following a pattern of abuse that quickly became standard. "While much of the strength of these stories came from their highly repetitive nature, predicated as they were on the fundamental model of the *imitatio Christi*," writes Grig, "martyr narratives also, inevitably, sought to 'outdo' each other with more impressive miracles and nastier tortures, to produce effective religious heroes in an era of intense religious competition."[26] In fact, all late antique female martyrs had their deaths elaborated and distorted within the male literary imagination. Their stories were extremely popular, "retold with gusto," and in the retelling, "horrors became more horrible, even as triumph over pain, decay, and fragmentation became more impressive and more improbable," as Tracy observes.[27] Male clerics and scribes created these virgin martyrs; they also progressively grew the grotesque details of their labored deaths—tales that reached a peak of grisly detail not in late antiquity at all but in the Counter-Reformation and again in the nineteenth century, when Cristina's festival began to assume the shape it has today.[28] The Counter-Reformation produced a spasm of grotesque paintings and sculpture of the tortured female body, sometimes rendered graphically, sometimes (less frequently in Italian Renaissance art) only hinted at through the reduction of the torture to a single small iconographic feature, such as Agatha's breasts held aloft on a plate or Apollonia holding her tooth with pliers.[29] Their tortures were

---

25. Grig, "Torture and Truth," 322.

26. Grig, "Torture and Truth," 322.

27. Tracy, *Torture and Brutality*, 38, quoting C. Bynum, *Fragmentation and Redemption: Essays on Gender and the Human Body in Medieval Religion* (New York: Zone Books, 1992), 269.

28. It is not clear when the passion plays of Bolsena were first performed; although they give the impression of originating in the Middle Ages, the earliest posters I could find for the event dates to 1817 and 1827. See Moscani, *Cristina di Bolsena Culto e Iconographia*, 182–83.

29. See Helen Hills, "Demure Transgressions: Portraying Female 'Saints' in Post-Tridentine Italy," *Early Modern Women* 3 (2008): 153–207.

well-known enough that the viewers of these images could quickly be led into a meditation on these virgin martyrs' suffering. No longer counter-hegemonic, these examples of suffering became important reminders of a key Catholic virtue for its own sake.

Late antique martyrological legend fixates on two elements: the purity and chastity of the virgin martyr's flesh, and men's strenuous and continuous determination to defile it. There is graphic sexual torture that cannot be rape (because that would destroy the martyr's prized virginity) but that instead takes the form of mutilation, usually of the breasts and often the tongue. These elements remained puissant into the Middle Ages, where martyrologies enjoyed a renewed popularity.[30] Historian Robert Mills writes of the medieval legends: "The saint's body is imagined in the throes of extreme sexualized violence—her breasts, too, are removed—while she simultaneously remains inviolate and sexually pure. This conveys an essential and ubiquitous hagiographic paradox: the juxtaposition of violence and virginal impermeability."[31] As Ambrose declared of Agnes already in the fourth century, "She both remained a virgin and obtained martyrdom" (*Virg.* 1.2).

The "pornography of power" (to use a term from Brent Shaw) that so clearly emerges from the stories of late antique saints such as Cristina, Apollonia, Agnes, and Agatha expresses and refracts troubling male anxieties of female despoliation.[32] Chastity is a virtue but a double-edged sword. Agnes's chastity is "good" inasmuch as she resists the punishments enacted on her by her male pagan adversaries—attempts to force her into prostitution and subjection to the male gaze—but it is also dangerous, in that it transforms her, as Virginia Burrus has said so well, from a virgin into a *virago*, a mistress of sexual continence who allows no domestica-

---

30. There is a wealth of outstanding scholarship. In addition to the work of Tracy already cited, see Beth Craciolo, "Female and Male Martyrs in the South English Legendary," in *"A Great Effusion of Blood"? Interpreting Medieval Violence*, ed. Mark D. Meyerson, Daniel Thiery, and Oren Falk (Toronto: University of Toronto Press, 2004), 147–63 (esp. 158); Jocelyn Wogan-Browne, *Saints' Lives and Women's Literary Culture c. 1150–1300: Virginity and Its Authorisations* (Oxford: Oxford University Press, 2001); Kathleen Coyne Kelly, *Performing Virginity and Testing Chastity in the Middle Ages* (London: Routledge, 2000).

31. Robert Mills, *Suspended Animation: Pain, Pleasure, and Punishment in Medieval Culture* (New York: Reaktion Books, 2006).

32. Brent Shaw, "Body/Power/Identity: Passions of the Martyrs," *JECS* 4 (1996): 273.

tion.[33] Cristina, similarly, not only uses her sharp tongue to "smart mouth" her father and her torturers, but even uses her severed tongue as a weapon: silenced, she directs her fury to blinding the male gaze by throwing it at her torturer. Cristina, too, is a *virago*. We see in the martyrologies of Agnes and Cristina, as with our other late antique female saints, refractions of men anxious about other men's gaze and their own loss of sexual power, played out in the wanton narrative destruction of women's lily-white flesh. Beneath it all, the ideal female saint must be *dismembered* as well as remembered. It is an unspoken rule.

There has been a good deal of excellent feminist scholarship on torture in late antique martyrologies; alongside Perkins, Burrus, and Grig, we must acknowledge also the outstanding work of Kate Cooper and L. Stephanie Cobb.[34] All these studies illuminate well the female martyr's deployment of social power through suffering, as well as calling out the apparent Christian scribal obsession with power struggles, articulated primarily through the virginal female body. One sees the shadow of Michel Foucault here in these contemporary insights into the interplay of bodies, discourse, and power. As Perkins writes, "torture ... although experienced as pain, is always intended to be interpreted as power."[35]

Yet at some point in our analyses Foucault may lead us astray. Foucault's pronouncements on torture ("a technique ... not an extreme expression of lawless rage"; "torture must be spectacular"; "in the 'excesses' of torture, a whole economy of power is invested"[36]) are useful when we think about actual judicial torture itself; but different rules apply when torture is merely a narrative trope. Elaine Scarry's work on torture in modern authoritarian regimes—much cited by scholars of late antiquity—similarly theorizes a historical reality, which is essentially and crucially different from narrative representation.[37] Thus an oft-cited article by Maureen Tilley analyzing

---

33. Virginia Burrus, "Reading Agnes: The Rhetoric of Gender in Ambrose and Prudentius," *JECS* 3 (1995): 25–46.

34. Kate Cooper, "The Voice of the Victim: Gender, Representation, and Early Christian Martyrdom," *BJRL* 80 (1998): 147–57; L. Stephanie Cobb, *Dying to Be Men: Gender and Language in Early Christian Martyr Texts* (New York: Columbia University Press, 2008).

35. Perkins, *Suffering Self*, 117.

36. Michel Foucault, *Discipline and Punish: The Birth of the Prison*, 2nd ed., trans. Alan Sheridan (New York: Vintage, 1995), 33–52.

37. Elaine Scarry, *The Body in Pain: The Making and Unmaking of the World* (New York: Oxford University Press, 1985).

Christian ascetics and martyrs, for instance, makes the error of failing to distinguish between constructed narrative and history. On the logic of torture, for example, Tilley writes, "But the torturers in the stories of martyrs—and in the present—still keep torturing long after these ostensible goals are achieved. Why? Because their real goal is not merely the control of an individual but the restructuring of society."[38]

We must be careful here. The torturers of Cristina's legend, as in other late antique martyrologies, have no real goal, because they are only flat characters. We must not attribute to them personhood and motives. That is, as feminist literary critic Mieke Bal has pointed out, to make the fatal flaw of confusing character with person.[39] The natural desire of feminist scholars (myself included) to give the victim back her voice in the phenomenon of early Christian martyrdom ought not to occlude a reality: the tortures that Cristina endures stretch the limits of our ability to take her narrative too seriously, at least as it lays claim to historical truth. Cristina's narrative is "full of improbabilities," as medieval historian Sherry Reames notes.[40] As she points out, others before her have had difficulties taking seriously this "collection of unconvincing and pointless marvels" and "childish fables."[41] I do not wish to be as dismissive as the nineteenth-century gentlemen scholars who made these remarks; at the same time, I do not think we are served by mistaking narrative for history. My goal is not to downplay torture as less than monstrous. Christian martyrs did exist, and documents such as the Passion of Perpetua or the letters of Ignatius give us insight into what they faced and what they thought. But Cristina's world was always fictive, illuminated through a host of manuscripts produced well after the time of persecutions was past. The shifting details of her tortures, along with their gradual accretion and fantastical details, should remind us that in her case, what ought

---

38. Maureen Tilley, "The Ascetic Body and the (Un)making of the World of the Martyr," *JAAR* 59 (1991): 468.

39. Mieke Bal, "Sexuality, Sin and Sorrow: The Emergence of the Female Character," in *Women, Gender and Religion: A Reader*, ed. Elizabeth A. Castelli and Rosamond C. Rodman (New York: Palgrave, 2001), 157.

40. Sherry L. Reames, "Christina of Bolsena: Introduction," in *Middle English Legends of Women Saints* (Kalamazoo, MI: Medieval Institute Publications, 2003), 223–25.

41. *The Lives of the Saints, Originally Compiled by the Rev. Alban Butler*, ed., rev., and suppl. Herbert Thurston, SJ, and Donald Attwater (London: Burns, Oates & Washbourne, 1932), 7:337–38.

to occupy us are determining the dynamics and social consequences of male, clerical fantasies concerning the female body, and male anxieties about its integrity, preservation, and inherent otherness.

Cristina on Stage

If we have some sense as to what the late antique and medieval authors/ redactors of Cristina's legend were about as they drew her character, we might now consider its placement in one specific historical context: Tuscany of 2016. The context calls for the legend's reinterpretation and for the reconceptualization of Cristina's body.

First, we might consider the strange hybridity of the Bolsena passion play. Is it a true theatrical performance or a religious ritual? Like medieval passion plays performed directly outside a church, the Bolsena performances uncomfortably straddle conceptual categories. The tableaux have meaning integrally tied to the Catholic Church; they are enacted under particular, ritualized conditions: annually on the same day, always outside the church, always involving a procession of deity and her clergy. The performances are marked at their initiation and conclusion by formal, special religious services. Cristina's martyrology and the Bolsena passion play aim for the same goals: verisimilitude, manipulating the audience's emotions, bolstering Christian faith. In these ways, the spectacle constitutes religious ritual.

At the same time, enthusiastic civic participation and the perforation of local identities into a sacred story make the passion play more theater than religious ritual. A clue is the Cristinas themselves, who are selected for their aesthetic appeal and visual homogeneity—purely secular considerations—rather than, say, because of their piety or displays of exemplary Christian behavior. Cristina is multiplied five times in the bodies of five adolescent girls, chosen not for their piety or attempts at purity but for their long brown hair and lithe bodies—embodiments of heteronormative beauty, at once sexualized and desexualized in their long, white, loose robes, soaked through with ersatz blood. Were this ritual, one would hope that the person in the center of the performance might have prepared differently, have been selected differently, and experience the rite as something more than several moments of standing still in a cotton shift in front of an audience. Or perhaps she does. I should not presume.

Perhaps the distinction between theater and ritual is a modern one, at any rate; theater and ritual were once entwined, at least in the ancient Greek context. In a provocative article, theater historian and theorist Rebecca Schneider ponders the difference. "In the theater," she writes, "as opposed to much religious ritual, one achieves 'suspension of disbelief' rather than, strictly speaking, 'belief.' Rather than achieving belief (Marlon Brando *is* Stanley and Stanley *does* rape Vivien Leigh who *is* Blanche), we achieve a facsimile, an almost but not quite. Not belief, but not not belief."[42] Perhaps this is useful for thinking through the Bolsena performances. Through the principle of the suspension of disbelief, these girls *are* Cristina, just as the tortures *are* real. The spectacles of Bolsena are not about belief, but (to paraphrase Schneider), they are also not not about belief. The power of the cult of the saints to shape Catholic faith and practice has birthed this performance and given it its visual and dynamic power, and yet, the spectacles take place on the street, in the neighborhoods, and not within the church. The *theatron*—the "place for viewing"—in Bolsena is a secular space that is penetrated, temporarily, by double instantiations of Cristina: the first through the still body of a girl, the second through the stiff wooden effigy of Cristina brought out of the church and into the *contrada*.

Yet despite Cristina's procession out of her church and the tableaux unfolding under her gaze, there is no question that we are witnessing theater, not religious ritual, because our suspension of belief never tilts into belief. There is no embodied ritual practice in this performance; the Cristinas woodenly act out their suffering from faked torture, and although a mythic time is evoked, no one falls headlong into it. If there are Catholic faithful in the crowd, drawn into an ancient and annually rehearsed narrative of the pathos of martyrdom and the torturing of a pure Christian virgin by evil men, they are invisible in the surging crowd calling out to their friends on stage, attempting to make them laugh.

I made the initial argument here that Perkins's analysis of the suffering martyr who co-opts and inverts social values through the power gained by enduring torture is incisive and useful, but that this modern performance in Bolsena takes us beyond what texts and the discourse of Christian martyrdom can achieve. If the church once controlled how to cite Cristina's body as an idealized performance of virtue and virginity, the power of this citation has waned for Italy's largely secular youth. We might consider

---

42. Rebecca Schneider, "'Judith Butler' in My Hands," in *Bodily Citations: Religion and Judith Butler* (New York: Columbia University Press, 2006), 234–35.

again, for a moment, how the Bolsena Cristina differs from the Cristina of medieval legend.

Let us return to Cristina's severed tongue. In the medieval legends, this mutilation signified the male mania for silencing an unruly woman. The tearing out of Cristina's tongue makes narrative sense in the medieval legends of silencing a mouthy girl, but in the context of the Bolsena play, where Cristina never speaks nor even seems to want to, that particular torture is rendered senseless. It is merely sadistic. Similarly, while the central drama in the medieval legends of Cristina center on her relationship with her father, the Bolsena scenes omit her father altogether. Missing is the hint (or overt depictions!) of domestic violence. On the one hand, perhaps this is a good thing: domestic abuse should not be normalized. On the other hand, one wonders whether the father is absent from this scenario just because, narratively (and hence, visually), Cristina bests him, and such behavior is not appreciated in modern Italian society. In the absence of the father character, Cristina has lost her unruly woman status entirely, becoming instead the model of feminine submissiveness. It is troubling, I think, that the Cristina of medieval legend was far more of a nasty woman, to pick up on modern American political parlance, than the Cristina of 2016. Are we really moving forward in terms of sexual equality?

Cristina's Festival and Secular Subversion

"The martyr *Acts* refuse to read the martyrs' broken bodies as defeat, but reverse the reading, insisting on interpreting them as symbols of victory over society's power," writes Perkins. She continues, "By rejecting that they experienced pain or defeat, Christians rejected the power structures surrounding them, and rejected the social order these supported."[43] Perkins is very right about these stories in their ancient context. Our Bolsena play, however, reframes the issue. The message is no longer the victory of the church made vicariously (and paradoxically) through the broken, suffering body of a young female. Cristina on stage still suffers, stoically, to symbolize the triumph of the church and the moral virtues it promotes. But the church of 2016 is differently situated; Italy's measurable move away from church attendance—particularly among the younger generations

---

43. Perkins, *Suffering Self*, 117.

(notably, those who participate most actively in the Bolsena performances)—reframes ancient Cristina's battle against the secular authorities of the state in a different light. In the particular stages of this legend, the town fights back.

As I have noted, the decision to render Cristina's martyr spectacle as a series of *tableaux vivants* stands in vivid contrast to her medieval martyrologies, where Cristina is characterized primarily through her forceful subjectivity and power of speech. Although the tortures remain consistent, Cristina in Bolsena shows no pluckiness, no defiance, and certainly no eloquence. She does not talk back; indeed, she comes across as a barely animate living doll—a voodoo doll, perhaps?—both mute and blind, unseeing. These human bodies, perhaps ironically, are more passive than Cristina's passing wooden body. They do not move; they remain fixed in their sufferings, expressionless, gazing out unblinking into nothing, while their flesh is tortured. The only virtue on display here is the endurance of pain, but it has no redemptive or transformative effect for society.

But we miss something if we focus solely on Cristina's body. It is only the center of the spectacle, and the periphery is just as striking. Cristina's dazzling white figure is framed, on these stages, by ordinary townspeople who dress as her visual counterpoints. The scene of Cristina's baptism, for instance, is offset visually by two dozen townspeople dressed in leather, spikes, and chains, with demon horns and tails. Hell, to the Bolsenese, looks like a New York City S&M club in 1984. Other stage scenes feature similarly scantily clad actors, in leather bustiers and gold lamé loincloths.

The frank embrace of eroticism in these scenes is perhaps their most startling feature. The eye is drawn not only to the beautiful young Cristinas, so chastely covered while they are being boiled or drowned or mutilated, but also to the bare-chested, tanned, and oiled bodies of beautiful young men who surround her. The men of the town prepare for their physical exposure by months of devotion in the gym honing their sculpted muscles, removing all traces of body hair, and wearing clothing that would ordinarily only be suitable at the beach. The men wrap their tattooed, muscled bodies onstage with leather straps and spikes; in further staged displays of homoeroticism, muscle-bound young men pull other men with dog collars and chains. In front of this cheerful, sexualized performance, the wooden effigy Cristina—visiting town from the sanctuary of her church—watches. Out in the world now, she "sees" the citizens of Bolsena as they would only be on the beach or, better, in the bedroom. During her festival, though, they parade on the steps of her church and before the saint's eyes. They have queered the festival, by complicating an already complex narrative with homoerotic overtones. One might ask: What does Cristina see? What pleases her? What draws our eye—Cristina's white robes, or the supple, nearly naked bodies of the male performers? Which gives us more pleasure? Where is our desire?

In her beautifully eloquent article on Agnes, Virginia Burrus notes that Agnes and many of her sisters are transformed through narrative from *viragines* into *virgins*.[44] Cristina, too, is transformed from a *virago* to a femininely docile *virgo*, just not in her medieval legends, but now. And why does this happen? Burrus reminds us: "It is the articulation not of female but male identity that lies at the heart of these texts' concerns."[45] In essence, the Bolsena plays hint at the same mechanism, *doubly instantiated*: overshadowing Cristina's figuration as the docile virgin (already a construction that favors male systems of power) are the exuberant displays of Italian masculinity that easily co-opt our gaze. Burrus, again: "I suggest we take careful note of the masculine self-representation of fourth-century Christian orthodoxy, recognizing further the distinctive assertiveness and ambiguity of the emerging Christian rhetoric of masculinity."[46] *Plus ça change, plus c'est la même chose*: in 2016 Italy, conceptions of social power no longer lie in rhetoric, or in chastity, or even in enduring suffering, but in the transformation of the male body that comes from dozens of bench presses. Onstage, as in civic life, masculine self-representation adumbrates the saintly Cristina. While the church dictates or oversees the key religious elements of the performance—the static narrative, as well as the display of chaste virginity as a key virtue—any positive moral lesson to be gleaned from a suffering saint is not only lost on its modern Italian audience; it is actively framed by the exuberant display of more secular values.

Cristina's festival is an interesting case of an ecclesiastical literary imagination refracted through the sensibilities of ordinary people. They do not reject the misogynistic violence of a text; to the contrary, they hijack it, turning it into a form of play. While this is absolutely a serious performance, it is also not: the crowd jokes and cajoles, attempting to break the serious demeanor of the silent, still actors, trying to make them move or laugh. In a civic, amateur performance such as Bolsena's, the individual

44. Burrus, "Reading Agnes," 26.
45. Burrus, "Reading Agnes," 28.
46. Burrus, "Reading Agnes," 29.

cannot ever be overwritten by the character she plays; she remains constantly recognizable as a person and not (just) a character. Casting features elaborate inside jokes: inversions or duplications of civic and theatrical roles; families participating onstage together as families or as enemies; lovers and neighbors and friends jumbled and juxtaposed. These social relationships, transformed into play within the passion performance, constitute a language that can be read only by the Bolsenese themselves.

In essence, Bolsena's spectacle can be seen as deeply subversive—not of the essence of social power, which remains resolutely phallic in its orientation, but of Christian moral power over the secular state; while it draws on the same power as true torture (the display of the real, writhing snakes, or the showing of Cristina's bloody tongue, held aloft by her torturer) to demonstrate the power of the state over the individual, it is also clear that this is all smoke and mirrors. The church, in essence, has little hold here: it controls only the base narrative of a tortured girl and her ultimate exaltation to heaven. In the hands of Bolsena's townspeople, a late antique hagiography becomes a wild spectacle of competing power, exuberant sexuality, and subversive play.

Bibliography

Achilli, A., and Q. Galli. *Riti, feste primaverili e il Lago di Bolsena: Atti del convegno tenutosi a Bolsena il 7-8 giugno 1986*. Viterbo: Cultura Subalterna, 1988.

Bal, Mieke. "Sexuality, Sin and Sorrow: The Emergence of the Female Character." Pages 149–73 in *Women, Gender and Religion: A Reader*. Edited by Elizabeth A. Castelli and Rosamond C. Rodman. New York: Palgrave, 2001.

Burrus, Virginia. "Reading Agnes: The Rhetoric of Gender in Ambrose and Prudentius." *JECS* 3 (1995): 25–46.

Bynum, C. *Fragmentation and Redemption: Essays on Gender and the Human Body in Medieval Religion*. New York: Zone Books, 1992.

Carletti, Carlo, and Vincenzo Fiocchi Nicolai. *Die Katakombe von der Heiligen Christine in Bolsena*. Vatican City: Pontifical Commissione di Archeologia Sacra, 1989.

Cobb, L. Stephanie. *Dying to Be Men: Gender and Language in Early Christian Martyr Texts*. New York: Columbia University Press, 2008.

Cooper, Kate. "The Voice of the Victim: Gender, Representation, and Early Christian Martyrdom." *BJRL* 80 (1998): 147–57.

Craciolo, Beth. "Female and Male Martyrs in the South English Legend-ary." Pages 147–63 in *A Great Effusion of Blood"? Interpreting Medieval Violence.* Edited by Mark D. Meyerson, Daniel Thiery, and Oren Falk. Toronto: University of Toronto Press, 2004.

Delehaye, Hippolyte. "Vita S. Danielis Stylitae." *Analecta Bollandiana* 32 (1913): 121–229.

Foucault, Michel. *Discipline and Punish: The Birth of the Prison.* 2nd ed. Translated by Alan Sheridan. New York: Vintage, 1995.

Grig, Lucy. "Torture and Truth in Late Antique Martyrology." *Early Medieval Europe* 11 (2002): 321–36.

Gwara, Scott, ed. *Aldhelmi Malmesbiriensis Prosa de virginitate: Cum glosa latina atque anglosaxonica.* 2 vols. CCSL 124, 124a. Turnhout: Brepols, 2001.

Hills, Helen. "Demure Transgressions: Portraying Female 'Saints' in Post-Tridentine Italy." *Early Modern Women* 3 (2008): 153–207.

Kelly, Kathleen Coyne. *Performing Virginity and Testing Chastity in the Middle Ages.* London: Routledge, 2000.

The Lives of the Saints, Originally Compiled by the Rev. Alban Butler. Edited, revised, and supplemented by Herbert Thurston, SJ, and Donald Attwater. London: Burns, Oates & Washbourne, 1932.

Mills, Robert. *Suspended Animation: Pain, Pleasure, and Punishment in Medieval Culture.* New York: Reaktion Books, 2006.

Moscani, Marcello. *Cristina di Bolsena Culto e Iconographia.* Bolsena: Parroco della Basilica di Santa Cristina, 2002.

Norsa, Medea. "Martirio di Santa Cristina nel cod. Messin. 29." *Studi Italiani di Filologia Classica* 19 (1912): 316–27.

Perkins, Judith. *The Suffering Self: Pain and Narrative Representation in the Early Christian Era.* London: Routledge, 1995.

Potter, David. "Martyrdom as Spectacle." Pages 53–88 in *Theater and Society in the Classical World.* Edited by Ruth Scodel. Ann Arbor: University of Michigan Press, 1993.

Reames, Sherry L. "Christina of Bolsena: Introduction." Pages 223–25 in in *Middle English Legends of Women Saints.* Kalamazoo, MI: Medieval Institute Publications, 2003.

Scarry, Elaine. *The Body in Pain: The Making and Unmaking of the World.* New York: Oxford University Press, 1985.

Schneider, Rebecca. " 'Judith Butler' in My Hands." Pages 225–52 in *Bodily Citations: Religion and Judith Butler.* New York: Columbia University Press, 2006.

Shaw, Brent. "Body/Power/Identity: Passions of the Martyrs." *JECS* 4 (1996): 269–312.

Tilley, Maureen. "The Ascetic Body and the (Un)making of the World of the Martyr." *JAAR* 59 (1991): 467–79.

Tracy, Larissa. *Torture and Brutality in Medieval Literature: Negotiations of National Identity*. London: Boydell & Brewer, 2012.

Wogan-Browne, Jocelyn. *Saints' Lives and Women's Literary Culture c. 1150–1300: Virginity and Its Authorisations*. Oxford: Oxford University Press, 2001.

Alienated Identity in the Acts of Thomas

Jennifer A. Glancy

The opening scene of the Greek version of the third-century Acts of Thomas finds the apostles gathered in Jerusalem, dividing the regions of the world into missionary districts.[1] Judas Thomas, also identified as Didymos, or twin, rejects his assignment of India. He argues that as a Hebrew he will not be effective in proclaiming the truth to the Indians. Even an apparition of the Lord (*kyrios*) fails to convince Thomas to accept his allotment. That is, until Thomas is sold to a traveling merchant by the Lord, who writes out a bill of sale: "I, Jesus, son of the carpenter Joseph, declare that I have sold my slave, Judas by name, to you, Abban, a merchant of Gundaphorus, king of the Indians." When Abban asks Judas whether Jesus is his master (*despotēs*), Judas affirms that Jesus is his master (*kyrios*), simultaneously accepting both his identity as slave and his mission territory in India (Acts Thom. 2).

From the outset, then, the Acts of Thomas focuses on *identity*, in multiple senses of the word. In its most basic sense, identity refers to selfhood or personal identity, what makes a person unique—what makes me me, what makes you you. From antiquity, musings about personal identity have extended to questions about spatiotemporal continuity, including such questions as how to account for persistence of identity from infancy through maturity into senescence. From Enlightenment philosopher

---

1. The Greek text of the Acts of Thomas is thought to reflect a text tradition as old or older than the extant Syriac text, the probable language of composition. My analysis is based primarily on the Greek text in Richard A. Lipsius and Max Bonnett, eds., *Acta Apostolorum Apocrypha*, 2 vols. in 3 (repr., New York: Hildesheim, 1990). English quotations are based on J. K. Elliott, "The Acts of Thomas," in *The Apocryphal New Testament: A Collection of Apocryphal Christian Literature in an English Translation Based on M. R. James* (Oxford: Clarendon, 1993), 439–511, a translation I have adapted.

David Hume's designation of the self as a bundle of sensations to queer theorist Judith Butler's interpretation of the self as performative, modern Western thought has plumbed questions of individual identity.[2] However, as contemporary philosopher Kwame Anthony Appiah argues, individuality cannot be sustained apart from collective identity—"the idea of identity already has built into it a recognition of the complex interdependence of self-creation and sociability."[3] Academics have thus become additionally accustomed to writing about identity in terms of group affiliation or identity position, such as race, gender, and social status.

These competing senses of identity factor into my analysis of the narrative of the Acts of Thomas. My analysis is additionally informed by studies of the development of Christian identity in the first centuries of Christianity.[4] Particularly important are Judith Perkins's *Roman Imperial Identities in the Early Christian Era* and Judith Lieu's *Christian Identity in the Jewish and Graeco-Roman World*. For Perkins, the apocryphal acts "provide valuable sources to view how Christians understood and positioned themselves vis-à-vis and in dialogue with other members of their complex and highly mobile society." Through such fictions, Perkins argues, Christians promoted their "cultural identity and position."[5] Lieu acknowledges key paradoxes, including the vexed relationship of corporate and individual identity—"separable, interdependent, or derivative one from the other"—and the tension between sameness and change inherent in identity formation.[6]

In the Acts of Thomas, constancy proves a greater challenge than metamorphosis. Arguing that early Christian writings construct Christian identity as racial identity, Denise Buell comments on the contemporary supposition that race is inherited and thus immutable within a per-

---

2. David Hume famously considers identity in *A Treatise of Human Nature*; Judith Butler introduces performative identity in *Gender Trouble: Feminism and the Subversion of Identity* (New York: Routledge, 1990).

3. Kwame Anthony Appiah, *The Ethics of Identity* (Princeton: Princeton University Press, 2005), 17.

4. Scholarly literature on identity in early Christianity continues to burgeon. These notes are necessarily selective. In addition to literature cited as immediately relevant, I have been influenced by Benjamin H. Dunning, *Aliens and Sojourners: Self as Other in Early Christianity* (Philadelphia: University of Pennsylvania Press, 2009).

5. Judith Perkins, *Roman Imperial Identities in the Early Christian Era*, RMCS (London: Routledge, 2009), 116.

6. Judith M. Lieu, *Christian Identity in the Jewish and Graeco-Roman World* (Oxford: Oxford University Press, 2004), 12.

son's lifetime. However, both ancient and modern treatments of race at times presume otherwise. Buell contends that early Christian racial logic depended on compulsory mutability, summarized by the dictum, "if one can change, one can or must change."[7] Buell notes that racial mutability might be conceived "as either evolutionary (one's essence being fully revealed or distorted …) or substitution (that certain factors fundamentally alter one's identity)."[8] The Acts of Thomas supplies instances of both.

Compulsory mutability suffuses the Acts of Thomas. As Lieu demonstrates, instability of identity is characteristic of the culturally complex situation of ancient Christianity. Shifting identities in the Acts of Thomas additionally play a strategic narrative role. Emphasizing the centrality of mutable identities to ancient fiction, Tim Whitmarsh writes, "Narrativity—the condition of narrative possibility—demands detour, deviation, difference." As a result, "Narrative raises the question of difference, both in terms of spatiality (travel is a metaphor for estrangement) and temporality (how does time transform us?)."[9] In the Acts of Thomas, narrative enactment of identity is volatile. Not only are characters within the story tripped up by the likeness between Thomas and his twin, Jesus—the reader is likely to be as well. However, as Thomas travels from Jerusalem to India and crosses boundaries including those of language, family formation, and social status, the text's insistence on acquisition of a Christian identity as the only route to authentic selfhood remains a constant.

In the Acts of Thomas, identity is both tested and expressed through polymorphy. The animal characters are unusual in that their identity does not shift over the course of the narrative. For human characters, identification with Jesus supplants corporate identification according to geography, language, race/ethnicity, social and legal status, wealth, and marital status. For the follower of Jesus, true identity is epitomized, not without ambiguity, as radical twinning with the *kyrios* Christ, a peculiar identity with alterity at its heart.

---

7. Denise Kimber Buell notes ethical liabilities to this position, as joining the new race is presented as precondition for full humanity. See Buell, "Early Christian Universalism and Modern Forms of Racism," in *The Origins of Racism in the West*, ed. Miriam Eliav-Feldon, Benjamin Isaac, and Joseph Ziegler (Cambridge: Cambridge University Press, 2009), 121.

8. Buell, "Early Christian Universalism," 115.

9. Tim Whitmarsh, *Narrative and Identity in the Ancient Greek Novel: Returning Romance* (Cambridge: Cambridge University Press, 2011), 254.

1. Corporate Identity

Appiah muses that the contemporary fixation on race and gender as sources of identity "reflects the conviction that each person's identity—in the older sense of who he or she truly is—is deeply inflected by such social features."[10] The Acts of Thomas complicates this conviction, highlighting a multiplicity of socially inflected identities only to downplay their ultimate import for personal identity. In the Acts of Thomas, the corporate identity that proves definitive is identification with Christ.

Geography and Language

It is widely agreed that the Acts of Thomas was composed in third-century-Edessa, a locale that Annette Yoshiko Reed argues shapes the text's distinctive perspective on the "ways local, regional, religious, and imperial identities took shape in interaction with one another."[11] How did the world look from Edessa, she asks, from a Hellenized city near the eastern border of the Roman Empire? Reed proposes that the literature associated with Edessa decenters a dichotomized view of the ancient world as divided between a clearly defined East and a clearly defined West.

Stress on the importance of language and place for racial/ethnic identity is especially strong in the opening sequences of the text, beginning with the opening scene of Thomas's sale as slave. In the Greek version, the merchant Abban and his newly purchased slave embark from Jerusalem, a peculiar detail given the absence of navigable water there. The Syriac version stresses the importance of place for identity when the bill of sale identifies Jesus with reference to place—"from the village of Bethlehem, which is in Judea" (Acts Thom. 2). Although the Acts of Thomas trades on the importance of place for identity, little concern is evinced for getting geographic details right.[12] One detail that has attracted considerable

---

10. Appiah, *Ethics of Identity*, 65.

11. Annette Yoshiko Reed, "Beyond the Land of Nod: Syriac Images of Asia and the Historiography of 'the West,'" *HR* 49 (2009): 50–51.

12. So James F. McGrath, "History and Fiction in the *Acts of Thomas*: The State of the Question," *JSP* 17 (2008): 297–311. McGrath offers a more defensible assessment than Reed, who writes that the representation of India in the text is characterized by "verisimilitude … unmatched by its Greek and Latin counterparts" ("Beyond the Land of Nod," 64).

scholarly attention is the name of the king who authorizes the purchase of Thomas. In the search for the historical Gundaphorus, pride of place is given to suggestive numismatic evidence seeming to substantiate the claim that Gundaphorus was a Parthian king in northern India.[13]

More important than scattered references to proper names or vague knowledge of multiple kingdoms in India is the text's insistence on the difficulties a native speaker of a Semitic language from the Levant might encounter in communicating with Indians. Oddly, once the apostle arrives in India, the issue of language recedes. The last scene in which linguistic competence figures at the level of plot takes place en route to India, in a city called Andrapolis, where the apostle is first called "a stranger, a man coming from a foreign land" (4). The apostle encounters a Hebrew flute girl who plays a pivotal role in his project of evangelization.[14] When Thomas prophesies the imminent destruction of a cupbearer who has arbitrarily struck him, the flute girl is the only one who understands his words, spoken in Hebrew, and thus the only one to appreciate that prophecy has been fulfilled when the cupbearer is immediately killed by a lion and ripped apart by dogs. She spreads the word about Thomas's prophecy, a report quickly reaching the king's ears and catalyzing conversion of the king's household.[15]

Gary Reger notes the irony that although Thomas cites his Hebrew identity as a reason not to accept a mission to India, that very identity is essential to this inaugural instance of evangelization.[16] Reger cites the flute girl's connection with a fellow Hebrew as an instance of the kinds of mundane social networking integral to the narrative world of the Acts of Thomas—"social strands of connection by virtue of family, class, occupation, ethnicity, language, and social position."[17] For Reger, there is a larger irony that Thomas's preaching relativizes the very social networks enabling the success of his mission "in favour of a radically different kind

---

13. McGrath, "History and Fiction," 299–301; Reed, "Beyond the Land of Nod," 63–64.

14. Gary Reger, "On the Road to India with Apollonius of Tyana and Thomas the Apostle," *Mediterranean Historical Review* 22 (2007): 263.

15. Andrew S. Jacobs's suggestion that the king is "catechized by his (former?) slave-girl" stretches the textual evidence. See Jacobs, "A Family Affair: Marriage, Class, and Ethics in the Apocryphal Acts of the Apostles," *JECS* 7 (1999): 137.

16. Reger, "On the Road to India," 259.

17. Reger, "On the Road to India," 266.

of network whose nodes were, in some ultimate sense, not on earth, but in heaven."[18]

Although as a travel narrative the Acts of Thomas draws the reader's attention to the role of geography and language in constituting racial/ethnic identity, such identity turns out to be of passing importance in relation to a true identity contingent on relationship to Christ. Social definition of identity remains relevant to the narrative of the Acts of Thomas, but the text is less concerned with the otherness or strangeness of Indians than with the otherness or strangeness of the apostle, whose identity as foreign/strange/Hebrew serves as trope for the otherness/strangeness of an earthly sojourn for anyone whose destiny is heavenly, an otherness expressed simultaneously in terms of a migrant social identity and in terms of polymorphy and twinship.

Gender, Family, and Sex

Just as the apostle discovers his true identity in relationship to his Lord, so too do those he evangelizes, a process seen with elite converts who reject social identities defined through marriage, family ties, and reproduction.[19] Again, the Acts of Thomas calls attention to social identity only to redefine identity in terms of relationship with Christ.

The first to repudiate "filthy intercourse" (Acts Thom. 12) are the daughter of the king of Andrapolis and her bridegroom, whom the king has required Thomas to bless on the occasion of their marriage. After the apostle withdraws, the bridegroom approaches the nuptial chamber and sees his bride alone with Jesus, appearing as Thomas, already complicating questions of identity. Jesus clears up the confusion, at least in part, saying, "I am not Judas Thomas, I am his brother" (11). He then dissuades the bride and bridegroom from consummating their union.[20] Bride-

---

18. Reger, "On the Road to India," 266. Given that Thomas is enslaved, it is problematic to suggest, as Reger does, that Thomas benefits socially from "association with a merchant."

19. Richard Valantasis, "The Question of Early Christian Identity: Three Strategies Exploring a Third Genos," in *A Feminist Companion to the New Testament Apocrypha*, ed. Amy-Jill Levine with Maria Mayo Robbin, FCNTECW (Cleveland: Pilgrim, 2006), 71.

20. Of the episode of the nuptial chamber Jacobs writes, "A couple turns away from an upper-class marital union upon learning its moral deficiencies, and instead enters into a spiritualized marriage in turn subordinated to their new 'kinship,' in

groom and bride renounce their expected identities as husband and wife, the bride telling her father the king that she chooses instead a "different marriage" (14). She announces, "I had no conjugal intercourse with a temporary husband ... because I have been united to the true husband" (14). The bridegroom rejoices because through Jesus he has come to know his own identity, "to know who I was and who and how I now am, that I may become again what I was" (15).[21]

The second half of the Acts of Thomas is dominated by the apostle's interactions with Mygdonia, wife of Charisius, and other elite Indians who encounter Thomas as a result of Mygdonia's conversion. As Perkins notes, Charisius is "incredulous" that his wife would favor a poor and ugly man such as Thomas.[22] Seeking to dissuade his wife from her newfound attachment—which he perceives not as an attachment to Jesus but to the strange/foreign sorcerer Thomas—Charisius repeatedly invokes her identity as a noblewoman. He asks, "Why did you not observe the decency becoming a free woman?" (89). Even Mygdonia calls attention to her old identity when, preparing for baptism, she begs her nurse, Marcia, to have regard "for my liberty" (120). But the text overwrites Mygdonia's identity as elite woman with a new identity as follower of Jesus.

Charisius appeals to Mygdonia by citing his own high status, in explicit contrast to the low status of the stranger/foreigner he believes has captured his wife's heart—"I am far more handsome than that sorcerer. I have riches and honor, and everybody knows that none has such a family as mine" (116).[23] However, the one Mygdonia loves is not, as Charisius believes, the Hebrew sorcerer Thomas: "But he whom I love is heavenly and shall bring me also into heaven. Your riches shall pass away, and your beauty shall be destroyed" (117). Clinging to his princely identity, Charisius resists the kind of personal change the Acts of Thomas proposes as necessary for eternal life. Attempting to denigrate Thomas's masculinity, Charisius instead

---

which their 'brethren' could as easily be slaves as kings" ("Family Affair," 134–35). I am more hesitant than Jacobs to perceive social critique in the text.

21. My analysis relies on Richard Valantasis, "The Nuptial Chamber Revisited: The *Acts of Thomas* and Cultural Intertextuality," *Semeia* 80 (1997): 264.

22. Perkins, *Roman Imperial Identities*, 119.

23. Despite Charisius's jabs at Thomas, I agree with Helen Rhee's insistence that sexual abstinence is more central to the Acts of Thomas than rivalry between apostle and elite male. See Rhee, *Early Christian Literature: Christ and Culture in the Second and Third Centuries* (London: Routledge, 2005), 133–36.

diminishes himself by identification with a social status that is temporal and corruptible. Hence Mygdonia's verdict, "You are a bridegroom who pass away and are destroyed, but Jesus is the true bridegroom, remaining immortal in eternity" (124).

Legal Status: Slavery

The Acts of Thomas ironically highlights dimensions of social identity that are understood differently by readers and by characters in the tale. Seen as a stranger or foreigner by Indians, Thomas is a stranger in an alien world, his true home in heaven. Rejecting their roles as wives destined to perpetuate family lines, elite women redefine their identities through union with an eternal bridegroom. Thomas acknowledges that he is a slave and thus confesses his identity as slave of the lord/master (*kyrios*)—a slave who carries the price of his own redemption, already paid by the *kyrios* (Acts Thom. 3).

A talking colt draws attention to Thomas's identity as a truly free slave: "Twin brother of Christ ... who, though free, has been a slave, and being sold, has brought many to freedom, kinsman of the great race which condemned the enemy and redeemed his own" (39). In her article "Animal Voices," Perkins proposes that in the apocryphal acts talking animals represent "a Christian intervention in a wider cultural discussion taking place in the period about human self-understandings and identity."[24] In the ancient world, slaves were often dehumanized by assimilation to animals. In the apocryphal acts, Perkins suggests, "the speaking animal figures the innate ability of all those people society has constructed 'as if' animals."[25] In the Acts of Thomas, talking animals include not only the ass colt but also a serpent and a wild ass.[26] Perkins notes that when a wild ass develops a voice to challenge Thomas to perform an exorcism, Thomas recollects

---

24. Judith Perkins, "Animal Voices," *R&T* 12 (2005): 385.

25. Perkins, "Animal Voices," 389. I am more guarded than Perkins in my assessment of social critique in the apocryphal acts. Despite criticism of slaveholding, there are no expectations for slaveholders to free slaves or otherwise modify their behavior before joining the community. See Jennifer A. Glancy, "Slavery in Acts of Thomas," *Journal of Early Christian History* 2 (2012): 3–21.

26. Janet E. Spittler argues plausibly that the ass's colt and wild asses are "typologies of the human being, representing two models of the embodied soul." See Spittler, *Animals in the Apocryphal Acts of the Apostles: The Wild Kingdom of Early Christian Literature*, WUNT 247 (Tübingen: Mohr Siebeck, 2008), 222.

that Christ underwent a series of status degradations on behalf of humanity (80).[27]

The incident of the wild asses is immediately followed by the appearance of the elite Mygdonia, her curiosity leading her to hear the apostle. Borne on a litter by slaves, jostled by the crowd, Mygdonia sends for more slaves to beat back the crowd. Thomas offers a beatitude for those who are laden with burdens like "irrational/wordless [alogois] beasts, because those who have authority over you think you are not human like themselves" (83). As Thomas continues to preach, no one is more taken by his message than Mygdonia, who throws herself at his feet, saying that her way of life has reduced her to the likeness of irrational/wordless (alogois) animals (87).[28] What does it mean to be human, the text implicitly asks, implying that persons are animalized not by legal status but by sinful behavior, which has the capacity to reduce a person to a status even lower than that of a wild ass.

Mygdonia's husband, Charisius, conjectures that his rival Thomas may be a runaway slave (100), speculation recalling Thomas's initial resistance to a mission in India. Ironic focus on Thomas's identity as slave again surfaces during a period of imprisonment before his execution when King Misdaeus interrogates the apostle. Are you free or slave, asks Misdaeus, and the apostle identifies himself as a slave of one "over whom you have no authority." Misdaeus assumes that Thomas has run away. Thomas clarifies that he had been sold by his master to serve in India. Misdaeus asks, "Who is your lord [despotēs]?" Thomas replies, "My Lord [kyrios] is your master [despotēs], and he is Lord [kyrios] of heaven and earth" (163). The scene returns to the work's opening identification of Thomas as slave, an identification working throughout the narrative on two levels—as legal status, as indicator of relationship to his Lord.

Thomas and Jesus are figured as slave and lord/master, but also as twins. Indeed, as the twin of one hymned as assuming the form of a slave (Phil 2:7), Thomas must also be a slave, or so hints the wild ass in his address to Thomas—"Twin brother of Christ ... fellow worker of the Son of God, who, though free, has been a slave, and being sold, has brought

<hr />

27. Perkins, "Animal Voices," 389. See also István Czachesz, "Speaking Asses in the Acts of Thomas: An Intertextual and Cognitive Perspective," in *The Prestige of the Pagan Prophet Balaam in Judaism, Early Christianity, and Islam*, ed. George H. von Kosten and Jacques Reiten (Leiden: Brill, 2008), 275–85.

28. Perkins, "Animal Voices," 390.

many to freedom" (Acts Thom. 39).[29] So when an imprisoned Thomas gives thanks because he has become "a stranger and a slave … and a prisoner and hungry and thirsty and naked" (145), he has become truly the twin of Christ, who promised that his followers would see him naked and hungry and in prison (Matt 25:35–45). In the Acts of Thomas, this radical twinning is at once a constant threat to the apostle's identity on a spatio-temporal plane and the secret of his true identity.

2. Polymorphy and Racial Mutability

Scholarly discussions of social identities in the Acts of Thomas tend to shy away from attention to polymorphy, including the doubling of Jesus and Thomas; discussions of polymorphy tend to ignore the dynamics of corporate identity. I argue that the central exposition of Christian identity in the Acts of Thomas requires us to consider both social identities and the peculiarities of spatiotemporal identity exemplified by polymorphy and compulsory mutability. Those peculiarities include the radical twinning of Jesus and Thomas. Often considered primarily through the lens of Christology, polymorphy in the Acts of Thomas is not confined to Christ. I turn first to other instances of shape shifting and race alteration that offer distinctive perspectives on Christian identity. The Acts of Thomas likens acquisition of a Christian identity to metamorphosis, to deliberate choosing of one's own race, nature, or kinship.

The work of Thomas, purchased as a slave for King Gundaphorus, as a celestial carpenter for an earthly monarch occupies the first scenes set in India; the second half of the Acts of Thomas narrates stories of the circles around Mygdonia. In between, a cluster of stories returns in multiple ways to questions of identity: questions about what it means to have a true self, about beauty and the appearance of beauty, about whether genealogies are given or chosen, about spatiotemporal continuity, and of racial affiliation. The tales are characterized by compulsory mutability, to use Buell's phrase.

In the first of these tales Thomas confronts a serpent who has killed a beautiful young man (Acts Thom. 30–38). Recognizing Thomas as Jesus's twin, the serpent confuses the agency of the two: "I know that you are the twin brother of Christ and always reduce our race [or nature, *physin*] to

---

29. Monika Pesthy, "Thomas, the Slave of the Lord," in *The Apocryphal Acts of Thomas*, ed. Jan N. Bremmer, Studies on Early Christian Apocrypha 6 (Leuven: Peeters, 2001), 67.

nothing" (31). The man resurrected by Thomas likewise associates Thomas and Jesus in an especially strong way, implying that Thomas is not limited in space, complicating any simple sense of the apostle's identity: "For you are a man having two forms, and wherever you wish, you are found" (34).

In a parallel way, the text focuses attention on the identity of the serpent. Jesus asks, "Tell me, of what seed [*sporas*] and of what race [*genous*] are you" (31), then demands, "Show now the nature [*physin*] of your father" (33). The serpent locates himself as "son of him who sits on the throne which is under heaven" and "kinsman to him who is outside the ocean, whose tail lies in his mouth," taking credit for tempting Eve, inciting Cain, casting the angels to earth, hardening Pharaoh's heart, provoking Herod, inflaming Judas, and an impressive resume of other bad behavior. The serpent's identity is expressed racially and genealogically, but his genealogy has as much to do with deeds as paternity, his race a matter not only of inheritance but also of performance.[30]

The young man is caught between two possible genealogies, two possible races, two possible identities. He says that he has "destroyed that kinsman of the night, who forced me to sin by his own practices; but I found, however, that kinsman of mine who is the light" (34). In the apostle's response, it is clear that it is up to the young man whether he will ultimately choose to be kin to the night or to the light and that his identity—indeed his genealogy—will be revealed through his choices.

Another tale compounds the text's play with identity, physical (un) attractiveness, and compulsory mutability (Acts Thom. 42–50). A beautiful woman begs the apostle for help. For five years she has been the sexual target of a demon. When the demon first approached her she was already on an encratite track, refusing marriage. The demon first appeared as a troubled young man to the woman and as an old man to the woman's female slave. The woman was further disturbed when she realized the demon had appeared in two forms to her (43)—and then the nightly abuse began. The woman begs Thomas to free her so that she might return to her "original nature [*physin*] and receive the gift which has been granted to my kinfolk" (43).

Thomas decries the wickedness of the demon: "O hideous one who subjects the beautiful ones! Oh polymorphous one—he appears as he

---

30. The serpent's story is immediately followed by a tale in which an ass colt reveals his own genealogy. The colt's race seems as much a matter of deeds—a willingness to serve God—as of inheritance (Acts Thom. 39–41).

wishes, but his being [*ousia*] cannot be changed!" (44). The demon appears, visible only to Thomas and the woman, his voice apparently heard by all.[31] The demon in turn calls attention to Thomas's kinship with Jesus—"For you are altogether like him, as if you had him for a father" (45). The demon observes that Jesus had been deceptive in his physical form, appearing to be impoverished and unattractive in form.[32] Jesus's physical ugliness was a disguise, but the demon's ugliness is a clue to his evil nature. Having invoked the demon as polymorphous, Thomas goes on to call Jesus polymorphous (47). Spatiotemporal identity is thus threatened by multiple guises, guises that may either be *dis*guises or reveal true identities.

In a story in which a woman is restored to life (Acts Thom. 51–61), the apostle claims both that Jesus appears continually and that he is invisible to eyes, claims borne out by the woman's response to the apostle. On being raised, she asks Thomas, "Where is your companion?" (54), later referring to Jesus as the one "like you" (57). The tale she relays of her time among the dead features a frightening excursion to a place of punishment, guided by an ugly black man.[33] Viewing a place of fiery wheels, souls hung from the wheels, the guide tells the woman that the souls share her nature or race (*homophyloi*; 55). However, there is a contest over her soul, as Christ—recalled as the one who resembles Thomas—identifies her as a sheep that has strayed (57).

I turn in the next section to the implications of the many forms of Christ and Thomas, including their twinship. In the Acts of Thomas, however, polymorphy is not an exclusively christological category, as demons are similarly prone to multiple forms. References to the polymorphy of Christ and of demons appear frequently in stories highlighting choices human beings make regarding their nature/race and kinship, their affiliation, in a strong sense. These stories underscore the question of identity—who I am, who we are. Identity is revealed in change and in the choices one makes.

---

31. Rhee argues that Christ's polymorphy "corresponds to different levels of perception"—so, apparently, does demonic polymorphy (*Early Christian Literature*, 85).

32. Rhee suggests that in the Acts of Thomas the incarnation should be seen in the wider context of polymorphy (*Early Christian Literature*, 86).

33. There is also a later appearance by a demonic black man (Acts Thom. 64). Nonetheless, as the Acts of Thomas constructs race, blackness seems less salient than quality of one's deeds. For wider socioliterary context, see Gay L. Byron, *Symbolic Blackness and Ethnic Difference in Early Christian Literature* (London: Routledge, 2002).

Embracing an identity through affiliation with Christ may involve res-
toration of one's nature, as suggested by the woman who begs Thomas to
restore her original nature, or a repudiation of one's nature, as suggested
by the woman who affiliates with Christ after witnessing the torments of
damned souls who share her nature. In either case, forging a Christian
identity requires change.[34] I have argued that the Acts of Thomas calls
attention to dimensions of racial/ethnic identity, including place of origin
and language, yet ultimately implies that identity transcends such provi-
sional categories. It turns out, however, that kinship, genealogy, and race
are crucial to identity in the Acts of Thomas—but a kinship that is chosen,
and a nature that is an artifact of deeds.

3. Twinned Identity

The apostle refers twice to Jesus as polymorphous (Acts Thom. 48, 153),
a term he also applies to a demon (44), as we have seen. In the Acts of
Thomas Christ's polymorphous capability is expressed by his propensity
for appearing in the guise of his twin, Thomas, the apostle's second reference to Jesus as polymorphous even elicited by a report in which recent
converts mistake Jesus for Thomas (151–153). Scholarly discussion of
polymorphy in the Acts of Thomas importantly and appropriately focuses
on christological dimensions.[35] However, identification of Christ and
Thomas as twins additionally has implications for the identity of the apostle. The tropes of polymorphy and twinship are as important for notions of
Christian identity as they are for Christology.

Appearances of Christ as Thomas and Thomas as Christ trouble the
self-identity of both Savior and apostle. "I am not Judas Thomas, I am
his brother," says the Lord (11). "I am not Jesus, but I am his slave," the
apostle later instructs (160). The confusion is understandable. In several
instances, Jesus's ability to appear as Thomas gives him entrée to a setting
or allows him to intervene on behalf of his followers, such incidents creating narrative confusion as identities are sorted out, propelling the plot.

---

34. Compare Buell's analysis of racial change in terms of either evolution or substitution ("Early Christian Universalism," 115).

35. For varying approaches, see, for example, David R. Cartlidge, "Transfigurations of Metamorphosis Traditions in the Acts of John, Thomas, and Peter," *Semeia* 38
(1986): 66; Rhee, *Early Christian Literature*, 86; Paul Foster, "Polymorphic Christology: Its Origin and Development in Early Christianity," *JTS* 58 (2007): 67, 94.

For example, when the bridegroom of the daughter of the king of Andrapolis sees his bride alone with Jesus, he at first believes his bride to be in
conversation with the stranger Thomas (11). In another episode, Jesus
confuses even his twin when he appears as Thomas to usher Mygdonia
and other women into the prison where Thomas himself is incarcerated,
eliciting from the apostle the ejaculation, "Glory to you, polymorphous
Jesus!" (151–153).

However, not all references to the doubling of Savior and apostle
advance the plot. We have already considered the sequence of stories
in which Thomas rescues those under the dominion of demons, stories
that repeatedly muddle the identity of the twins. The young man raised
from the dead observes that Thomas—not Jesus—has two forms (34);
the demon who habitually sexually abused a woman likens the apostle
to the Son of God (45); the woman raised from the dead associates Jesus
and Thomas, even inferring that Thomas had protected her in the post-
mortem place of punishment (55). These episodes suggest that Thomas's
identity cannot be apprehended without coming to terms with his relationship with Jesus.

Finally, just as Jesus can appear as Thomas, so Thomas can manifest
himself as the Savior. Mygdonia is on her way to visit Thomas in prison
when he approaches her on the street. She does not recognize him, mistaking him for a prince, "for a great light went before him" (118), light
elsewhere associated with the presence of Jesus (27, 153).

David Konstan comments that the twins seem almost "conceived as
the mortal and divine aspects of a single self," a formulation catching the
degree to which the identities of both Jesus and Thomas are twinned.[36]
In her sweeping treatment of early Christian identity, Lieu proposes "a
rudimentary definition of identity, that it involves ideas of boundedness,
of sameness and difference, of continuity, perhaps of a degree of homogeneity, and of recognition by self and by other."[37] The most basic sense
of identity—what makes me me, what makes you you—is complicated
by the relationship between Thomas and Jesus. What makes Thomas
Thomas turns out to be his relationship to Jesus—as slave, as twin, as
other self. As a result, even the basic identity of spatiotemporal continuity is fraught. Both Jesus and Thomas are able to manifest themselves in

---

36. David Konstan, "Acts of Love: A Narrative Pattern in the Apocryphal Acts,"
JECS 6 (1998): 30.

37. Lieu, *Christian Identity in the Jewish and Graeco-Roman World*, 12.

multiple places under multiple guises. Throughout the work, Thomas is known as a stranger or foreigner, and he is, ultimately, a stranger even to himself. As Jesus's twin, Thomas's union with him is unique. However, at the same time, Thomas repeatedly leads those he encounters into their own unions with Jesus, a relationship clearing the way to discovery or recovery of true personal identity.

4. Conclusions

What does the Acts of Thomas contribute to early Christian understandings of identity?[38] Perkins argues that the apocryphal acts help us understand how ancient Christians negotiated cultural identities. We see this process of negotiation in the Acts of Thomas, as group identities are acknowledged and redefined—foreignness epitomized not by geographical migration but by alienation from the world, physical marriage rejected in favor of union with an incorruptible bridegroom, freedom figured as slavery to a heavenly *kyrios*. Lieu's analysis of early Christian identity foregrounds key paradoxes, including the vexed relationship of corporate and individual identity and the tension between sameness and change inherent in identity formation, paradoxes pervading the Acts of Thomas. Some passages imply that to become Christian is to acquire a new identity. Other passages imply that to become Christian is to restore an original nature. The tension remains unresolved, a narrative device rich with generative theological ambiguity.

In the Acts of Thomas, the Christian is a foreigner or a stranger in the world, but the Christian is equally *other* to himself or herself. True self-identity in the Acts of Thomas requires doubling, identification with a heavenly other. The otherness of Christian identity that surfaces in some other early Christian writings thus finds unique expression in the complex narrative of the Acts of Thomas, where self-identity is itself grounded, paradoxically, in alterity.

---

38. The so-called Hymn of the Pearl appears in one Greek and one Syriac manuscript of Acts of Thomas. Given both space constraints and the hymn's uncertain relationship to the prose narrative, I do not include analysis of the poem. I would argue, however, that the hymn reinterprets identity categories while exploring the concept of mutable personal identity, with memory emerging as an essential component of identity.

Bibliography

Appiah, Kwame Anthony. *The Ethics of Identity*. Princeton: Princeton University Press, 2005.

Buell, Denise Kimber. "Early Christian Universalism and Modern Forms of Racism." Pages 109–31 in *The Origins of Racism in the West*. Edited by Miriam Eliav-Feldon, Benjamin Isaac, and Joseph Ziegler. Cambridge: Cambridge University Press, 2009.

Butler, Judith. *Gender Trouble: Feminism and the Subversion of Identity*. New York: Routledge, 1990.

Byron, Gay L. *Symbolic Blackness and Ethnic Difference in Early Christian Literature*. London: Routledge, 2002.

Cartlidge, David R. "Transfigurations of Metamorphosis Traditions in the Acts of John, Thomas, and Peter." *Semeia* 38 (1986): 53–66.

Czachesz, István. "Speaking Asses in the Acts of Thomas: An Intertextual and Cognitive Perspective." Pages 275–85 in *The Prestige of the Pagan Prophet Balaam in Judaism, Early Christianity, and Islam*. Edited by George H. von Kosten and Jacques Reiten. Leiden: Brill, 2008.

Dunning, Benjamin H. *Aliens and Sojourners: Self as Other in Early Christianity*. Philadelphia: University of Pennsylvania Press, 2009.

Elliott, J. K. "The Acts of Thomas." Pages 439–511 in *The Apocryphal New Testament: A Collection of Apocryphal Christian Literature in an English Translation Based on M. R. James*. Oxford: Clarendon, 1993.

Foster, Paul. "Polymorphic Christology: Its Origin and Development in Early Christianity." *JTS* 58 (2007): 66–99.

Glancy, Jennifer A. "Slavery in Acts of Thomas." *Journal of Early Christian History* 2 (2012): 3–21.

Hume, David. *A Treatise of Human Nature*. London, 1738.

Jacobs, Andrew S. "A Family Affair: Marriage, Class, and Ethics in the Apocryphal Acts of the Apostles." *JECS* 7 (1999): 105–38.

Konstan, David. "Acts of Love: A Narrative Pattern in the Apocryphal Acts." *JECS* 6 (1998): 15–36.

Lieu, Judith M. *Christian Identity in the Jewish and Graeco-Roman World*. Oxford: Oxford University Press, 2004.

Lipsius, Richard A., and Max Bonnett, eds. *Acta Apostolorum Apocrypha*. 2 vols. in 3. Reprint, New York: Hildesheim, 1990.

McGrath, James F. "History and Fiction in the Acts of Thomas: The State of the Question." *JSP* 17 (2008): 297–311.

Perkins, Judith. "Animal Voices." *R&T* 12 (2005): 385–96.

———. *Roman Imperial Identities in the Early Christian Era*. RMCS. London: Routledge, 2009.

Pesthy, Monika. "Thomas, the Slave of the Lord." Pages 65–73 in *The Apocryphal Acts of Thomas*. Edited by Jan N. Bremmer. Studies on Early Christian Apocrypha 6. Leuven: Peeters, 2001.

Reed, Annette Yoshiko. "Beyond the Land of Nod: Syriac Images of Asia and the Historiography of 'the West.'" *HR* 49 (2009): 48–87.

Reger, Gary. "On the Road to India with Apollonius of Tyana and Thomas the Apostle." *Mediterranean Historical Review* 22 (2007): 257–71.

Rhee, Helen. *Early Christian Literature: Christ and Culture in the Second and Third Centuries*. London: Routledge, 2005.

Spittler, Janet E. *Animals in the Apocryphal Acts of the Apostles: The Wild Kingdom of Early Christian Literature*. WUNT 247. Tübingen: Mohr Siebeck, 2008.

Valantasis, Richard. "The Nuptial Chamber Revisited: The *Acts of Thomas* and Cultural Intertextuality." *Semeia* 80 (1997): 261–76.

———. "The Question of Early Christian Identity: Three Strategies Exploring a Third Genos." Pages 60–76 in *A Feminist Companion to the New Testament Apocrypha*. Edited by Amy-Jill Levine with Maria Mayo Robbin. FCNTECW. Cleveland: Pilgrim, 2006.

Whitmarsh, Tim. *Narrative and Identity in the Ancient Greek Novel: Returning Romance*. Cambridge: Cambridge University Press, 2011.

Ephesus, *Loca Sancta*:
The Acts of Timothy and Religious Travel
in Late Antiquity

Meira Z. Kensky

Introduction

At the beginning of her important study of the late antique practice of pilgrimage to holy people, Georgia Frank states, "The first step for any pilgrim lands not on the road, but somewhere in the imagination."[1] Before one hits the road, one hits the books or hears the stories. Stories about holy people and holy places proliferated and were even written to invite—or entice—people to visit. This essay argues that the Acts of Timothy was written in the fifth century CE as part of an attempt not only to revitalize the waning ecclesiastical fortunes of Ephesus but to affix this once-great metropolis, now in the shadow of Constantinople, firmly on both the literal and imaginative maps of potential religious travelers. By examining the details of this curious text, we can see how it establishes Ephesus as a critical place in the fabric of early Christian memory and even sketches out an itinerary for travelers who would visit the city.

By all accounts, the Acts of Timothy is a strange text. Not quite hagiography, not quite martyrology, not quite apocryphal acts, this short, difficult-to-date piece has almost no real content and, as such, has been largely ignored by scholars since the height of the Bollandist era. The text

---

A version of this paper, "Timothy in Ephesus? 1 Timothy, the Acts of the Apostles, and the *Acts of Timothy* Reconsidered," was presented at the Ancient Fiction and Early Christian and Jewish Narrative section of the 2015 Annual Meeting of the Society of Biblical Literature in Atlanta.

1. Georgia Frank, *The Memory of the Eyes: Pilgrims to Living Saints in Christian Late Antiquity* (Berkeley: University of California Press, 2000), 1.

itself, edited by Hermann Usener in 1877, exists in both Greek and Latin versions, with the Latin having some notable variations, including the superscription, which gives the author as Polycrates, bishop of Ephesus in the second century.[2] This past decade saw more interest in the text, as Claudio Zamagni produced a critical edition of the Greek manuscripts in 2007, and most recently Cavan Concannon published a new English translation of the text based mostly on Zamagni's edition of the Greek manuscripts, with some reference to the Latin.[3]

Following the introductory lines, which give the date of Timothy's martyrdom and an explanation of why the text is justified and valuable, the text basically consists of two main sections. The first, longer section (ll. 3–11[4]) goes into detail about the relationship between Timothy and John and how each came to be at Ephesus. The Acts of Timothy establishes Timothy as the first bishop of Ephesus and explains how John showed up in the city after shipwreck and arranged the Synoptic Gospels from a bunch of loose-leaf pages that the other disciples could not figure out how to put together, and then why he decided to write his own gospel based on the information that he "wiped off of the divine bosom" (ἐκ τοῦ θείου στήθους ἀναμαξάμενος), following which he was banished from Ephesus and exiled to Patmos.[5] The second section (ll. 12–16) details Timothy's death during the Katagogia festival, in which Timothy was beaten to death

---

2. Hermann Usener, *Natalicia regis augustissimi Guilelmi imperatoris Germaniae ab Universitate Fridericia Guilelmia Rhenana [...] Insunt Acta S. Timothei* (Bonn: Programm der Universität Bonn, 1877). Discussion of the manuscript variants can be found in Claudio Zamagni, "Passion (ou Actes) de Timothée: Étude des traditions anciennes et edition de la forme BHG 1487," in *Poussières de christianisme et de judaïsme antiques: Études réunies en l'honneur de Jean-Daniel Kaestli et Éric Junod*, ed. A. Frey and R. Gounelle (Prahins: Publications de l'Institut Romand des Sciences Bibliques, 2007), 359–64; see also Cavan Concannon, "In the Great City of the Ephesians: Contestations over Apostolic Memory and Ecclesial Power in the *Acts of Timothy*," *JECS* 24 (2016): 419–46; Concannon, "The Acts of Timothy," in *New Testament Apocrypha: More Noncanonical Scriptures*, ed. Tony Burke and Brent Landau (Grand Rapids: Eerdmans, 2016), 396–401.

3. Zamagni, "Passion (ou Actes) de Timothée," 341–75; Concannon, "Acts of Timothy," 396–401.

4. Here I follow Concannon in using Zamagni's line numbering. All translations from Acts of Timothy are my own unless otherwise noted.

5. The Acts specifically directs the reader that they can find much of this information about John's activities in Ephesus in the writings of Irenaeus (ll. 26–27).

by masked men carrying clubs;[6] the way the Christians in the city took his still-breathing body to a peaceful place to die and buried him in a place called Pion (where the text says his *martyrion* now stands); and the return of John to the city, who took over the Christian community there until the time of Trajan.

Readers looking to this text for information about or stories of the activities of Timothy, that is, for this text to look like other apocryphal acts, will be greatly disappointed. Though the text repeatedly calls Timothy "most holy" and gives a brief description of Timothy's parentage (cf. Acts 16:1–3), it only vaguely says that Timothy had a great reputation in terms of teaching, miracles, healings, and conduct (Acts Tim. 5) before proceeding to detail John's shipwreck and evangelistic activities. When Timothy finally takes center stage in the second section, he literally says one thing and then dies. Coming to the middle of the *embolos*, the main artery of the city, he cries, "Men, Ephesians, do not go mad with idols but know the truly living God" (13), following which he is immediately murdered.[7] There are very few acts of Timothy in the Acts of Timothy. Theodor Zahn concluded that our author did not actually know a single tradition about Timothy, while Usener argued that our author took most of his information from a hypothesized "Ephesian History," no evidence of which has ever been found.[8] Timothy Barnes argued, "The sole and transparent aim of this fictitious confection is to present Timothy as the first bishop of Ephesus."[9]

---

6. Presumably *phalloi* sticks, as found in the Dionysiac festivals, called ῥόπαλα in the Greek and Latin here (discussed further below). See also Eric Csapo, "Comedy and the *Pompe*: Dionysian Genre-Crossing," in *Greek Comedy and the Discourse of Genres*, ed. Emmanuela Bakola, Lucia Prauscello, and Mario Telò (New York: Cambridge University Press, 2013), 40–80.

7. Csapo, describing this scene, notes that "we are told that he achieved a grizzly, if poetic martyrdom, beaten to death by the *phallos*-sticks of the pagan faithful, a martyrdom so delightfully Dionysian, that one would sooner be tempted to shelve Timothy with Orpheus and Pentheus than with Lawrence and Anthony" ("Comedy and the *Pompe*," 63).

8. See Hippolyte Delehaye, "Les Acts de Saint Timothee," in *Anatolian Studies Presented to William Hepburn Buckler*, ed. W. M. Calder and Joseph Keil (Manchester: Manchester University Press, 1939), 77–84.

9. Timothy D. Barnes, *Early Christian Hagiography and Roman History* (Tübingen: Mohr Siebeck, 2010), 302.

This is not, however, a sufficient explanation, since it fails to account for the entire second section of the text, which describes Timothy's violent death at the hands of *phalloi*-wielding Dionysiacs at the Katagogia festival. The presence of the second section and the precision with which it attempts to fix the date of Timothy's death and the spot of his *martyrion* on the Pion clearly indicates that something besides Timothy's episcopal authority and primacy is in view.[10] A much more plausible scenario is to understand the text as part of an Ephesus revitalization project, undertaken as an attempt to revitalize the city and invest it with meaning during the waning ecclesiastical and economic fortunes of Ephesus in the fifth century CE in the shadow of *Nova Roma* right down the road.[11] Rather than understanding the Acts of Timothy as an attempt to claim Ephesus for Timothy, we should understand this text as an attempt to claim not only Timothy but also John *and the creation of the tetraevangellium itself* for Ephesus, part of a strategy to assert Ephesus's continuing relevance, sacrality, and vibrancy in order to lure pilgrims and other religious travelers and tourists to the city.

In what follows, I will discuss three particular issues that lend themselves to this understanding of the text: the focus on *textuality* that we see especially in the first section, as the text presents itself and establishes Ephesus as central to the creation of the sacred library; the presentation of Ephesus as *loca sancta*, sanctified by the blood of Timothy, and the relevance of this for travelers; and, looking outward, the broader relationship between texts and pilgrims that could stand behind a text such as this. We see in the Acts of Timothy a conscious concern to invest Ephesus with site-specific meaning, and to weave the city's history with the history of earliest Christianity and with the texts that make up its sacred library. The Acts of Timothy promotes

---

10. This text is also late, postdating Eusebius's assertion that Timothy was the first bishop of Ephesus (*Hist. eccl.* 3.4, information he clearly obtained from the Pastoral Epistles, since in the same section he states that Titus was appointed bishop of Crete, information unattested anywhere other than the Letter to Titus). The text refers to Lystra as a city in the Lyconian province (μία τῆς Λυκαόνων ἐπαρχίας; *una Lycaoniae praefecturae*), and as Delehaye noted early on, Lyconia did not become a province until 374, establishing this as the terminus a quo (Delehaye, "Les Acts de Saint Timothee," 74). The text would not then seem to *need* to have been written *just* to claim that Timothy had been the first bishop of Ephesus, even if this is part of the aims of the text.

11. So Kensky, "Timothy in Ephesus?" Cavin Concannon has also reached these conclusions about the text's historical background and presents them in detail in "In the Great City of the Ephesians," 419–46.

Ephesus as a holy place, worthy of visit and veneration, and is one of several texts, including the Acts of John by Prochorus and the Syriac *History of John in Ephesus*, that work to construct Ephesian edifices in the imagination.[12]

This Text, Those Texts, This City

The beginning of the Acts of Timothy self-consciously presents itself as a new text, situates itself within the sacred library of early Christianity by means of textual hyperlinks and cross-referencing, and goes into detail about the circumstances behind the material compilation of the four gospels, an activity it places squarely as happening in Ephesus.

After a superscription fixing the date of Timothy's martyrdom, the text begins by offering an explanation for its composition: "We know many histories and biographies, recording the morals, relationships and deaths of god-loving and holy men, from which they have made them famous to subsequent generations; therefore, it is not alien to justice and we, wishing to do such a thing, hasten to hand down to memory the life, relationships, and death of Timothy the holy apostle and first bishop of the great metropolis of the Ephesians" (Acts Tim. 2–3).[13] This somewhat generic-sounding

---

12. This is not dissimilar to how Cyril of Jerusalem actively promoted his city in the fourth century, when Jerusalem found itself with somewhat waning fortunes. Brouria Bitton-Ashkelony describes Cyril of Jerusalem as an active promoter of his city in the fourth century, explaining that he "had good reason to be frustrated," because "he lived in an era when Christianity had already marked its triumph by locating its collective memory in his city and sanctifying its near landscape, with masses of pilgrims flocking to the city's grandiose new churches. In such an atmosphere he might well have expected the status of his city to be enhanced; yet its universal ecclesiastical status remained inferior. Indeed, the seventh canon of Nicaea (325), while decreeing the succession of honor of the bishop of Jerusalem, still acknowledged Caesarea as the metropolitan see in Palestine." See Bitton-Ashkelony, *Encountering the Sacred: The Debate on Christian Pilgrimage in Late Antiquity* (Berkeley: University of California Press, 2005), 57. This is similar to the situation Ephesus found itself in a hundred years later as it waned in importance next to Constantinople's rising star. Though it was one of the major centers of early Christian activity, with lineage tracing to both Paul and John, it was eclipsed by the rootless but glamorous Constantinople. Not only did Constantinople become more and more popular, but Ephesus was officially demoted below it at the Council of Chalcedon in 451, the end result of a process that began with the third canon of the Council of Constantinople in 381.

13. A notable manuscript variant is that some manuscripts read "patriarch" instead of "bishop" throughout the text. Concannon discusses the use of the politically

preface is self-consciously textual. Speaking in the first-person plural, the authors explain their decision to write this text by demonstrating their knowledge of *other* texts (histories and biographies) that celebrate the lives of "god-loving and holy men."[14] These texts have made their subjects famous "to subsequent generations," so they are justified in producing their own text "to hand down to memory" traditions about Timothy.

Acknowledgment of the work of others is certainly a standard topos in historiographical prefaces, as is the use of the first person.[15] These prefaces are not as common in martyrological narratives, which are found in multiple genres and thus lack generic uniformity,[16] but a similar justification for writing appears in the Passion of Perpetua and Felicitas:

---

charged word *patriarch*, arguing "that the Acts of Timothy would go out of its way to name the first bishop of the city a patriarch suggests that a subtle argument was being made in favor of Ephesus's broader standing," and that the fact that the Paris manuscript, which Usener relied on, does not include this terminology shows that "the title of patriarch was a contested aspect of the narrative's transmission" ("In the Great City of the Ephesians," 339–40).

14. Concannon's translation of this line emphasizes the composers of the texts rather than the texts themselves: "We know that many have put in writing the stories" ("Acts of Timothy," 402). This obscures the fact that the Greek highlights the texts, not the people: ἴσμεν πολλοὺς ἱστορίας τε καὶ βίους ... συγγραψαμένους.

15. We see this in Luke 1:1–4 ("Since many have undertaken ... it also seemed good to me to write to you"), and this is a common feature of Greek historiography, the bibliography on which is extensive. See, for example, H. J. Cadbury, "Commentary on the Preface of Luke," in *The Beginnings of Christianity*, ed. F. J. Foakes-Jackson and K. Lake (London: Macmillan, 1922), 1:489–510; Donald Earl, "Prologue-Form in Ancient Historiography," *ANRW* 1.2:843–56; Terrance Callan, "The Preface of Luke-Acts and Historiography," *NTS* 31 (1985): 576–81; Gregory E. Sterling, *Historiography and Self-Definition: Josephos, Luke-Acts, and Apologetic Historiography*, NovTSup 64 (Leiden: Brill, 1992); Loveday Alexander, *The Preface to Luke's Gospel*, SNTSMS 78 (Cambridge: Cambridge University Press, 1993); Clare K. Rothschild, *Luke-Acts and the Rhetoric of History*, WUNT 2/175 (Tübingen: Mohr Siebeck, 2004); David E. Aune, "Luke 1.1–4: Historical or Scientific *Prooimion*?," in *Paul, Luke and the Graeco-Roman World: Essays in Honour of Alexander J. M. Wedderburn*, ed. Alf Christophersen, Carsten Claussen, Jörg Frey, and Bruce Longenecker, JSNTSup 217 (New York: T&T Clark, 2002), 138–48; Sean A. Adams, "Luke's Preface and Its Relationship to Greek Historiography: A Response to Loveday Alexander," *JGRCJ* 3 (2006): 177–91.

16. For recent discussion on issues of genre related to martyrological literature, see Michal Beth Dinkler, "Genre Analysis and Early Christian Martyrdom Narratives: A Proposal," in *Sybils, Scriptures, and Scrolls*, ed. Joel Baden, Hindy Najman, and Eibert Tigchelaar (Leiden: Brill, 2017), 1:314–36.

The deeds recounted about the faith in ancient times were a proof of God's favour and achieved the spiritual strengthening of men as well; and they were set forth in writing precisely that honour might be rendered to God and comfort to men by the recollection of the past through the written word. Should not then more recent examples be set down that contribute equally to both ends? For indeed these too will one day become ancient and needful for the ages to come, even though in our own day they may enjoy less prestige because of the prior claim of antiquity. (Pass. Perp. 1.1–2 [Musurillo])[17]

Here the Passion engages in a lengthy explanation for why "recent examples" of the faith should have their lives recorded for future generations, noting that they will "become ancient and needful" in future times, even though people may be less interested in them now. The Acts of Timothy, reflecting a later date (later even than the "subsequent generations" it notes), says that it hastens to record the life of Timothy because *other such texts* have been so successful at increasing the renown of its subjects. It thus "is not alien to justice" (οὐχ ἔξω τοῦ δικαίου) for them to do so as well.[18] The Acts of Timothy thus presents itself as a new text and includes a somewhat strongly worded justification for its composition.[19]

More importantly, this preface establishes the text's deliberate promotional intent. It specifically mentions the functions and effects of these other texts, that is to say, the renown they bring to the subjects they celebrate, and establishes that the author wants to promote Timothy, identified here as "the holy apostle and the first bishop of the great metropolis of the Ephesians" (Acts Tim. 2) in this same manner. The explicit rationale for writing, therefore, highlights the intended effect of the text—attention/fame to Timothy—but it seems to be secondary to the real goal, which is to bring attention/fame to the metropolis itself. As Concannon notes,

---

17. See also Martyrdom of Pious the Presbyter 1; Martyrdom of Marian and James 1.4.

18. This unusual phrasing seems like a stronger justification for writing than the more placid "it is more fitting to remember" (μᾶλλον μεμνῆσθαι προσήκει) from the Martyrdom of Pious the Presbyter, though not as officious (and self-righteous?) as the preface to the Martyrdom of Saints Montanus and Lucius, where the author declares that "it is by the force of this reasoning that love and a sense of obligation have urged us to write this account" (1 [Musurillo]).

19. Concannon's choice to translate this as "It is right" obscures the phrasing and its deviance from more established formulae.

the text repeatedly refers to Ephesus with the adjective λαμπρὰ, "radiant" or "splendid," and calls Ephesus "this" city multiple times in the narrative (e.g., 4, 7, 14, 15).[20] In praising Ephesus thus, the text paints a picture for its readers of an Ephesus worthy of their attention, and, as I will explain further, a worthwhile stop on any traveler's itinerary.

Following the preface, readers are then told that they can learn all about Timothy's miraculous deeds, teachings, and healings from "those things which are variously said about him in the Acts of the holy Apostles" (Acts Tim. 5). This then is the third group of texts mentioned in the Acts of Timothy, following the histories and lives from the preface. By situating itself relative to these other literary corpora, the text invites readers to locate themselves in a distinctly Christian textual universe. This attempt to bolster itself by referencing other books in the sacred library is a late antique form of the hyperlink. By establishing these connections, the text asks readers to add what follows into their landscape of the past, fixing not only Timothy but also *this text about Timothy* firmly into their cultural memory. It is not an overstatement to say that this text is trying to wedge itself into the sacred library of early Christian traditions (though it may be doing so in a clumsy manner).

This textual hyperlinking continues as the text turns its attention to John and his activities at Ephesus. "It is just for us to state," the text continues, "that the same most-holy apostle Timothy was not only an eyewitness and hearer of the apostle Paul, the holy and famous apostle, but also of the famous theologian John, who rested on the chest of the great God and our savior Jesus Christ" (6). The text then proceeds to explain that John showed up in the city after shipwreck, explicitly stating that the reader can find much of this information about John's activities in Ephesus in the writings of Irenaeus (7).[21] Though Irenaeus is explicitly mentioned, the writer here implicitly alludes to the material about Paul and his activities in Ephesus from Acts of the Apostles, as well as also possibly Paul's own literary corpus. These hyperlinks situate the Acts of Timothy to these other narratives, creating a network of relationships that encourage readers to put this text in the context of other now-sacred literature.

---

20. See Concannon, "In the Great City of the Ephesians," 425.

21. Note that John's shipwreck near the coast of Ephesus is narrated in full in the Acts of John by Prochorus, and thus this mention represents yet another hyperlink to existing narratives.

Nowhere is this more evident than in what comes next, when the text interrupts the narrative about the relationship between John and Timothy to provide critical information about the composition and compilation of the gospels:

> Indeed, those following the apostles of our Lord Jesus Christ, since they did not know how to put together these sporadically collected papers they had in various languages about wonders done by our lord Jesus Christ, coming to Ephesus they brought them, by agreement, to John, the much-lauded theologian. Who, after considering everything and starting from them, placing the things said by them in the three gospels, copied them out in the order of Matthew, Mark, and Luke, placing their names on the gospels. But finding them to have traced out the economy of the incarnation, he himself theologized those things which he had wiped off of the divine bosom [ἐκ τοῦ θείου στήθους ἀναμαξάμενος] which were not said, adding the divine miracles poorly covered by them in summaries. After this, he placed his own name on this kind of collection or gospel. (8–9)[22]

The text thus claims that the Synoptic Gospels were put together by John *at Ephesus* from a bunch of loose-leaf pages that the other disciples could not figure out how to put together. This establishes Ephesus's critical place in the formulation of the sacred library. Ephesus is, here, the location of the compilation of the Gospels of Mark, Matthew, and Luke and also the location of the composition of John's Gospel with its esoteric source material. Not only, then, does the Acts of Timothy attempt to wedge itself into the library and impress itself on the landscape of the past; it attempts to give an origin story for the foundational narratives of that very library (or, in the language of popular culture, to "retcon" the library itself).

By establishing Ephesus as the place of the redaction of the gospels, the composition of the Fourth Gospel, and the place of "thrice-blessed" and "most-holy" Timothy's martyrdom, the Acts of Timothy thus stacks or doubles associations with Ephesus.[23] Scott Fitzgerald Johnson notes that "doubling of holy figures at the same site is a key factor in the emergent association of Christian saints with specific places."[24] This doubling makes

---

22. Thanks to Duncan McRae for assistance with this translation.

23. Scott Fitzgerald Johnson, *Literary Territories: Cartographical Thinking in Late Antiquity* (New York: Oxford University Press, 2016), 39–40.

24. Johnson, *Literary Territories*, 94.

Ephesus a very attractive location for religious travelers, as it is established as the location of not one but several pilgrimage-worthy events. Additionally, the text places Ephesus in not one but *two* apostolic columns. According to Johnson, "the emergent concept of the Christian *loca sancta* ('holy places' or 'Holy Land') is inextricably linked to *sortes apostolorum* in the fourth and fifth centuries, as pilgrims, ascetics, and emperors alike were looking for authenticated loci of supernatural power, preferably in the Levant, on which to hang their hats."[25] Though not the Levant, here Ephesus is firmly fixed in the apostolic geography, linked to John, Timothy, and Paul. Religious travelers could hang multiple hats here, coming to see where Timothy died and was buried, but also the very place where their sacred texts were put together. The Acts of Timothy intends for its readers to head toward Ephesus in their minds, to be followed by heading to Ephesus with their very selves.

Here, in This Place

The second section of the Acts of Timothy is characterized by even more geographical specificity, as the reader is placed in the middle of the action, moving around the city itself. In particular, there are four instances where the narrative attempts to locate the reader. First, in describing the brutal activity of the Katagogia revelers, the narrative explains that "they did not stop committing unfated murders and pouring out a throng of blood in the distinguished places of the city [ἐν τοῖς ἐπισήμοις τῆς πόλεως τόποις]" (Acts Tim. 12). When Timothy makes his one-sentence stand against the celebrants, he speaks "in the midst of the *embolos*" (13), the main artery of the city. After Timothy is beaten, the servants of God take Timothy to "the mountain of this radiant metropolis, situated on the opposite side of the harbor" (14). And when he dies, they take his body to "a place called Pion, where now stands his most holy martyrion" (14). These geographical markers invite readers to see sacred history unfolding in the urban landscape and thus participate in sacralizing the city of Ephesus, turning it from territory that was at best neutral (and at worst idolatrous) into holy space. As Sabine MacCormack explains, "What made certain parts of space holy was a human impact: worship, possibly the remains of a holy human being, and the

---

25. Johnson, *Literary Territories*, 67.

unfolding of sacred history."[26] By describing Timothy's last stand and specifying the locations of his blood, last breath, and remains, the text invites readers to see the urban topography of Ephesus as sacred space, and lays out a way for them to come experience it intimately through pilgrimage.[27]

First, the Acts of Timothy paints a vivid picture of the events surrounding Timothy's martyrdom in a scene that draws on the pagan history of Ephesus. Though no mention is made of Artemis, the subject of Ephesus's most famous devotions, iconography, and temple (torn down under the authority of John Chrysostom in 400 CE), the opening lines of the section ask readers to recall what Ephesus was like before the rise of Christianity: "When these things were thus in these ways, and the bishopric was inhabited piously and nobly by Timothy, often called most holy, the early idolatry of the Ephesians still held remnants among those living at that time" (Acts Tim. 12).[28] In this case, the "early idolatry" of the Ephesians takes the form of a popular festival called Katagogia. The text describes the practitioners gruesomely:

> for certain days putting on unseemly cloaks over themselves, covering their faces with masks in order that they would not be recognized, and carrying cudgels and images of idols and calling out certain chants, lawlessly attacking both free men and notable women, they did not stop committing unfated murders and pouring out a throng of blood in the

---

26. Sabine MacCormack, "*Loca Sancta:* The Organization of Sacred Topography in Late Antiquity," in *Blessings of Pilgrimage*, ed. Robert G. Ousterhout (Urbana: University of Illinois Press, 1990), 17–18.

27. As Béatrice Caseau explains, pilgrimage practices "changed the notion of space for Christians. As they traveled to the shrines of the saints, they created a sacred geography. The location of churches where the saints were buried went from being neutral to being sacred." See Caseau, "Sacred Landscapes," in *Late Antiquity: A Guide to the Postclassical World*, ed. G. W. Bowersock, Peter Robert Lamont Brown, and Oleg Grabar (Cambridge: Harvard University Press, 1999).

28. For discussion of Artemis, see Rick Strelan, *Paul, Artemis, and the Jews in Ephesus*, BZNW 80 (Berlin: de Gruyter, 1996); Guy McLean Rogers, *The Mysteries of Artemis of Ephesos* (New Haven: Yale University Press, 2013). Artemis also loomed large in literary presentations of Ephesus; see Christine Thomas, "At Home in the City of Artemis: Religion in Ephesos in the Literary Imagination of the Roman Period," in *Ephesos, Metropolis of Asia*, ed. Helmut Koester, HTS (Valley Forge, PA: Trinity Press International, 1995), 81–118.

distinguished places of the city [ἐν τοῖς ἐπισήμοις τῆς πόλεως τόποις] as if
they were doing something necessary and profitable for their souls. (12)

Here the human denizens of Ephesus are portrayed as particularly savage,
disguising themselves in order to attack and murder citizens without being
recognized, even in the "distinguished places of the city."

We might be tempted to dismiss this characterization of the festival
as wholly polemical, designed to disparage and denigrate non-Christian
practices and practitioners, but enough evidence survives from antiquity to
support the basic outlines of this description. We know that the Katagogia
festival was associated with Dionysus. In Priene, Dionysus was worshiped
as Dionysus Katagogius; an inscription from Priene lays this out clearly:
ἱερήσεται δὲ καὶ τοῦ Διονύσου τοῦ καταγωγίου.[29] Masks in particular were
associated with the Dionysian cults. Rick Strelan explains that "the mask
functioned as a symbol of transition, and transition was at the heart of the
Dionysian cult...; he is the 'double-god' of life and death.... Masks 'identified' the wearer with the god, the powers, and the creatures of the ritual."[30]
Likewise the cudgels, ῥόπαλα in the Greek (Latin *ropala*), are most likely
the *phallos* sticks carried by Dionysiac celebrants. Csapo explains that
the *phallos* sticks seem to have functioned in both song and dance, which
might befit the Acts of Timothy's description of "certain chants" above.[31]

In addition, we know that that the Katagogia was celebrated at Ephesus,
and Richard Oster has laid out the "abundant" evidence for the veneration of
Dionysus at Ephesus, including the important fact that the month Lenaeon,
"sacred for the Dionysia," was part of the Ephesian calendar.[32] Epigraphic
and numismatic evidence attests to the continued influence and veneration

---

29. IPriene 174. 5, cited in Strelan, *Paul, Artemis, and the Jews in Ephesus*, 123.
See also Fritz Graf, "Gods in Greek Inscriptions," in *The Gods of Ancient Greece: Identi-
ties and Transformations*, ed. Jan Bremmer and Andrew Erskine, Edinburgh Leventis
Studies 5 (Edinburgh: Edinburgh University Press, 2010), 67.

30. Strelan, *Paul, Artemis, and the Jews in Ephesus*, 123, citing David Wiles, *The
Masks of Menander: Sign and Meaning in Greek and Roman Performance* (Cambridge:
Cambridge University Press, 1991), 113; and Marcel Detienne, *Dionysos at Large*,
trans. Arthur Goldhammer (Cambridge: Harvard University Press, 1989), 2.

31. For discussion of the connections between *phallos* sticks and Dionysiac cel-
ebrations, as well as the iconographic associations of Dionysus and *phallos* sticks, see
Csapo, "Comedy and the *Pompe*," esp. 59–64.

32. Richard Oster, "Ephesus as a Religious Center under the Principate," *ANRW*
2.18.3:1673.

of Dionysus.[33] It is possible that the Bacchic festival that met Marc Antony at Ephesus in 41 BCE (Plutarch, *Ant.* 24) was a Katagogia. Inscriptional evidence attests to the Katagogia at Ephesus.[34] Strelan notes that archaeologists have discovered a statue group of Dionysus in Ephesus at the crossroads of the Curetes Street (the Embolos) and the Marble street, "dedicated in 92–93 CE as a reminder to the Ephesians of the *Katagogia.*"[35] There is no reason to doubt that the Katagogia was celebrated in Ephesus with masks, singing, and sticks, in much the way the Acts of Timothy describes it.

Additionally, the part of the description in the Acts of Timothy that seems most polemical—the violence—is also partially corroborated by other instances of the festival's celebration. Eric Csapo notes that verbal aggression "is well-attested" for the Pompe and other Dionysiac festivals, and even a "certain amount of physical aggression was also tolerated and expected."[36] Csapo points to an incident found in Demosthenes, in which he talks about the violence inflicted by one leather strap–carrying Ctesicles at the festival (who pled not-guilty to violent assault because he was under the influence of the Pompe and drunkenness), and to the revealing comment by a scholiast to Demosthenes, who said that men were in the habit of wearing felt caps under their masks to protect themselves from the impact of physical blows.[37] Csapo explains that in Athens, "decorum and good order from any semi-organized group of young men was so far from being expected that the Athenians created boards of 'Wardens (*epimeletai*) of the *Pompe*,'" whose task seems to have been to make sure that the choruses of *phalloi*-wielding drunk men did not riot and lose control.[38] It is not inconceivable that a Katagogia festival could have resulted in the type of violence that the Acts of Timothy describes, even if the way the Acts of Timothy describes it is clearly polemical.[39]

---

33. Oster, "Ephesus as a Religious Center under the Principate," 1674.

34. See Isabelle Tassignon, "Dionysos et les Katagôgies d'Asie Mineure," in *Homo religiosus: Dieux, fêtes, sacré dans la Grèce et la Rome antiques*, ed. A. Motte and C.-M. Ternes (Turnhout: Brepols, 2003), 82. Oster points, for example, to an inscription that specifically attests to the celebration of the Katagogia, found in D. Knibbe, "Epigraphische Nachlese," *JÖAI* 47 (1964–1965): 29–30. See further M. P. Nilsson, *The Dionysiac Mysteries of the Hellenistic and Roman Age* (New York: Arno, 1975).

35. SEG 35:1116, cited in Strelan, *Paul, Artemis, and the Jews in Ephesus*, 123.

36. Csapo, "Comedy and the *Pompe*," 61.

37. Csapo, "Comedy and the *Pompe*," 62.

38. Csapo, "Comedy and the *Pompe*," 62.

39. We should note also that Ephesus was no stranger to riots and mob violence,

This verisimilar portrait of the Katagogia paints a picture of the distinguished city under attack. The brutal way in which the Acts of Timothy describes the activities of the revelers invites the readers not only to imagine themselves caught in the midst of the action in the crowded city but also to see Ephesus itself as being victimized. Her "distinguished places," a phrase which seems to refer to the centers of civic, cultic, and political life, are now distinguished by a throng of bloodshed, desecrated by the actions of this unruly mob. The Acts of Timothy not only calls attention to numerous unnamed victims; it presents the city itself—including its most honorable areas—as under attack. Just as the Egyptian hagiographies make sense of the liminal zones of the wilderness, the "spaces of beasts," the Acts of Timothy imagines pre-Christian Ephesus as the site of the savage, masked, club-wielding idolaters, polluting its innermost sanctuaries with blood, only sanctified by the blood of the most holy Timothy.[40] Timothy's heroic action not only demonstrates his ability to testify to God in the midst of such critical danger; it reveals his great love for the city, of which he is overseer. Ephesus is thus redeemed by Timothy's action, her places distinguished again by his bloodshed in the name of God.

It is thus significant that the main action takes place on the Ephesian *embolos*. According to Clive Foss, the *embolos* was "the center of late antique Ephesus," lined by buildings, statues, and colonnades, which formed entrances to shops, and official decrees.[41] The *embolos* was eleven

---

and it may not have been hard for readers to imagine a group of hooligans—even religious hooligans—wreaking havoc on the city. According to Clive Foss, in late antique Ephesus, "One of the greatest causes of civil disturbance was religion. Different sects would riot to assert their beliefs, followers of rival bishops were ready to use violence in support of their candidates, and crowds of monks were always available to join in the disturbances, or lead them." See Foss, *Ephesus after Antiquity: A Late Antique, Byzantine, and Turkish City* (Cambridge: Cambridge University Press, 1979), 17. Foss points in particular to the riots that occurred when Proclus, the patriarch of Constantinople (434–446), imposed Basil as bishop over the city, and in 451 when John was chosen over a rival. Foss actually describes the Ephesians as "a population quick to indulge in acts of violence" (*Ephesus after Antiquity*, 41). That religious rioting here causes the death of Timothy, and that the most prominent rioting in Ephesus in the fifth century was part of the ongoing rivalry between Ephesus and Constantinople, may be very crucial background to this text.

40. David Frankfurter, "Hagiography and the Reconstruction of Local Religion in Late Antique Egypt: Memories, Inventions, and Landscapes," *CHRC* 86 (2006): 23.

41. Foss, *Ephesus after Antiquity*, 66.

meters wide, paved with marble, and part of it was closed to wheel traffic, open only to pedestrians, which explains its abundance of graffiti. When Timothy makes his stand in the center of the *embolos*, he is entering into the heart of civic and daily commercial life, the main artery of the city.[42] In terms of verisimilitude, this busy, bustling avenue would have been a great place to try to reach a great number of inhabitants—but also an easy place to get knocked down in the midst of a throng of *phalloi*-wielding revelers.[43] Beyond the verisimilitude, however, the *embolos* represented the lifeblood under the city, a place on any visitor's travel itinerary. Now it is specifically linked to the testimony and death of a Christian martyr associated with Ephesus's apostolic history. The *embolos* is thus sacralized by the text. It is not difficult to imagine that the authors are anticipating that readers may want to come see this for themselves. Lined with statues, dedicatory inscriptions, and both imperial and provincial decrees, the *embolos* was a well-traversed pedestrian mall, a major center for commerce, and easily accessible—much to recommend itself to late antique travelers. Now, it is distinguished by being the place of Timothy's bloodshed.

Moreover, the *embolos* was a great place for religious travelers to shop. The street boasted colonnades, which provided entrance to a large number of stores. It seems likely that the text imagines that when visiting the *embolos* to see the site of Timothy's martyrdom, religious travelers will want to shop for souvenirs and to collect mementos and *eulogiai* of their travels. Perhaps one or more of those shops might have trafficked in souvenirs related to the apostolic heritage of the city. We know that eventually pilgrims to Saint John's Basilica would take home *ampullae* filled with the site's unique manna, and it is not difficult to imagine that such material objects may also have been for sale in the city's commercial district. Souvenirs related to other Ephesus-based martyrs—such as Timothy—could also have been available for travelers. Even texts may have been available for purchase. We know that Egeria collected texts on her travels, and others probably did so as well. Egeria shows a special concern for acquiring texts

---

42. For extensive discussion of the *embolos*, see Foss, *Ephesus after Antiquity*, 65–69; see also J. Keil, *Führer durch Ephesos* (Vienna: Österreichisches Archäologisches Institut, 1964), 121–24; A. Bammer, "Zur Topographie und Städtebaulichen Entwicklung von Ephesos," *JÖAI* 46 (1961–1963): 136–57.

43. Close to the place where archaeologists have discovered a statue group with an inscription reminding the Ephesians to celebrate the Katagogia (see Strelan, *Paul, Artemis, and the Jews at Ephesus*, 123).

on site. Pointing to Egeria's comments on acquiring the best possible version of the letters between Abgar and Jesus while at Edessa, Johnson notes that "for Egeria and others like her, the closer to the physical source she can find a text, the better—and, significantly, she is more prone to distrust her own text, collected earlier and perhaps less complete, than the text of the bishop or tour guide trying to promote his city in the presence of a wealthy matron and her entourage."[44] While there is no evidence that Egeria purchased her text—she was much more likely to have been gifted it—other religious travelers who did not have her resources or whose patronage was not as desirable might have needed to purchase their own copies.

The Acts of Timothy might have been an easy text for a traveler to acquire. It is a short text, well designed for portability or to be included among other material. It would certainly lend itself to tiny copies. We know from John Chrysostom that some women wore miniature codices of the gospels around their necks, a practice that continued at least until the fifth century.[45] Not all miniature codices contained gospels; eight out of the fifty-five extent miniature codices contained apocryphal works.[46] Stephen Davis discusses two tiny copies of the Acts of Thecla, one from fifth-century Oxyrhynchus and one from fourth-century Antinoopolis, arguing that "such pocket codices of the ATh would have been eminently portable; they would have lent themselves well to the needs of pilgrim travel."[47] It is possible that the short length of the Acts of Timothy indicates that the text was designed for precisely this purpose.

The *embolos* is not the only major Ephesian landmark mentioned by the text. After Timothy's blood is spilled *right there* on the pedestrian mall, the believers then take his body to an area opposite the harbor, another major Ephesian landmark.[48] After he gives up his spirit, which

---

44. Johnson, *Literary Territories*, 88.

45. Stephen Davis points to the reference to this practice in one of the letters of fifth-century Egyptian monk Isidore of Pelusium. See Davis, "Pilgrimage and the Cult of St. Thecla in Late Antique Egypt," in *Pilgrimage and Holy Space in Late Antique Egypt*, ed. David Frankfurter, RGRW 134 (Leiden: Brill, 1998), 331.

46. See Harry Gamble, *Books and Readers in the Early Church* (New Haven: Yale University Press, 1995), 235–36, cited in Davis, "Pilgrimage and the Cult of St. Thecla in Late Antique Egypt," 331 n. 103.

47. Davis, "Pilgrimage and the Cult of St. Thecla in Late Antique Egypt," 332.

48. When discussing the province of Asia, the *Expositio totius mundi et gentium*, a fourth-century survey of the Roman Empire, specifically mentions Ephesus's harbor: "Asia is outstanding among all provinces and has innumerable cities, indeed very great

presumably occurred three days after his fatal wounding (Acts Tim. 16), he is then interred on Mount Pion, which is the modern Panayirdağ. This was supposedly the burial site of Hermione (the daughter of Philip) and Mary Magdalene.[49] This was also the location of the cave of the Seven Sleepers of Ephesus, and as a result "a large complex of mausolea and chapels" grew up around this site, the beginning of the construction of which dates at least to the reign of Theodosius II and possibly even to Theodosius I.[50] Another Theodosius, the sixth-century pilgrim, after describing the tradition of the Seven Sleepers in Ephesus, notes almost as an afterthought that "Ibi est sanctus Timotheus, discipulus sancti Pauli" (*De terra sancta* 34). The importance and reputation of the tomb of the Sleepers clearly outclassed any Timothy *martyrion*, but given the number of shrines that apparently blossomed on this site, it might be notable that the only other one that Theodosius mentions is Timothy's.[51] The association of Timothy with Mount Pion seems to have been driven by the growing sanctity and importance of the hill in Ephesus and provided pilgrims with another reason to visit.

Additionally, Mount Pion literally looms over the city.[52] It is thus significantly closer to the heart of Ephesus than Ayasoluk, where John was

---

ones and many on the sea. Two of these must be mentioned: Ephesus, which is said to have an outstanding harbor, and likewise Smyrna, itself a splendid city" (quoted in Foss, *Ephesus after Antiquity*, 7). For discussion of the literary and archaeological evidence, see Heinrich Zabehlicky, "Preliminary Views of the Ephesian Harbor," in Koester, *Ephesos, Metropolis of Asia*, 201–16.

49. Including Aristobulus, Paul of Thebes, and local Ephesian martyrs; see Foss, *Ephesus after Antiquity*, 84.

50. Foss, *Ephesus after Antiquity*, 84–85.

51. Foss also draws our attention to the fact that this site is adjacent to the Roman necropolis, "on a mountain which seems to have had particular sanctity," and suggests that "it is not therefore inconceivable that the whole mountain had religious associations far older than Christianity, and that the legends, not only of the Seven Sleepers but of the saints mentioned above, were attached to it because it was holy rather than vice versa" (Foss, *Ephesus after Antiquity*, 86). David Frankfurter discusses this phenomenon with regard to Victor Turner's theory of the "Archaic Pilgrimage," "that oft-noted phenomenon in Christianity whereby native ('pagan') holy sites or practices are reconsecrated and even revitalized during the process of conversion." See Frankfurter, "Introduction: Approaches to Coptic Pilgrimage," in Frankfurter, *Pilgrimage and Holy Space in Late Antique Egypt*, 7.

52. Foss describes the hill as "steep and massive with three peaks ranging from 105 to 155 meters" (Foss, *Ephesus after Antiquity*, 46).

interred and where Justinian eventually constructed the great basilica. To be sure, Ayasoluk was the location of the Artemision, at the end of the Sacred Way, but it was "barren and isolated,"[53] far from the action, and inhospitable to pilgrims until Justinian constructed the aqueduct to bring water from the Arcadiane. Mount Pion, however, was *right there*, easily accessible, and its presence was felt throughout the city. Pilgrims could feel the proximity of the sanctity without trekking all the way out to Ayasoluk; they could experience this sense of presence as they went about all of their activities in the city. The association of Timothy with Mount Pion made Timothy's presence a part of all the areas of the city, whenever anyone looked up. Timothy died *right here*, was buried *right there*. The Acts of Timothy brings out this "right there" quality, which contributes to the sacred geography of Ephesus.

In fact *all* of the sites mentioned in the Acts of Timothy have this "right there" quality. The "right there" quality establishes correspondences between major Ephesian landmarks and sacred narrative. Pilgrims visiting Ephesus can mark out these landmarks with ease and establish connections with them. The last activities of Timothy are thus written into the geography of the city itself. In the Acts of Timothy, bodies move throughout the main areas of the city, from the "distinguished places," where innocent blood is spilled, to the *embolos*, the area near the harbor, and finally Mount Pion. The text thus places signposts at crucial Ephesian locations where the blood and body of Timothy (and others) were found. Though this is not quite the Via Dolorosa, and no concrete indications suggest that pilgrims traced a route around the city, the text contributes to the creation of a mental map of the city. Visiting Ephesus, a pilgrim could see and experience the city anew by locating Timothy in its stones and mountains. No longer the site of the Katagogia of Dionysus, the city becomes the site of the *anagogia* of Timothy. The text asks readers to see the city anew and presents concrete associations for the pilgrims it hopes will follow.

Texts and Pilgrims

Ephesus needed the boost that these religious travelers could bring, as it was dealt several blows in the fourth and fifth centuries CE when its fortunes diminished with the rise of Nova Roma right down the road.

---

53. Foss, *Ephesus after Antiquity*, 46.

Ephesus was stripped—literally—of its apostolic heritage.[54] In 356 Constantius translated Timothy's relics from Ephesus to the Church of the Holy Apostles in Constantinople.[55] Paulinus of Nola (who credits Constantine himself with the translation) specifically explains that Andrew and Timothy's bones were chosen to endow Constantinople with an apostolic pedigree that could rival Rome: "so Constantinople now stands with twin towers, vying to match the hegemony of great Rome, and more genuinely rivalling the walls of Rome through the eminence that God bestowed on her, for He counterbalanced Peter and Paul with a protection as great, since Constantinople gained the disciple of Paul and the brother of Peter" (19.329).[56] Timothy's relics helped to establish Constantinople as equal to Rome and thus served a highly visible political purpose.[57] The by-product, though, was the loss of Ephesus's material claims to Timothy.

Ephesus was also stripped of her claims to Mary. Vasiliki Limberis, in her discussion of the Council of Ephesus in 431, carefully traces how Ephesus lost its power and prestige to Constantinople, and how the council, while ostensibly deliberating over the cult of the Theotokos, was really over claims of episcopal primacy.[58] The story of Mary, and the location of her later life and death, became currency in the power struggle. While there had been a tradition that Mary had accompanied John to Ephesus and died there, ultimately the tradition that she lived and died in Jerusalem won out and became the official story. The legends that located Mary's

---

54. Several of the extent medieval Greek manuscripts include a description of this translation. Full discussion of the Greek manuscripts can be found in Zamagni, "Passion (ou Actes) de Timothée," 346–64.

55. This date is very well attested in multiple sources; see *Consularia Constantinopolitana* 356; 357; Chronicon Paschale 542$_{7-11}$; Jerome, *Chron.* 356; 357; *Vir. ill.* 7; Theodorus Lector, *Hist. eccl.* 2.61.

56. Translated by P. G. Walsh, *The Poems of St. Paulinus of Nola*, ACW 40 (New York: Newman, 1975). Cyril Mango calls Paulinus, who places the date at 357, "weak on facts" and also suggests that he deliberately confused Constantine with Constantius perhaps to provide sanction for the practice of moving relics. See Cyril Mango, "Constantine's Mausoleum and the Translation of Relics," *BZ* 83 (1990): 53.

57. This was also one of the first instances of such translation. Though the earliest recorded translation was that of Babylas from Antioch to Daphne (a distance of five miles) in 351–354, since the move was so geographically limited, this was unlikely to have captured widespread attention (Mango, "Constantine's Mausoleum," 52).

58. Vasiliki Limberis, "The Council of Ephesos: The Demise of the See of Ephesos and the Rise of the Cult of the Theotokos," in Koester, *Ephesos, Metropolis of Asia*, 321–40.

death in Jerusalem and saw her relics transferred to Constantinople helped to secure the prominence of Constantinople over Ephesus in the cult of the Virgin, part of the program of the legitimation of the see and authority of Constantinople.[59] Mary was thus "firmly dissociated" from Ephesus.[60]

Ephesus had lost the bones of Timothy and now the claim to Mary as well. However, it still had its claim to John. Karen Britt has argued that Ephesus's waning fortunes were a crucial part of the background of the construction of the Basilica of Saint John in Ephesus under Justinian. Britt convincingly demonstrates that it was Hypatius, the sixth-century CE archbishop of Ephesus, who was the driving force and influence behind the building of the basilica, part of an overall program designed to build up the reputation and prestige of Ephesus and to establish it as a center of pilgrimage. Ephesus had not been able to take advantage of the growing pilgrimage industry in part because of inhospitable terrain and a lack of fresh water on what is now Ayasoluk, the site of John's *martyrion*. Ultimately, as part of the large-scale construction of the basilica, Justinian funded an aqueduct to bring water to the site. Procopius, extolling the beneficence of Justinian, describes the site of John's *martyrion* as "lying on a steep slope hilly and bare of soil and incapable of producing crops, even should one attempt to cultivate them, but altogether hard and rough."[61] Just as important to the lack of pilgrims as the run-down nature of the site was the brilliance of Constantinople just down the road, a far more attractive draw. If Hypatius wanted to enhance Ephesus's grandeur and attraction, he needed to provide pilgrims with an outstanding reason to come to Ephesus, and he drew on his close relationship with the imperial family to make this happen.[62]

---

59. "The legends gave Constantinople exclusive rights to Mary's relics, further sanctifying and legitimating the new Rome with the holiest of all presences.... Because Mary's death was located once and for all in Jerusalem, Ephesos lost its claim to her presence and holiness" (Limberis, "Council of Ephesos," 340).

60. Karen C. Britt, "How to Win Pilgrims and Influence Emperors: A Historical Reinterpretation of the Byzantine Church of St. John at Ephesus," *JECS* 64 (2012): 145.

61. Procopius, *De aedificiis* 5.1.4, quoted in Britt, "How to Win Pilgrims and Influence Emperors," 140–41.

62. Hypatius was successful; graffito on a marble column of the church by an early visitor attest to this, as do a large number of clay *ampullae*, pilgrims' flasks, discovered in the area. Legends grew about the healing properties of the site and about magical flour (called *manna*), expelled from the site and carried away as relics by pilgrims. By the end of the sixth century, Gregory of Tours tells us that "today his sepulcher

Buildings take a long time. Stories, however, can take root much more quickly; it is much easier to build edifices in the imagination, "palaces of paragraphs."[63] Texts—especially short, easily portable ones—could circulate quickly and thus represented a far faster way to try to attract visitors. Concannon calls the Acts of Timothy a "narrative intervention in Constantinople's eclipsing of Ephesian authority," placing the text in the context of Ephesus's ecclesiastical diminishment in the fourth and fifth centuries.[64] Beyond attempting to boost Ephesus's ecclesiastical standing (which may ultimately have been a lost cause), though, the text has a practical purpose in mind: bring religious travelers to the city. The economic advantages of this would greatly benefit the city, especially since one of the main stops on a traveler's itinerary—the famous temple of Artemis—was crossed off[65] in 400 when it was torn down under Chrysostom's authority. Once sites became destinations, services and subsidiary economies developed around them. As Rebecca Stephens Falcasantos explains, "pilgrimage sites are religious marketplaces; they require staff to care for sites and pilgrims; and they invite secondary industries, from food and hospitality to trinkets and guide work."[66]

---

throws up manna like flour, from which blessed relics carried away throughout the whole world, guarantee safety to the diseased." See PL 71.730, quoted in Britt, "How to Win Pilgrims and Influence Emperors," 140. Britt suggests that the *ampullae* were produced as vessels for the manna.

63. Lin-Manuel Miranda, "Burn," performed by Philippa Soo, Atlantic Records B0135P6PZA, 2015, CD.

64. Concannon, "In the Great City of the Ephesians," 439.

65. Pun intended. Ephesus was not only facing competition from Constantinople but also continued to face competition from Smyrna. According to Foss, "Ephesus had a natural rival in Smyrna, a city only two days' journey away, which also flourished as a great port and center of trade and industry. Competition between the two cities was expressed in the second and third centuries by struggles over the use of honorary titles, such as that of First and Greatest Metropolis of Asia. The rivalry and ill-feeling continued in Late Antiquity. An inscription set up in Ephesus in 441 condemned some 'wicked Smyrnaeans' for an unspecified offense. The action of the Council of 451 was another step in the quarrel: the bishop of Smyrna was made independent of the Metropolitan of Ephesus, though not given equality with him, for the church of Smyrna was assigned no subordinate bishops of its own. In the reign of Justinian, the government was obliged to interfere once again the age-old dispute for priority, and another inscription was set up in Ephesus.... It was only the decline of Ephesus as a harbor in the Middle Ages which finally gave greater prominence to Smyrna" (Foss, *Ephesus after Antiquity*, 6).

66. Rebecca Stephens Falcasantos, "Wandering Wombs, Inspired Intellects: Christian Religious Travel in Late Antiquity," *JECS* 25 (2017): 113. Falcasantos points

We know that texts about the lives of martyrs and saints were read by pilgrims while visiting their shrines and *martyria*. The writings of Egeria demonstrate that one of the activities she engaged in at pilgrimage sites was reading texts about the saint or martyr's activities and death. Johnson notes that when Egeria traveled, her first act was "to go to the local church associated with the famous personality and read related texts in situ."[67] Johnson argues that reading a text on site was one of Egeria's primary reasons for visiting a shrine. He also demonstrates that she was an avid collector of such texts, looking forward to bringing new or more authentic versions home with her. For Johnson, Egeria chose her destinations based on what she had read and what she hoped to take back with her. It was not just glittering buildings or legends in the abstract that motivated her travels; it was her access to the written word and her desire to acquire as much textual knowledge as she could.

Egeria's practice of reading texts on site and being motivated to travel based on her reading was not confined to the Holy Land, as she visited the shrine of Thomas in Edessa and the shrine of Thecla in Seleucia. We know also that Egeria planned a visit to Ephesus. After visiting the *martyrion* of Thecla in Seleucia, Egeria headed to Constantinople and arrived there in June or July 384. She writes that her next destination is Asia, and particularly Ephesus to visit the *martyrion* of John (23.10).[68] It is not much of a stretch to imagine that Egeria's trip to Ephesus was motivated by her reading of John's activities in the Acts of John, some version of which is thought to have been in circulation already in the late second century.[69] She cannot have been motivated by the grandeur of the *martyrion*, since the *martyrion* at the time was literally nothing to write home about.[70] This is in line with Egeria's visits elsewhere. Johnson explains,

---

to the necessity of wealthy patrons to construct large-scale projects; it is certainly possible that the Acts of Timothy hopes to attract the attention of such donors.

67. Scott Fitzgerald Johnson, "Apostolic Geography: The Origins and Continuity of a Hagiographic Habit," *DOP* 64 (2010): 7; Johnson, *Literary Territories*, 82.

68. Trans. John Wilkinson, *Egeria's Travels*, 3rd ed. (Oxford: Aris & Phillips, 1999), 142.

69. For discussion, see Pieter J. Lalleman, *The Acts of John: A Two-Stage Initiation into Johannine Gnosticism* (Leuven: Peeters, 1998).

70. In her discussion of Ephesus, Egeria makes no mention of a *martyrion* of Timothy here, or any other reason for heading to Ephesus. This does not mean that there was *no* cult of Timothy in Ephesus at this time, but it does suggest that if there was it was not well known outside the city, and certainly not popular enough to attract

in the case of both Thomas and Thekla, there is a textual component
to Egeria's pilgrimage. Stories she has read about these saints motivate
her to seek out the places where they are honored. Furthermore, in both
cases she either produces a text that she owns related to the apostle or
takes away a text to add to her collection. Both visits are described by
Egeria herself as being off the beaten path; she emphasizes the special
care she took to visit them in person.[71]

It was Egeria's *reading* that set her route, and she was most likely not alone
in this practice. As Johnson explains, "Egeria's mode of interacting with
holy sites is not unique, and her approach seems to betoken an almost
obsessive archiving instinct that, coupled with the adoption of 'sacred
tourism,' disseminated Christian knowledge widely and rapidly."[72]

Part of the reason behind the composition of the Acts of Timothy,
therefore, was to give pilgrims an additional reason to visit Ephesus and
an itinerary to follow once they got there—from the distinguished places,
to the *embolos*, the harbor, and Mount Pion. The superabundant way in
which the text refers to Timothy ("most holy," "most laudatory," "thrice-
blessed") belies an attempt to persuade readers of Timothy's worthiness as
an object of veneration. The way the text praises the city and establishes
its critical position in the formation of the sacred library strongly suggests that the text is trying to fix this city firmly on the mental landscape
of its readers. Timothy is worth venerating, and the city is worth knowing
intimately. Travelers—especially, perhaps, travelers to Constantinople—
should take the time to see Ephesus, easily accessible by land or sea.[73]

---

pilgrims. In fact, Egeria's silence here about Timothy may be significant: we know that
in Constantinople, Egeria visited "all the churches," and "the tombs of the apostles"
(23.9), which almost certainly means the Church of the Holy Apostles with its relics
of Timothy, Andrew, and Luke. Had Egeria known of a tradition of Timothy's martyrdom and cult at Ephesus, it seems likely that she would have mentioned it here. This
does not seem to be on her radar.

71. Johnson, *Literary Territories*, 82–83.

72. Johnson, *Literary Territories*, 88.

73. The good news for travelers and for those who would promote religious travel
to Ephesus was that the city was well-situated and equipped to handle an influx of
visitors. Ephesus boasted a well-known and critical seaport and was a major center
on the trade route to Alexandria, an important economic engine for the city. Foss
argues that Ephesus's economic importance was not diminished by the foundation
of Constantinople, since it "thereafter lay on the main route of shipping between the
capital and the eastern provinces" (Foss, *Ephesus after Antiquity*, 7). Foss notes that

Conclusion

Texts and stories created vivid associations for readers and auditors, who were inspired to travel to visit holy people and holy places. Ephesus, eclipsed by the rootless but glamorous Constantinople, needed to fix itself firmly in the minds of late antique Christians. Texts could help make this a reality. Writing about the fifth-century Life and Miracles of Thecla, Johnson notes that the fifth-century text roots Thecla firmly in Seleucia and highlights the "local flavor" of the text, which he calls the "patriographical" element, "because the literary argument of rooting Thekla in Seleukeia brings praise for the city and the region where she resides."[74] Here we see a similar—though much shorter—attempt to root Timothy in Ephesus. The Acts of Timothy does not seem, moreover, to be the only text produced in this time period with these goals in mind. A similar attempt to root John to Ephesus is evident in contemporaneous literature. Prochorus's fifth-century *Acts* includes a significant amount of Ephesus-related material, including a parallel tradition about the shipwreck that brought John there (14), an extensive series of episodes involving the place of Artemis and a nearby bathhouse (14–32), and a series of events surrounding the temple of Artemis, including its destruction (32–44).[75] The text places the composition of John's Gospel at Patmos rather than Ephesus but includes John's instructions to send the papyri to Ephesus (154–158). Though the circumstances behind the composition are unclear, this text clearly reflects strong associations of John with Ephesus and could be another example of a text edited to promote Ephesus and increase pilgrimage activity to the city, especially if understood as part of a larger project eventually including the construction of the basilica. The extensive Syriac *History of Saint John* at Ephesus may also be part of this same project, as it clearly reflects strong desire to

---

at the Council of Ephesus in 431 an imperial official praised Ephesus by saying, "We have chosen Ephesus as a city easily accessible to those who come by land or sea, bounteously providing all useful local and imported products to its inhabitants." This is deliciously ironic, since this was the very same council that stripped Ephesus of its ecclesiastical power and influence, but it clearly points to Ephesus's prime location and easy accessibility for travelers.

74. Johnson, *Literary Territories*, 66.

75. On the dating and contents of this text, see R. Alan Culpepper, *John the Son of Zebedee* (Columbia: University of South Carolina Press, 1994), 204–22.

detail John's activities in the city, including its major landmarks. Notable also is that we see here another tradition involving the composition of the Gospel of John, here firmly located in Ephesus, as Peter and Paul make a special visit to Ephesus together to convince John to write his gospel (59). The development of this web of traditions involving John, the composition of the gospel, and the temple of Artemis saw new currency in the fifth century, possibly related to the actual destruction of the temple of Artemis in 400 and certainly to the overall project to place Ephesus more firmly on the map of early Christian travelers. Texts were crucial commodities in the growing pilgrimage industry. If Ephesus wanted to attract religious travelers—or patronage from wealthy or influential figures—she would need to win them using multiple tactics, and one of them seems to have been the production of texts. These texts could attract the attention of wealthy patrons or bishops, many of whom were actively involved in promoting the cult of the martyrs.[76]

Jonathan Z. Smith explains that "place is best understood as a locus of meaning."[77] In this text Ephesus is overlaid with new meaning, as the great metropolis becomes concretized as the site of the compilation of the gospels and of the martyrdom of "most holy" and "thrice-blessed" Timothy. Even as Constantinople can boast Timothy's remains, Ephesus can boast Timothy's blood and breath. Timothy did not give his life for Constantinople; Timothy gave his life opposing those who would pour out blood in the most holy places of Ephesus. By spilling out Timothy's own blood in the city, the text sacralizes the city in a most visceral way. Discussing sacred landscapes in late antiquity, Beátrice Caseau points to a line in Prudentius (fifth century CE), who, writing about the relics of Paul and Peter at Rome, says, "Tiber separates the bones of the two and both its banks are consecrated as it flows between the hallowed tombs" (*Peristephanon* 12.29, trans. H. J. Thompson)." The city was made sacred by the martyrs; our text sacralizes Ephesus in this same way, its distinguished places made holy

---

76. For example, Bitton-Ashkelony discusses how for Basil of Caesarea and Gregory of Nyssa, "the promotion and institutionalization of the cult of the martyrs was an integral part of their ecclesiastical activities" (*Encountering the Sacred*, 43). For broader discussion of the role of bishops in the cult of the martyrs, see Ramsey MacMullen, *Christianity and Paganism in the Fourth through Eighth Centuries* (New Haven: Yale University Press, 1999), 119–24.

77. Jonathan Z. Smith, *To Take Place: Towards Theory in Ritual* (Chicago: University of Chicago Press, 1987), 28.

again by Timothy's blood.[78] *Hic locus est*—here is the place where Timothy's blood was spilled, where his body was laid, where John compiled the gospels. Ephesus's urban topography is reimagined as *loca sancta*, the place of Timothy's martyrdom and of the composition of the *tetraevangelium*. Don't you want to come see it for yourself?

Bibliography

Adams, Sean A. "Luke's Preface and Its Relationship to Greek Historiography: A Response to Loveday Alexander." *JGRCJ* 3 (2006): 177–91.

Alexander, Loveday. *The Preface to Luke's Gospel*. SNTSMS 78. Cambridge: Cambridge University Press, 1993.

Aune, David E. "Luke 1.1–4: Historical or Scientific *Prooimion?*" Pages 138–48 in *Paul, Luke and the Graeco-Roman World: Essays in Honour of Alexander J. M. Wedderburn*. Edited by Alf Christophersen, Carsten Claussen, Jörg Frey, and Bruce Longenecker. JSNTSup 217. New York: T&T Clark, 2002.

Bammer, A. "Zur Topographie und Städtebaulichen Entwicklung von Ephesos." *JÖAI* 46 (1961–1963): 136–57.

Barnes, Timothy D. *Early Christian Hagiography and Roman History*. Tübingen: Mohr Siebeck, 2010.

Bitton-Ashkelony, Brouria. *Encountering the Sacred: The Debate on Christian Pilgrimage in Late Antiquity*. Berkeley: University of California Press, 2005.

Britt, Karen C. "How to Win Pilgrims and Influence Emperors: A Historical Reinterpretation of the Byzantine Church of St. John at Ephesus." *JECS* 64 (2012): 137–74.

Cadbury, H. J. "Commentary on the Preface of Luke." Pages 489–510 in vol. 1 of *The Beginnings of Christianity*. Edited by F. J. Foakes-Jackson and K. Lake. London: Macmillan, 1922.

Callan, Terrance. "The Preface of Luke-Acts and Historiography." *NTS* 31 (1985): 576–81.

Caseau, Béatrice. "Sacred Landscapes." In *Late Antiquity: A Guide to the Postclassical World*. Edited by G. W. Bowersock, Peter Robert Lamont Brown, and Oleg Grabar. Cambridge: Harvard University Press, 1999.

---

78. See Caseau, "Sacred Landscapes."

Concannon, Cavan. "The Acts of Timothy." Pages 396–401 in *New Testament Apocrypha: More Noncanonical Scriptures*. Edited by Tony Burke and Brent Landau. Grand Rapids: Eerdmans, 2016.

———. "In the Great City of the Ephesians: Contestations over Apostolic Memory and Ecclesial Power in the *Acts of Timothy*." *JECS* 24 (2016): 419–46.

Csapo, Eric. "Comedy and the *Pompe*: Dionysian Genre-Crossing." Pages 40–80 in *Greek Comedy and the Discourse of Genres*. Edited by Emmanuela Bakola, Lucia Prauscello, and Mario Teló. New York: Cambridge University Press, 2013.

Culpepper, R. Alan. *John the Son of Zebedee*. Columbia: University of South Carolina Press, 1994.

Davis, Stephen. "Pilgrimage and the Cult of St. Thecla in Late Antique Egypt." Pages 303–39 in *Pilgrimage and Holy Space in Late Antique Egypt*. Edited by David Frankfurter. RGRW 134. Leiden: Brill, 1998.

Delehaye, Hippolyte. "Les Acts de Saint Timothee." Pages 77–84 in *Anatolian Studies Presented to William Hepburn Buckler*. Edited by W. M. Calder and Joseph Keil. Manchester: Manchester University Press, 1939.

Detienne, Marcel. *Dionysos at Large*. Translated by Arthur Goldhammer. Cambridge: Harvard University Press, 1989.

Dinkler, Michal Beth. "Genre Analysis and Early Christian Martyrdom Narratives: A Proposal." Pages 314–36 in vol. 1 of *Sybils, Scriptures, and Scrolls*. Edited by Joel Baden, Hindy Najman, and Eibert Tigchelaar. Leiden: Brill, 2017.

Earl, Donald. "Prologue-Form in Ancient Historiography." *ANRW* 1.2:843–56.

Falcasantos, Rebecca Stephens. "Wandering Wombs, Inspired Intellects: Christian Religious Travel in Late Antiquity." *JECS* 25 (2017): 89–117.

Foss, Clive. *Ephesus after Antiquity: A Late Antique, Byzantine, and Turkish City*. Cambridge: Cambridge University Press, 1979.

Frank, Georgia. *The Memory of the Eyes: Pilgrims to Living Saints in Christian Late Antiquity*. Berkeley: University of California Press, 2000.

Frankfurter, David. "Hagiography and the Reconstruction of Local Religion in Late Antique Egypt: Memories, Inventions, and Landscapes." *CHRC* 86 (2006): 13–37.

———. "Introduction: Approaches to Coptic Pilgrimage." Pages 3–48 in in *Pilgrimage and Holy Space in Late Antique Egypt*. Edited by David Frankfurter. RGRW 134. Leiden: Brill, 1998.

Gamble, Harry. *Books and Readers in the Early Church*. New Haven: Yale University Press, 1995.

Graf, Fritz. "Gods in Greek Inscriptions." Pages 55–80 in *The Gods of Ancient Greece: Identities and Transformations*. Edited by Jan Bremmer and Andrew Erskine. Edinburgh Leventis Studies 5. Edinburgh: Edinburgh University Press, 2010.

Johnson, Scott Fitzgerald. "Apostolic Geography: The Origins and Continuity of a Hagiographic Habit." *DOP* 64 (2010): 5–25.

———. *Literary Territories: Cartographical Thinking in Late Antiquity*. New York: Oxford University Press, 2016.

Keil, J. *Führer durch Ephesos*. Vienna: Österreichisches Archäologisches Institut, 1964.

Knibbe, D. "Epigraphische Nachlese." *JÖAI* 47 (1964–1965): 29–30.

Lalleman, Pieter J. *The Acts of John: A Two-Stage Initiation into Johannine Gnosticism*. Leuven: Peeters, 1998.

Limberis, Vasiliki. "The Council of Ephesos: The Demise of the See of Ephesos and the Rise of the Cult of the Theotokos." Pages 321–40 in *Ephesos, Metropolis of Asia*. Edited by Helmut Koester. HTS. Valley Forge, PA: Trinity Press International, 1995.

MacCormack, Sabine. "*Loca Sancta*: The Organization of Sacred Topography in Late Antiquity." Pages 7–40 in *Blessings of Pilgrimage*. Edited by Robert G. Ousterhout. Urbana: University of Illinois Press, 1990.

MacMullen, Ramsay. *Christianity and Paganism in the Fourth through Eighth Centuries*. New Haven: Yale University Press, 1999.

Mango, Cyril. "Constantine's Mausoleum and the Translation of Relics." *BZ* 83 (1990): 51–62.

Miranda, Lin-Manuel. "Burn." Performed by Philippa Soo. Atlantic Records B0135P6PZA. 2015. CD.

Musurillo, Herbert. *Acts of the Christian Martyrs*. Oxford: Clarendon, 1972.

Nilsson, M. P. *The Dionysiac Mysteries of the Hellenistic and Roman Age*. New York: Arno, 1975.

Oster, Richard. "Ephesus as a Religious Center under the Principate." *ANRW* 2.18.3:1673.

Rogers, Guy McLean. *The Mysteries of Artemis of Ephesos*. New Haven: Yale University Press, 2013.

Rothschild, Clare K. *Luke-Acts and the Rhetoric of History*. WUNT 2/175. Tübingen: Mohr Siebeck, 2004.

Smith, Jonathan Z. *To Take Place: Towards Theory in Ritual.* Chicago: University of Chicago Press, 1987.

Sterling, Gregory E. *Historiography and Self-Definition: Josephos, Luke-Acts, and Apologetic Historiography.* NovTSup 64. Leiden: Brill, 1992.

Strelan, Rick. *Paul, Artemis, and the Jews in Ephesus.* BZNW 80. Berlin: de Gruyter, 1996.

Tassignon, Isabelle. "Dionysius et les Katagôgies d'Asie Mineure." Pages 81–100 in *Homo religious: Dieux, fêtes, sacré dans la Grèce et la Rome antiques.* Edited by A. Motte and C.-M. Ternes. Turnhout: Brepols, 2003.

Thomas, Christine. "At Home in the City of Artemis: Religion in Ephesos in the Literary Imagination of the Roman Period." Pages 81–118 in *Ephesos, Metropolis of Asia.* Edited by Helmut Koester. HTS. Valley Forge, PA: Trinity Press International, 1995.

Usener, Hermann. *Natalicia regis augustissimi Guilelmi imperatoris Germaniae ab Universitate Fridericia Guilelmia Rhenana [...] Insunt Acta S. Timothei.* Bonn: Programm der Universität Bonn, 1877.

Walsh, P. G. *The Poems of St. Paulinus of Nola.* ACW 40. New York: Newman, 1975.

Wiles, David. *The Masks of Menander: Sign and Meaning in Greek and Roman Performance.* Cambridge: Cambridge University Press, 1991

Wilkinson, John, trans. *Egeria's Travels.* 3rd ed. Oxford: Aris & Phillips, 1999.

Zabehlicky, Heinrich. "Preliminary Views of the Ephesian Harbor." Pages 201–16 in *Ephesos, Metropolis of Asia.* Edited by Helmut Koester. HTS. Valley Forge, PA: Trinity Press International, 1995.

Zamagni, Claudio. "Passion (ou Actes) de Timothée: Étude des traditions anciennes et edition de la forme BHG 1487." Pages 359–64 in *Poussières de christianisme et de judaïsme antiques: Études réunies en l'honneur de Jean-Daniel Kaestli et Éric Junod.* Edited by A. Frey and R. Gounelle. Prahins: Publications de l'Institut Romand des Sciences Bibliques, 2007.

Jesus's Sense of Sin

David Konstan

In this paper, I propose a radical redefinition of Jesus's conception of sin, as it is revealed to us in the gospels and certain other canonical texts of the New Testament, in particular the Acts of the Apostles. My thesis is that in the gospels, sin, that is, *hamartia*, is understood as the failure to trust in Jesus's capacity to perform miracles and hence in his divinity, despite the manifest evidence of his supernatural abilities in the many wonders that he performs. Sin is thus a negative idea; by contrast, trust in Jesus's powers is the *conditio sine qua non* for the remission of sin and in turn guarantees salvation and eternal bliss in the afterlife. To be absolutely clear, sin, I am arguing, does not consist in any specific act of wrongdoing, not even in the violation of the commandments. Murder, incest, adultery, and the rest are not sins per se. With the coming of Jesus, sin, or the state of sin, is reconceived as a lack of confidence in the sure signs of Jesus's claim to be the son of God. That, and only that, is what Jesus (as he is represented in the gospels) meant by sin.

As I have indicated, I am considering only the uses of the Greek word *hamartia*, which is consistently rendered as "sin" in the King James Version of the Bible and in equivalent translations into other languages. Other Greek words are sometimes translated as "sin" (though not in the King James and related versions, such as the RSV), but wrongly so, since I believe that the vocabulary of the New Testament is precise in this regard. Those other terms, for example, *ponēron, kakon, rhadiourgia, adikia, anomia, skandalon, planē, halisgēma,* and *paraptōma,* may signify "an evil," "wickedness," "iniquity," "villainy," "badness," "injustice," "error," "slip," "pollution," or "transgression," and the like, and are so rendered in the King James Bible, but they are distinct from *hamartia* and are not to be confused with the New Testament idea of sin.

In classical Greek, the word *hamartia* signified most broadly something like "missing the mark," in the literal sense of failing to hit the target,
but it also had the moral connotation of "error" (which itself derives from
the Latin verb meaning "go astray"). The word is used very frequently in
the Greek translation of the Hebrew Bible, or LXX, where it has again a
wide range of applications. Here too, there is a distinction to be observed
between biblical uses and the way the term is employed in texts that have
not been influenced by Jewish or Christian conceptions. I first indicate the
nature of *hamartia* in Judeo-Christian literature generally, as distinct from
classical Greek, and then turn to its use in the gospels, where, I argue, the
conception of sin ascribed to Christ is new and specific. But Jesus's sense
of sin differs not only from previous uses but also from the way it was
subsequently employed by the church fathers and noncanonical Christian
works, where *hamartia* commonly signifies offenses against divine stric-
tures generally, in much the way the word *sin* is employed today. This is
why it is necessary to recover its unique meaning in the gospels themselves. I begin, then, by indicating the distinction between the biblical
sense of *hamartia* and its use in ordinary Greek texts, and then turn to the
more restricted sense found in the gospels.

Sin is a loaded term: it differs from a mere fault or error, as well as from
wrongdoing and crime, in that it bears a religious connotation or pen-
umbra in the Judeo-Christian tradition that associates it with penitence
and damnation—even damnation for all eternity. The extreme degree of
punishment of course arouses a profound apprehension, as does the sense
of estrangement from God that some modern theologians see as essential
to the concept of sin; as one writer on hamartiology puts it, "Sin separates
us from God (Is.59:1–2).... In our relationship with Him, therefore, sinful
behavior on our part alienates us from Him by definition."[1] But apart from
the intensity of divine retribution and the existential anxiety that a feeling of distance from God may arouse in those who are conscious of God's
presence or absence in their lives, what is it, if anything, that distinguishes
sin from the sense of guilt that even strictly secular people may experience
upon wronging others or failing to live up to their own moral standards?
Is there anything about sin that separates it as an act from wrongdoing
more generally?

---

1. Robert D. Luginbill, *Hamartiology: The Biblical Study of Sin* (Ichthys: Bible
Study for Spiritual Growth, n.d.), 118; online at https://tinyurl.com/SBL4217a.

There is no word in ancient Greek that specifically identifies sin as opposed to other terms that seem to fall within the same broad semantic sphere. For just this reason, it is necessary to provide a definition that succeeds in isolating a specifically biblical sense of the term *hamartia*, as opposed to its uses in Greek literature more generally. In a recently published paper, I ventured various possible differentiae that might single out *sin* from offenses recognized outside the biblical tradition, and so justify translating *hamartia* as "sin" uniquely when it appears in the Bible or other Jewish and Christian texts, as opposed to "fault," "transgression," or the like, as in the case, for example, of Aristotle's *Poetics*, where *hamartia* is commonly rendered as "flaw" in the expression "tragic flaw."[2] A definition of a specifically biblical sense of *hamartia* would also allow the possibility of distinguishing between uses of the term within the LXX and New Testament, where it might well be the case that uses vary and that the specifically biblical signification is not applicable to every occurrence of *hamartia* and the verbal form *hamartanō*.

It would be hard to locate the difference between the uses of *hamartia* in the Bible and ordinary Greek texts in the nature of the acts that are prohibited: murder, incest, adultery, and the like are equally condemned in both traditions. An alternative is to consider the offended party rather than the offense itself: in the Bible, a violation of the law is an affront to God, who promulgated and upholds the rules of comportment. But classical texts too recognize that wrongdoing may be a slight against a divinity. The *Odyssey* opens with a conversation on Mount Olympus, in which Zeus complains of the way humans blame the gods for their misfortunes: "It is from us, they say, that evils come, but they even of themselves, through their own blind folly, have sorrows beyond that which is ordained [σφῇσιν ἀτασθαλίῃσιν ὑπὲρ μόρον ἄλγε' ἔχουσιν]" (1.34).[3] As a case in point Zeus cites Aegisthus, who was slain by Orestes. But Aegisthus's fate was of his own doing, since he murdered Agamemnon and married his wife, and so brought evils on himself "beyond that which was ordained," even though Zeus had given him fair warning, "sending Hermes, the keen-sighted Argeiphontes, that he should neither slay the man nor woo his wife, for from Orestes shall come vengeance for the son of Atreus when once he has

---

2. See David Konstan, "Sin: The Prehistory," *Scandinavian Journal for Greek and Byzantine Studies* 3 (2017): 125–40.

3. Translations of Homer's *Odyssey* follow A. T. Murray, trans., *The Odyssey*, 2 vols., LCL (Cambridge: Harvard University Press, 1919).

come to manhood and longs for his own land. So Hermes spoke, but for all his good intent he prevailed not upon the heart of Aegisthus; and now he has paid the full price of all" (1.29–43). The phrase "blind folly" represents the Greek word *atasthaliai*, the plural of *atasthalia*, which Liddell, Scott, and Jones defines as "presumptuous sin, recklessness, wickedness."[4] In the present instance, then, why not translate *atasthaliai* as "sins"? After all, Zeus himself sent Hermes, his messenger, to warn Aegisthus not to murder Agamemnon; his deed would seem to be an act of willful disobedience to the chief god of the Greek pantheon.

But perhaps merely contravening a divine order or preference is not sufficient to qualify an act as a sin. Sin requires, it may be, a sense of a specifically religious code, as opposed to the legal canons that govern civic life. Even here, however, there are examples in classical literature that seem to fit the description. An instance is the well-known passage in Sophocles's *Antigone* where the heroine pronounces her allegiance to "the unwritten and secure laws of the gods" (ἄγραπτα κἀσφαλῆ θεῶν νόμιμα, 454–455):

> It was not Zeus who published me that edict, and not of that kind are the laws which Justice who dwells with the gods below established among men. Nor did I think that your decrees were of such force, that a mortal could override the unwritten and unfailing statutes given us by the gods. For their life is not of today or yesterday, but for all time, and no man knows when they were first put forth. Not for fear of any man's pride was I about to owe a penalty to the gods for breaking these. (450–460)[5]

Disobeying Creon's edict prohibiting the burial of Antigone's brother Polynices is an infraction of the law, given that Creon, as king, decides what is lawful. But since Antigone believes that the decree contradicts the divine injunction that relatives bury their dead, she regards it as invalid, or at any event less binding than the unwritten and enduring prescription of the gods. It is tempting to see a distinction here between the crime, if we may call it that, of disobeying Creon's decree and the violation of divine prescriptions, which might properly be regarded as a sin.

Nevertheless, there is, I think, a further dimension to the nature of sin in the Bible that does, I believe, separate it out even from the contravention

---

4. LSJ, s.v. "ἀτασθᾰλία."
5. I have slightly modified the translation of Richard C. Jebb, *The Antigone of Sophocles* (Cambridge: Cambridge University Press, 1902).

of divine law that Antigone so clearly enunciates. But to see this distinction clearly, we must think not so much of specific kinds of offenses or the source, human or divine, of the prohibition but rather of the script in which the act of sinning is, as it were, embedded. For sin in the gospels is defined not so much by the wrongful deed as such, taken as a momentary act in time, as by its relation to the possibility of forgiveness, which constitutes the outcome or conclusion of the narrative. This scenario is implicit or, most often, explicit in the references to sin in the gospels and Acts, as well as in Paul's letters: the focus is invariably on the remission of sin, which is consequent on faith in Jesus. This aftermath is part and parcel, I suggest, of the definition of biblical sin and what distinguishes this conception from offenses against divine prescriptions in classical literature: in a word, pagan gods do not forgive, or if they do, it is for strictly personal motives having nothing to do with faith. The idea of grace is entirely absent.

In the New Testament, the remission or *aphesis* of sin is associated with two fundamental terms: *metanoia* and *pistis*. *Metanoia* is traditionally rendered as "repentance" and may thus suggest that sin is particularly related to remorse on the part of the offender and not simply to trust in Jesus's powers. According to the Gospels of Mark (1:4) and Luke (3:3), John the Baptist "did baptize in the wilderness, and preach the baptism of repentance for the remission of sins" (KJV). We may compare Luther's version: "die Taufe der Buße zur Vergebung Sünden"; the Spanish Nueva Versión Internacional: "el bautismo de arrepentimiento"; the Italian Nuova Riveduta 2006: "un battesimo di ravvedimento." Now, *metanoia* in classical texts most often signifies a change of mind or the simple wish that things had turned out otherwise and only rarely connotes the sense of moral regret that we associate with remorse. One can regret leaving one's umbrella at home when it suddenly begins to rain, but we would not speak of remorse in this connection. In turn, we may feel remorse at having harmed another wrongly, supposing that we have an attack of conscience, whereas mere regret would seem too neutral a sentiment. There is, however, a considerable controversy over just how to translate *metanoia* and its cognates, as well as *metameleia*, in the Bible, and recent versions in a wide variety of languages have opted rather—and correctly, as I have argued—for "conversion" or something similar as the appropriate idea.[6]

---

6. On the translation of *metanoia*, see David Konstan, "Regret, Repentance, and Change of Heart in Paul: Metanoia in Its Greek Context," in *Paul's Greco-Roman Con-*

Thus, the Spanish La Palabra version has "un bautismo como signo de conversión," the Conferenza Episcopale Italiana translation reads "un battesimo di conversione," and the Gute Nachricht Bibel has "Kehrt um und lasst euch taufen!"—a rendering that is rejected for official Lutheran versions of the Bible, although permitted in the case of commentaries and learned discussions.

What is more, *metanoia* is closely associated in the Bible with *pistis*. In Acts, we read: "Paul said, 'John baptized with the baptism of *metanoia*, telling the people to believe [*pisteusōsin*] in the one who was to come after him, that is, in Jesus'" (19:4 NRSV). Here, in what is clearly an expansion of Luke 3:3, one might be inclined to take *metanoia* in the classical sense of a change of mind, which results in abandoning old beliefs in favor of the belief in Jesus. Again, when we read in Acts 10:43, "All the prophets testify about him that everyone who believes in him receives forgiveness of sins through his name" (NRSV), we may observe that belief here takes the place of *metanoia* as the condition of forgiveness, or as I would prefer to translate it, of the remission (*aphesis*) of sins. The words *metanoia* and *pistis* are placed in apposition in Acts 20:21, where Paul says: "as I testified to both Jews and Greeks about *metanoia* toward God and faith toward our Lord Jesus" (NRSV); the terms seem pretty much equivalent and suggest that the change of mind is to be understood precisely as the adoption of the new belief. There is a similar conjunction of belief with the verb *metamelomai* at Matt 21:32: "For John came to you in the way of righteousness, and you did not believe him [ἐπιστεύσατε], but the tax collectors and the harlots believed him; and even when you saw it, you did not afterward μετεμελήθητε and believe [πιστεῦσαι] him" (RSV).

Given that *metanoia* is so closely associated with *pistis*, it is crucial to determine with equal precision the sense of this latter term. The word *faith* today in religious contexts is understood to mean something like "belief," and this in two respects. As a state of mind, faith signifies a deeply rooted conviction that resists arguments to the contrary; it may even be regarded as transcending reason, relating to higher truths that are not susceptible to scientific demonstration. "Faith" may also refer to a doctrine or set of propositions that constitute the content of belief: one believes that something is the case, such as that there is a God, or that Christ died for

text, ed. Cilliers Breytenbach, BETL 277 (Leuven: Peeters, 2015) 119–33; Konstan, "Reue," RAC 28:1216–42.

our sins. As Teresa Morgan observes, in her magisterial and exhaustive study of the ancient terms at the time when the New Testament was being composed, these two aspects, which we may call the "what" of faith ("I believe this") and the "how" ("I believe in my heart"), are not part of the semantic range, or at best only marginally so, of the classical Latin word *fides* or the corresponding Greek word *pistis* (which is cognate with *fides* and with the English "bide").[7] Classical *fides* and *pistis* rather connote trust or confidence in another and also the reciprocal sense of trustworthiness: one trusts people or institutions that are reliable. What is more, as Morgan has convincingly shown, this is also the predominant sense of the terms in gospels, Acts, and the authentic letters of Paul. Morgan adds that, because trust is an intangible value, people tend to seek evidence for it or confirm it by referring to material signs such as handshakes, oaths, contracts, and divine portents, which serve as proofs of trustworthiness. The change of heart, then, that leads to the remission of sins is precisely the acquisition of confidence in Jesus's ability to work miracles, which is the sign of his divinity.

The core experience in the gospels, then, is the change of heart or conversion and the resulting confidence in the miracles, and hence the divinity, of Jesus; and this in turn is the condition for the remission of sins. What is more, reference to sin, that is, to the term *hamartia*, occurs almost exclusively precisely in this connection, that is, as a function of this trust. To take just a few examples, at Acts 2:38 we read: "Then Peter said unto them, 'Repent, and be baptized every one of you in the name of Jesus Christ for the remission of sins, and ye shall receive the gift of the Holy Ghost'" (KJV; Πέτρος δὲ ἔφη πρὸς αὐτούς· μετανοήσατε, καὶ βαπτισθήτω ἕκαστος ὑμῶν ἐπὶ τῷ ὀνόματι Ἰησοῦ Χριστοῦ εἰς ἄφεσιν ἁμαρτιῶν, καὶ λήψεσθε τὴν δωρεὰν τοῦ Ἁγίου Πνεύματος). Or again, at Acts 3:19: "Repent ye therefore, and be converted, that your sins may be blotted out" (KJV; μετανοήσατε οὖν καὶ ἐπιστρέψατε εἰς τὸ ἐξαλειφθῆναι ὑμῶν τὰς ἁμαρτίας), this coming immediately after Peter heals a lame man, in evidence of the divine gift bestowed on him. Or consider 10:43, Peter speaking to Cornelius about Jesus: "to him give all the prophets witness, that through his name whosoever believeth in him shall receive remission of sins" (KJV; τούτῳ πάντες οἱ προφῆται μαρτυροῦσιν, ἄφεσιν ἁμαρτιῶν λαβεῖν διὰ τοῦ ὀνόματος αὐτοῦ

---

7. See Teresa Morgan, *Roman Faith and Christian Faith: Pistis and Fides in the Early Roman Empire and Early Churches* (Oxford: Oxford University Press, 2015), 12–13, citing Augustine, *De trinitate* 13.2.5.

πάντα τὸν πιστεύοντα εἰς αὐτόν). At Mark 4:12 Jesus explains the para-
bles concerning sowing to the disciples, which, he says, are cryptic "that
seeing they may see, and not perceive; and hearing they may hear, and
not understand; lest at any time they should be converted, and their sins
should be forgiven them" (KJV; ἵνα βλέποντες βλέπωσι καὶ μὴ ἴδωσι, καὶ
ἀκούοντες ἀκούωσι καὶ μὴ συνιῶσι, μήποτε ἐπιστρέψωσι καὶ ἀφεθῇ αὐτοῖς
τὰ ἁμαρτήματα). Those who are not converted will not have their sins
forgiven. One further example, from Luke 7:36–50, the episode in which
Jesus dines at the home of a Pharisee, and a woman who is a sinner (v. 37:
καὶ ἰδοὺ γυνὴ ἐν τῇ πόλει ἥτις ἦν ἁμαρτωλός) kisses his feet and anoints him.
The Pharisee objects that Jesus, given that he is a prophet, ought to have
known "that she is a *hamartōlos*" (7:39 KJV; ὅτι ἁμαρτωλός ἐστι). Jesus
replies with the parable of a man who pardoned (ἐχαρίσατο, 7:42; also in
7:43; rendered as "forgave") two debtors, one owing five hundred denarii,
the other fifty: the remission of the larger debt is the greater benefit, and
since the woman gave more to Jesus than the others, he concludes: "Her
sins, which are many, are forgiven; for she loved much: but to whom little
is forgiven, the same loveth little" (7:47 KJV; ἀφέωνται αἱ ἁμαρτίαι αὐτῆς
αἱ πολλαί, ὅτι ἠγάπησε πολύ· ᾧ δὲ ὀλίγον ἀφίεται, ὀλίγον ἀγαπᾷ). In this
passage the remission of sins is associated with love (*agapē*) rather than
pistis, but in the following verses *pistis* takes the place of *agapē*: "And he
said unto her, Thy sins are forgiven. And they that sat at meat with him
began to say within themselves, Who is this that forgiveth sins also? And
he said to the woman, Thy faith hath saved thee; go in peace" (7:48–50
KJV; εἶπε δὲ αὐτῇ· ἀφέωνταί σου αἱ ἁμαρτίαι. καὶ ἤρξαντο οἱ συνανακείμενοι
λέγειν ἐν ἑαυτοῖς· τίς οὗτός ἐστιν ὃς καὶ ἁμαρτίας ἀφίησιν; εἶπε δὲ πρὸς τὴν
γυναῖκα· ἡ πίστις σου σέσωκέ σε· πορεύου εἰς εἰρήνην). Trust in Jesus, which
is equivalent to love for him, wipes sins away. This is the sense, I think, of
John 15:22: "If I had not come and spoken to them, they would not have
been guilty of sin, but now they have no excuse for their sin" (NRSV; εἰ μὴ
ἦλθον καὶ ἐλάλησα αὐτοῖς, ἁμαρτίαν οὐκ εἶχον· νῦν δὲ πρόφασιν οὐκ ἔχουσι
περὶ τῆς ἁμαρτίας αὐτῶν). If sin is the failure to believe in Jesus's divinity,
as revealed through his miracles, then until the coming of Jesus there can
have been no sin—wrongdoing, *ponēra*, *kaka*, for sure, but not sin in the
sense in which *hamartia* is predominantly used in the gospels.[8]

---

8. Contrast the interpretation of Albert Barnes, *Notes on the New Testament* (repr.,
Grand Rapids: Baker, 1949), 1313: "*Had not had sin*—This is evidently to be understood of the particular sin of persecuting and rejecting him. Of this he was speaking;

Now, I do not suppose that it comes as a great surprise that faith heals sins, or more precisely, on the interpretation of the key words that I have argued for, that conversion and trust in Jesus's divinity, as evidenced by his miraculous powers, are the condition for the remission of sin. What may be less evident, however, is that sin is mentioned in the Bible almost exclusively in connection with *pistis* and its power to earn forgiveness. Of course, there are many passages in which wrongdoing is mentioned independently of salvation. At Mark 7:1–8, the Pharisees criticize the disciples for not washing before eating, as ritual demands, and shortly afterwards Jesus declares that all foods are clean (7:19; καθαρίζον πάντα τὰ βρώματα). It is evil things that defile one, such as adultery, fornication, murder, theft, deceit, blasphemy, and pride, not foods and such: "For it is from within, from the human heart, that evil intentions come: fornication, theft, murder, adultery, avarice, wickedness, deceit, licentiousness, envy, slander, pride, folly. All these evil things come from within, and they defile a person" (7:21–23 NRSV; ἔσωθεν γὰρ ἐκ τῆς καρδίας τῶν ἀνθρώπων οἱ διαλογισμοὶ οἱ κακοὶ ἐκπορεύονται, μοιχεῖαι, πορνεῖαι, φόνοι, κλοπαί, πλεονεξίαι, πονηρίαι, δόλος, ἀσέλγεια, ὀφθαλμὸς πονηρός, βλασφημία, ὑπερηφανία, ἀφροσύνη· πάντα ταῦτα τὰ πονηρὰ ἔσωθεν ἐκπορεύεται καὶ κοινοῖ τὸν ἄνθρωπον;). There is no mention here of *metanoia*, *pistis*, or forgiveness: but neither is there

---

and though, if he had not come, they would have been guilty of many other sins, yet of this, their great crowning sin, they would not have been guilty." And this from John Calvin's *Commentary on John*, trans. William Pringle (Grand Rapids: Eerdmans, 1949), 2:86–87: "It may be thought that Christ intended by these words to say, that there is no other sin but unbelief; and there are some who think so. Augustine speaks more soberly, but he approaches to that opinion; for, since faith forgives and blots out all sins, he says, that the only sin that damns a man is unbelief. This is true, for unbelief not only hinders men from being delivered from the condemnation of death, but is the source and cause of all evils. But the whole of that reasoning is inapplicable to the present passage; for the word sin is not taken in a general sense, but as related to the subject which is now under consideration; as if Christ had said, that their ignorance is utterly inexcusable, because in his person they maliciously rejected God; just as if we were to pronounce a person to be innocent, just, and pure, when we wished merely to acquit him of a single crime of which he had been accused. Christ's acquittal of them, therefore, is confined to one kind of sin, because it takes away from the Jews every pretense of ignorance in this sin, of despising and hating the Gospel." Again, John Gill's *An Exposition of the New Testament*, 3 vols. (1746–1748): "*they had not had sin*; or been guilty of the sin of unbelief, in the rejection of the Messiah; not that they would have been without sin in any sense, or without any kind of sin, but without this particular sin."

mention of sin, if we take sin to be denoted specifically by *hamartia* in Greek. The various offenses catalogued by Jesus here are called *ponēra*, "evils" or "vicious acts"—bad things, to be sure, and condemned by Jesus as they are in the Hebrew Bible and for the most part also in Greek and Roman law. But they are not called *hamartiai* here. It is not, I think, overly nice, not to say finicky or pedantic, to insist on the strict lexical equivalence of *hamartia* and "sin" and hence to affirm that these acts, terrible as they are, are not to be regarded as sins. As I have noted, Greek has an ample vocabulary for errors or wrongs, all of which are to be found in the New Testament. But they occur predominantly in contexts that do not speak of forgiveness or salvation; when the forgiveness that is gained by *pistis* or confidence is in question, it is almost always *hamartia* and none of these other terms that is in play.

If this is right—and there are certain exceptions, or apparent exceptions, that have to be treated in a full analysis—and *hamartia* is almost entirely restricted to contexts that specify the remission of sins on the basis of *pistis*, then we may be justified in understanding sin as just the absence of that confidence in Jesus and his works.[9] Sin, then, is not simply a specific kind of offense or an offense against a divinity or divinely sanctioned code, but the condition of anyone who does not have trust in Jesus's capacity to work miracles and the divine gift that this implies. To be sure, such people of little faith are prone to doing wrong and committing those very *ponēra* that are forbidden by human and divine law. But sin in the strict sense is just that which is liable to remission as a consequence of conversion and trust in Jesus. It is in this regard that sin goes hand in hand with grace and pardon; more precisely, what distinguishes sin in the New Testament from classical conceptions of wrongdoing and error is its dialectical dependence on the possibility of remission through this particular kind of faith. It is only in such contexts, I suggest, that we are fully justified in translating any of the various terms for faults as "sin," and as it happens, the Greek word that occurs precisely in this script or pattern—and what is more, virtually only there—is *hamartia*.

As I have said, the sense of *hamartia* ascribed to Jesus in the gospels and some other passages in the New Testament was subsequently lost to sight, as *hamartia* came to signify wrongful acts generally, as does the Eng-

---

9. I treat these apparent exceptions in detail in the article I am preparing, "Sünde," *RAC* (forthcoming), in which I will cite the relevant passages more fully.

lish term *sin* and related words in other modern languages.[10] The process occurred in tandem with the emergence of new meanings associated with terms such as *metanoia*, now taken to signify repentance, and *pistis*, in the sense of "faith." We may reasonably ask why the sense of *hamartia* should have been so radically restricted in the gospels, in contrast to its use both in the LXX and in subsequent Christian literature. Although I cannot enter into a full exposition of the matter here, I suggest that the reason has to do with the extraordinary entry of God, or the divine, into the world represented by the presence of Jesus. The moment is decisive: it offers a unique opportunity of salvation by confidence in his works and hence in his divinity, or else damnation by a failure of such trust. Whatever sin may have meant in the past, that is, to Jews awaiting the arrival of the Messiah, it is now wholly reconfigured. Confidence in Jesus and his acts is everything. After his death—which he endured not for humankind's sins but rather to fulfill the prophecies of the Bible as he knew it—one could only believe in his powers via the texts that recorded his miracles. In the meantime, interpretations of his words and deeds led to an accumulation of doctrines that increasingly defined the content of Christianity and demanded belief on the part of the faithful. To sin now was to defy the pre-

---

10. See, for example, the Acts Thom. 38 for the easy shift between *hamartia* and other terms for wrongdoing: Τότε τὸ πλῆθος τῶν συναχθέντων ἀκοῦον ταῦτα ἐδάκρυεν καὶ ἔλεγεν τῷ ἀποστόλῳ· Ἄνθρωπε τοῦ θεοῦ, ὃν σὺ κηρύσσεις θεὸν ἡμεῖς οὐ τολμῶμεν λέγειν ὅτι αὐτοῦ ἐσμεν, ὅτι τὰ ἔργα ἡμῶν ἃ διεπραξάμεθα ἀλλότρια αὐτοῦ ἐστιν, μὴ ἀρέσκοντα αὐτῷ· εἰ δὲ σπλαγχνίζεται ἐφ' ἡμᾶς καὶ ἐλεεῖ ἡμᾶς καὶ ῥύεται παριδὼν τὰς προτέρας ἡμῶν πράξεις, καὶ ἀπὸ τῶν κακῶν ὧν διεπραξάμεθα ἐν πλάνῃ ὄντες ἐλευθεροῖ ἡμᾶς, καὶ οὐχ ὑπολογίζεται ἡμῖν οὐδὲ ὑπόμνησιν ἡμῶν ποιεῖται τῶν προτέρων ἁμαρτημάτων, γινόμεθα αὐτοῦ θεράποντες, καὶ τὸ θέλημα αὐτοῦ εἰς τέλος ἄξομεν. Ὁ δὲ ἀπόστολος αὐτοῖς ἀπεκρίνατο λέγων· Οὐ καταψηφίζεται ὑμῶν οὐδὲ λογίζεται ὑμῖν τὰς ἁμαρτίας ἃς ἐν πλάνῃ ὄντες διεπράξασθε, ἀλλὰ παραβλέπει ὑμῶν τὰ παραπτώματα ἃ κατὰ ἀγνωσίαν ἦτε πεποιηκότες ("Then the multitude of them that were gathered together hearing these things wept, and said unto the apostle: O man of God, the God whom thou preachest, we dare not say that we are his, for the works which we have done are alien unto him and not pleasing to him; but if he will have compassion on us and pity us and save us, overlooking our former deeds, and will set us free from the evils which we committed being in error, and not impute them unto us nor make remembrance of our former sins, we will become his servants and will accomplish his will unto the end. And the apostle answered them and said: He reckoneth not against you, neither taketh account of the sins which ye committed being in error, but overlooketh your transgressions which ye have done in ignorance," trans. M. R. James, *The Apocryphal New Testament, Being the Apocryphal Gospels, Acts, Epistles, and Apocalypses* [repr., Oxford: Clarendon, 1983]).

scriptions of the law—due, no doubt, to a failure of faith. But Jesus's own message was simpler: his presence was self-revealing and the supernatural quality of his acts unmistakable, and together they offered an immediate occasion for trust in his divinity. To experience this confidence was to gain the remission of one's sins; not to do so was to be in a state of sin, defined not just by the wrongs one had committed in life but by doubt concerning the nature Jesus. In the words of John Calvin—though he rejected this implication—"there is no other sin but unbelief."[11]

Bibliography

Barnes, Albert. *Notes on the New Testament*. Repr., Grand Rapids: Baker, 1949.

Calvin, John. *Commentary on John*. Translated by William Pringle. 2 vols. Grand Rapids: Eerdmans, 1949.

Gill, John. *An Exposition of the New Testament*. 3 vols. 1746–1748.

James, M. R. *The Apocryphal New Testament, Being the Apocryphal Gospels, Acts, Epistles, and Apocalypses*. Reprint, Oxford: Clarendon, 1983.

Jebb, Richard C. *The Antigone of Sophocles*. Cambridge: Cambridge University Press, 1902.

Konstan, David. "Regret, Repentance, and Change of Heart in Paul: Metanoia in Its Greek Context." Pages 119–33 in *Paul's Greco-Roman Context*. Edited by Cilliers Breytenbach. BETL. Leuven: Peeters, 2015.

———. "Reue." *RAC 28: 1216–42*.

———. "Sin: The Prehistory." *Scandinavian Journal for Greek and Byzantine Studies* 3 (2017): 125–40.

———. "Sünde." *RAC*. Forthcoming.

Luginbill, Robert D. *Hamartiology: The Biblical Study of Sin*. Ichthys: Bible Study for Spiritual Growth, n.d. https://tinyurl.com/SBL4217a.

Morgan, Teresa. *Roman Faith and Christian Faith: Pistis and Fides in the Early Roman Empire and Early Churches*. Oxford: Oxford University Press, 2015.

Murray, A. T. trans. *The Odyssey*. 2 vols. LCL. Cambridge: Harvard University Press, 1919.

---

11. Calvin, *Commentary on John*, trans. William Pringle, 2 vols. (Grand Rapids: Eerdmans, 1949), 2:86.

The Jewish Agave and Hera:
A Mimetic Reading of the Book of Judith

Dennis R. MacDonald

When I was asked to contribute to this volume, I immediately connected Judith Perkins with her ancient Jewish namesake, not simply because of the coincidence of the names but also because our Judith has long been a specialist in ancient religious fiction.

The book of Judith narrates the liberation of Judea from the Assyrians during the reign of Nebuchadnezzar (who actually was Babylonian; 605–562 BCE), but its date of composition likely was during the Hellenistic period (around 100 BCE, probably from Palestine). This study will argue that the author borrowed heavily from Greek poetry, most notably Euripides's *Bacchae* and Homer's *Il.* 14.[1] It then will apply the six relevant criteria of mimesis criticism to establish and interpret these imitations, and finally it will suggest the broader implications for understanding early Jewish fictions in Greek and their relevance to the composition of the gospels two centuries later.

Imitations of the Bacchae

1. Religious Persecution

1.1. Religious Persecution in the Bacchae

Euripides's tragedy begins with Dionysus alone on stage declaring why he has come to Thebes, his birthplace.

---

1. The superb commentary by Deborah Levine Gera mentions the influence of Homer, *Il.* 14, but surprisingly nothing about the influence of the *Bacchae*. See Gera, *Judith*, CEJL (Berlin: de Gruyter, 2014). Gera instead focuses on influences of Greek prose, especially Herodotus, Ctesias's *Persica*, and Xenophon's *Cyropaedia*.

> I have now come to the land of the Greeks for the first time,
> after having made those regions dance and having established my
> rites, so that a god might be revealed to mortals.
> Of the cities of Greece Thebes was the first one
> that I stirred to ululate, having clothed the women in fawnskin
> and placed the thyrsus in their hands, my ivied spear.
> Since my mother's sisters—whom one might least expect—
> were saying that Dionysus was not born from Zeus.
> ...
> For this reason I drove the women from their homes.
> They dwell in the mountains frenzied in mind.
> I forced them to take the tokens of my revelry. (*Bacch.* 20–27, 32–34)[2]

The tokens mentioned here include wreathes (στέφανοι) of ivy, tambourines (τύμπανα), cymbals (κύμβαλα), and thyrsi (fennel stalks wound with ivy and topped with pinecones). At the end of his opening speech, Dionysus addresses the chorus, or dancers, of maenads (crazed women).

> You who have left Mount Tmolus, defender of Lydia,
> my *thiasos* [band of female groupies], women whom from the barbarians
> I have brought here as my comrades in camp and march,
> take up the instrument native to the region of the Phrygians,
> tambourines [τύμπανα]. (55–59)

The god then leaves the stage, and the maenads dance and sing: "Soon all the land will dance, / when Clamor leads his thiasos / to the mountain" (114–116).

At first, the only Theban men to receive the god are Pentheus's grandfather Cadmus and the blind seer Tiresias, who warns him against violence against the maenads. Both old men are ready to join the women in their dances.

Despite Tiresias's warning, Pentheus insists on punishing the women.

> I hear of a new evil in the city.
> Our women abandon their homes
> in fake Bacchic ecstasy, scurry about in the wooded
> hills, and honor in dances some new daemon,
> Dionysus—whoever he is.
> At the center of their *thiasoi* stand full
> wine bowls. (216–222)

---

2. Unless otherwise noted, all translations are mine.

Pentheus already had used his authority to put an end to the madness of the maenads:

> Those whom I have seized, with their hands bound,
> my servants hold safely in the public jail;
> those still on the loose I will hunt from the hills.
>
> ...
>
> By securing them in iron nets,
> I will soon put a stop to this pernicious Bacchic activity.
>
> ...
>
> I'll chop his neck from this body,
> that one who says Dionysus is a god. (226–228, 231–232, 241–242)

Tiresias again responds:

> Receive the god into the land,
> pour libations, play the bacchant, and wreathe the head!
>
> ...
>
> I will not be convinced by your words and fight against the god. (312–313, 325)

1.2. Religious Persecution in Judith

The role of the god-fighter in the Jewish novel falls to Nebuchadnezzar's general Holofernes, who was ordered "to destroy all flesh, anyone who did not follow" the king's orders, such that "their wounded will fill their valleys and streams, and the river will be filled to overflowing with their dead" (Jdt 2:3, 8).

In order to appease Holofernes, the residents surrounding Judea "received [ἐδέξαντο] him, and their entire region received him with wreathes, dances, and tambourines [μετὰ στεφάνων καὶ χορῶν καὶ τυμπάνων]" (3:7). This passage alone should suffice to notify the reader of Dionysian connections. The women of Thebes worship the god of wine, wearing wreathes of ivy, dancing, and beating tambourines. Note also that Tiresias admonishes Pentheus, "receive [δέχου] the god into the land, / pour libations, play the Bacchant [by dancing], and wreathe [στέφου] the head" (*Bacch.* 312–313).

2. God-Fighting Begins

2.1. God-Fighting in the Bacchae

Pentheus then issues these orders to his soldiers:

> Scurry about the area and track down
> the effeminate stranger who introduces
> a new disease among the women and ruins their marriage beds.
> If you seize him, bring
> him here chained, so that by a judgment of stoning
> he may die. (*Bacch.* 352–357)

Before long, Theban soldiers bring the god in shackles.

2.2. God-Fighting in Judith

Despite the warm welcome from the Judeans, Holofernes persists in his murderous rage, because he has been ordered "to destroy all the gods of the land" (Jdt 3:8).

3. Prayers of the Faithful

3.1. Prayers of the Faithful in the *Bacchae*

After Pentheus incarcerates Dionysus, all male characters exit, leaving only the Lydian chorus, who pray for their god's rescue:

> Do you see [ἐσορᾷς], O child of Zeus,
> Dionysus, that your advocates
> are constrained by oppression?
> Lord, waving your gold-gleaming
> thyrsus, come down from Olympus
> and restrain the hubris of a murderous man! (*Bacch.* 550–555)

3.2. Prayers of the Faithful in Judith

> The people fell and worshiped the god and cried out, "Lord God of heaven,
> observe [κάτιδε] their arrogance and have mercy on the humiliation of our

people, and look upon [ἐπίβλεψον] the face of those who have sanctified themselves to you this day." (Jdt 6:18–19)

Particularly striking are the petitions in both works that the god observe the oppression and intervene against their arrogant and violent foes.

4. The Minatory Informant

4.1. The Minatory Informant in the Bacchae

A messenger reports to Pentheus what he has seen: at dawn the women were in the wild asleep, "soberly—not as you say / drunk from the wine-bowl" (*Bacch.* 686–687). When the women awoke, they performed the most amazing miracles, such as producing fountains of water and wine. "Had you been there, the god you now censure / you would approach with prayers on seeing such things" (712–713). The herder thus advises: "This god—whoever he may be—O master, / receive [δέχου] him into this city" (769–770).

4.2. The Minatory Informant in Judith

Holofernes calls for an informant, the Ammonite Achior, who narrates for him the history of divine protection of the Jews from Abraham, to the exodus, the conquest of Canaan, the exile, and the return to Judea. Here is his advice: "Now my lord master, … if there is no lawlessness in their ethnos, my lord should move along lest their Lord cover them with a shield and their God join them, and we become an object of scorn before all the earth" (Jdt 5:20–21).

5. The God-Fighter Ignores the Advice

5.1. Pentheus Ignores the Advice

Despite the messenger's report, Pentheus remains intent on ridding Thebes of this foreign scourge and again threatens to muster his troops against the reveling women in the wild. "We will go to war / with the bacchants!" (*Bacch.* 784–785). The god, however, warns: "I would rather sacrifice to him than kick against the goads, / a mortal raging against a god" (794–795).

5.2. Holofernes Ignores the Advice

Holofernes refuses to heed Achior's warning: Nebuchadnezzar "will dispatch his might and destroy them from the face of the earth, and their god will not rescue them" (Jdt 6:2). He then sends Achior into the Jewish camp to suffer the same violent fate as they.

6. Drunkenness and Beheading

6.1. Drunkenness and Beheading in the Bacchae

Dionysus then drives Pentheus mad, symbolized by double vision, a common result of drinking too much wine. The god then coaxes the demented king to spy on the women in the mountains, where they discover and attack him. The king tries desperately to reveal to his mother, Agave, who he is but in vain.

> She grabbed his left arm with a strong grip,
> planted her foot against the doomed man's ribs,
> and wrenched out the shoulder.
> ...
> One woman carried an arm,
> another a foot in its boot, and his ribs were bare
> from the tearing of the flesh; every woman with bloody
> hands played catch with Pentheus's flesh. (*Bacch.* 1125–1127, 1133–1136)

Agave then triumphantly carries his head back to Thebes atop her thyrsus, thinking that it is the head of a lion.

6.2. Drunkenness and Beheading in Judith

Judith agrees to drink privately with Holofernes in his bedroom, where "he kept drinking more quantities of wine than he ever had drunk in any one day since he was born" (Jdt 12:20). Before long, "Holofernes was conked out on his bed, for wine had overwhelmed him" (13:2). Then Judith

> came to the pillar of his bed, which was at Holofernes's head, she drew his short sword from it, and, approaching the bed, grabbed the hair of his head and said, "Lord God of Israel, strengthen me this day." And she struck his

neck twice with all her might and chopped off his head. His body rolled off the bed.... A little later she left and gave the head to her female slave. (13:6–9)

7. Heroines Return to Their Cities

7.1. Agave Returns to Thebes

Agave jabs her son's head atop a thyrsus descended from Mount Cithaeron and abandons the dancing maenads in the mountains (*Bacch.* 1139–1143). When she arrives within the gates, she praises Dionysus for her destruction of what she thinks was a lion (1144–1147). The chorus then receives her into their dance (1167: δέχεσθε; 1172: δέξομαι).

7.2. Judith Returns to Bethulia

Judith's female slave hides Holofernes's head in her food basket, and both women leave the Assyrian camp on pretense of going to prayer and ascend to the mountain Bethulia (Jdt 13:9–10). As she approached the gates, Judith praises her god "for his might against her enemies" (13:11; cf. 13:14). "The men of the city" run to the gate to meet her and "received [ὑπεδέξαντο]" her (13:12–13).

8. The Heroines Display the Heads

8.1. Agave Displays the Head of Pentheus

Agave next produces the thyrsus topped with Pentheus's head to the chorus (*Bacch.* 1173–1175) and later to the residents of Thebes: "Come and you will see [ἴδητε] the catch, / the beast we daughters of Cadmus have caught" (1203–1204).

8.2. Judith Displays the Head of Holofernes

"She took the head from the bag and said to them, 'See here [ἰδού] the head of Holofernes.... The Lord struck him down by the hand of a woman'" (Jdt 13:15).

9. Positive Responses to the Beheadings

9.1. Positive Responses to the Beheading in the *Bacchae*

The murder of Pentheus produces two polarized reactions. The persecuted maenads rejoice; the family of Cadmus, including Agave herself, ultimately laments. First the rejoicing.

Initially ecstatic at her presumed conquest, Agave boasts, "I will be called 'blessed [μάχαιρα] Agave'" (*Bacch.* 1180). The chorus responds, "O woman, I considered you blessed [εὐδαιμονίζω]" (1183; compare 1193: "I praise you").

9.2. Positive Responses to the Beheading in Judith

Ozias: "You, O daughter, are blessed [εὐλογητή] above all women on earth by god most high" (Jdt 13:18). Achior: "You are blessed [εὐλογημένη] in every tent in Judah and in every *ethnos*; whoever hears your name will be troubled" (14:7). Priests from Jerusalem "all blessed [εὐλόγησαν] her.... 'May you be blessed [εὐλογημένη] by the Almighty Lord forever'" (15:9–10).

10. Heroines Ask Authorities to Hang the Heads on City Walls

10.1. Agave Asks the Authorities to Hang the Head on the City Wall

Agave: Pentheus "should grab / and bring sturdy ladders to the houses / so that they can stake the head to the triglyphs," architectural ornamentation atop city walls (*Bacch.* 1212–1214). Again to Cadmus: "I bring in my arms, as you see, / the prize for valor, so that it might be hung up [ἀγκρεμασθῇ] at your home" (1238–1240).

10.2. Judith Asks the Authorities to Hang the Head on the City Wall

Judith: "Hear me, brothers, take this head and hang [κρεμάσατε] it on the battlements of your walls" (Jdt 14:1). Pentheus's head never makes it to the walls of Thebes, but "they hanged [ἐκρέμασαν] the head of Holofernes from the walls" of Bethulia (14:11).

11. Recognitions and Terror

11.1. Recognitions and Terror in the *Bacchae*

Agave gradually returns to her senses and recognizes, to her horror, that she has decapitated her son. Slaves then carry on stage a stretcher with the recoverable remains of Pentheus's body. Far from being blessed, Agave is "an unhappy sight" (ὄψιν οὐκ εὐδαίμονα; *Bacch.* 1232). In the end, Dionysus sends the entire house of Cadmus into exile.

11.2. Recognitions and Terror in Judith

When the Assyrians discover Holofernes's headless corpse (Jdt 14:15), they "rent their tunics, and their souls were terribly troubled" (14:19). In the end, they are forced to abandon their campaign against Judea.

Just in case the imitation of the *Bacchae* escaped the reader's notice, the author makes the parallels unmistakable in the following passage:

> Every woman of Israel ran en masse to see her and blessed her. And they formed a chorus [χορόν] of themselves for her. She took thyrsi in her hands and gave them to the women with her. And they wreathed [ἐστεφανώσαντο] with olive branches her and the women with her. And she went before all the people and led all the women in dancing. And every man of Israel followed in armor with wreaths [στεφάνων] and songs in their mouths. (Jdt 15:12–13)

Judith then sings.

> Begin with the tambourines [τυμπάνοις] to my God.
> Sing to my Lord with cymbals [κυμβάλοις].
> Tune up for him a new psalm.
> Exult and call on his name,
> for the Lord has crushed wars. (16:1–2)

Imitations of *Iliad* 14

Although the imitations of the *Bacchae* are extensive, scholars have recognized as well parallels with Hera's deception of Zeus in order to turn the Trojan War in favor of the Achaeans. In this case the parallels are sufficiently close to permit presentation in parallel columns.

Iliad 14	Judith 10–13
Hera decides to deceive Zeus in order to turn the battle in favor of the Achaeans (160).	Judith decides to deceive Holofernes in order to turn the battle in favor of the Judeans, especially those living in Judea.
"She went up into her room" (166). "There she entered" (169).	"She went up into her house, …
"First with ambrosia from her lovely body / she cleansed every stain and anointed herself richly with oil…. Having anointed her beautiful skin with it, / and combing her hair, she braided the bright tresses with her hand, / beautiful….	and she unwrapped the sackcloth she had been wearing, took off the garments of her widowhood, cleansed her body with water, anointed herself with costly myrrh, braided the hairs of her head, put on a tiara,
Then she clothed herself in an ambrosial robe that Athena / had made and smoothed, and put on many embroideries:" (170–171, 175–179) earrings and a veil, "She put on beautiful sandals" (186). "Then she placed around her body all of her finery [πάντα … κόσμον]" (187).	and put on her festive garments. And she took sandals for her feet and put on jewelry—bracelets, rings, and earrings— all of her finery [πάντα τὸν κόσμον; cf. Jdt 12:15: πάντι τῷ κόσμῳ τῷ γυναικείῳ]. And she beautified herself greatly for enticing the eyes of men, whoever might see her" (10:4).
"She left her chamber" (188).	"And she went out of the gate of the city" (10:6; cf. 12:16).
Hera goes to Mount Ida (292).	Judith goes to the Assyrian camp (10:11).
Zeus questions her: "Where are you going?" (292).	The guard questioned her: "Where do you come from? Where are you going?" (10:12; cf. 11:3).
Hera lies: she says she is going (ἔρχομαι) to patch up a domestic squabble between Oceanus and his wife, Tethys (300–310).	Judith lies: "I am going [ἔρχομαι] before Holofernes" to inform him how he can take Judea by force without losing a single man (10:13; cf. 11:6–19).
Zeus is smitten by her beauty (293–296).	The guards are smitten by her beauty (10:14; cf. 10:19, 23; 12:16).

Zeus invites her to his bed (313–314). After they make love, Sleep puts him to sleep.	Holofernes arranges for them to be alone at night and falls into a drunken sleep (13:1–2). Judith then beheads him (13:8–10).
As he sleeps, the Achaeans turn the Trojans from their ships.	In the ensuing battle, the Judeans rout the Assyrians from their land.

Testing for Mimesis

In several previous publications, several of which appear in the attending footnotes,[3] I employ a comparative methodology now known as mimesis criticism, at the heart of which are six criteria for establishing a text's literary imitation, or mimesis, of a model. The first two concern the cultural status of the proposed model or antetext.

Criterion 1. The criterion of *accessibility* assesses the likelihood that the author of the later text had access to the proposed antetext.
Criterion 2. *Analogy* determines whether other authors imitated the same mimetic model.

There can be little doubt that the *Bacchae* and *Il.* 14 satisfy these criteria. Courtney Friesen has argued for imitations of the former in many ancient texts, including those written by Jews, though he does not mention Judith.[4] Others have argued for the influence of the tragedy on 3 Maccabees.[5] I also

---

3. Dennis R. MacDonald, *The Homeric Epics and the Gospel of Mark* (New Haven: Yale University Press, 2000); MacDonald, *Does the New Testament Imitate Homer? Four Cases from the Acts of the Apostles* (New Haven: Yale University Press, 2003); MacDonald, *The Gospels and Homer: Imitations of Greek Epic in Mark and Luke-Acts*, NTGL 1 (Lanham MD: Rowman & Littlefield, 2014).

4. Courtney J. P. Friesen, *Reading Dionysus: Euripides' Bacchae and the Cultural Contestations of Greeks, Jews, Romans, and Christians*, Studien und Texte zu Antike und Christentum 95 (Tübingen: Mohr Siebeck, 2015).

5. J. R. C. Cousland, "Dionysus Theomachos? Echoes of the *Bacchae* in 3 Maccabees," *Bib* 82 (2001): 539–48; N. Clayton Croy, "Disrespecting Dionysus: 3 Maccabees as Narrative Satire of the God of Wine," in *Scripture and Tradition: Essays on Early Judaism and Christianity in Honor of Carl R. Holladay*, ed. Gail R. O'Day, Patrick Gray, and Carl R. Holladay, NovTSup 129 (Boston: Brill, 2008), 3–19.

have argued for extensive imitations in the Gospel of John, the Acts of the Apostles, and the Acts of Andrew.[6]

But no ancient book was more ubiquitous in ancient literary education than the *Iliad* (criterion 1). Furthermore, Hera's seduction of Zeus was a famous Homeric problem that generated many discussions and textual speculations. The Acts of Andrew likely contained an imitating parody of the episode.[7] The *Bacchae* and *Il.* 14 thus were accessible and imitated, but did they also inform the composition of Judith? Criteria 3–6 allow one to answer "yes."

> Criterion 3. *Density*: simply stated, the more parallels one can posit between two texts, the stronger the case that they issue from a literary connection.
>
> Criterion 4. The criterion of *order* examines the relative sequencing of similarities in two works. If parallels appear in the same order, the case strengthens for a genetic connection.
>
> Criterion 5. A *distinctive trait* is anything unusual in the targeted ante-text and the proposed borrower that links the two into a special relationship.
>
> Criterion 6. *Interpretability* asks what might be gained by viewing one text as a debtor to another. Why might an author have imitated the proposed model?

Deborah Levine Gera has argued that the author composed Judith around the year 100 BCE and created the fictional victory of the Judeans against the Assyrians/Babylonians to embolden Palestinian Jews to resist Hellenizing. The essay at hand has argued that this author modeled much of the book after two famous stories of powerful women in Greek poetry. To paraphrase the complaint of Julian the Apostate, he or she crafted arrows for his war against Hellenes with feathers plucked from their own

---

6. Dennis R. MacDonald, *The Dionysian Gospel: The Fourth Gospel and Euripides* (Minneapolis: Fortress, 2017); MacDonald, *Luke and Vergil: Imitations of Classical Greek Literature*, NTGL 2 (Lanham MD: Rowman & Littlefield, 2014), 11–65 (see also 205–10); MacDonald, "Lydia and Her Sisters as Lukan Fictions," in *A Feminist Companion to the Acts of the Apostles*, ed. Amy-Jill Levine, FCNTECW 9 (London: T&T Clark, 2004), 105–10; MacDonald, *Christianizing Homer: "The Odyssey," Plato, and "The Acts of Andrew"* (New York: Oxford University Press, 1994), 177–80.

7. MacDonald, *Christianizing Homer*, 134–41.

wings.[8] The heroine Agave and the goddess Hera seduced the author into imitating them to mock non-Jewish oppressors as powerless against a single Jewish widow. The author states this explicitly three times:

> Judith: "See here the head of Holofernes.... The Lord struck him down by the hand of a woman" (Jdt 13:15).
> An Assyrian officer: "A single woman has brought shame upon the house of king Nebuchadnezzar" (14:18).
> Judith again: "The Lord has foiled them by the hand of a woman, for their mighty man did not fall because of young men, nor did the sons of Titans strike him down, nor did tall giants oppose him, but Judith, the daughter of Merari undid him with the beauty of her face" (16:6), like the beauty of Homer's Hera.

Implications

Although the imitations of Greek poetry advocated here belong primarily to the cultural legacy of early Jewish compositions in Greek, they illumine three common objections to mimesis criticism in my previous books, especially those pertaining to the Gospel of Mark and Luke-Acts.[9] The first objects that my work favors the influence of Greek antetexts to the LXX and thus slights Jewish influence. The parallels argued for in this study—which could be amplified with respect to Tobit, 3 Maccabees, Josephus, and the Testament of Abraham—show that mimesis of Greek poetry was a thriving literary ploy among Jews themselves.

The second objects that the evangelists and their readers were insufficiently literate in Greek poetry to undertake and understand such sophisticated imitations, but the Greek of the book of Judith largely corresponds with that of the gospels and Acts. The third cavils that whereas Homer wrote in archaic Greek dactylic hexameters, the evangelists wrote in koine prose. This, of course, is precisely what one finds in Judith and other Jewish imitations of Homer and Greek tragedy.

---

8. Julian banned Christians from teaching because of their Christianizing Greek poetry, above all Homer. According to Theodoret, he complained that "'we are shot with arrows feathered from our own wings,' for they make war against us armed from our own books" (*Hist. eccl.* 3.4).

9. See note 2.

Bibliography

Cousland, J. R. C. "Dionysus Theomachos? Echoes of the *Bacchae* in 3 Maccabees." *Bib* 82 (2001): 539–48.

Croy, N. Clayton. "Disrespecting Dionysus: 3 Maccabees as Narrative Satire of the God of Wine." Pages 3–19 in *Scripture and Tradition: Essays on Early Judaism and Christianity in Honor of Carl R. Holladay.* Edited by Gail R. O'Day, Patrick Gray, and Carl R. Holladay. NovTSup 129. Boston: Brill, 2008.

Friesen, Courtney J. P. *Reading Dionysus: Euripides' Bacchae and the Cultural Contestations of Greeks, Jews, Romans, and Christians.* Studien und Texte zu Antike und Christentum 95. Tübingen: Mohr Siebeck, 2015.

Gera, Deborah Levine. *Judith.* CEJL. Berlin: de Gruyter, 2014.

MacDonald, Dennis R. *Christianizing Homer: "The Odyssey," Plato, and "The Acts of Andrew."* New York: Oxford University Press, 1994.

———. *The Dionysian Gospel: The Fourth Gospel and Euripides.* Minneapolis: Fortress, 2017.

———. *Does the New Testament Imitate Homer? Four Cases from the Acts of the Apostles.* New Haven: Yale University Press, 2003.

———. *The Gospels and Homer: Imitations of Greek Epic in Mark and Luke-Acts.* NTGL 1. Lanham MD: Rowman & Littlefield, 2014.

———. *The Homeric Epics and the Gospel of Mark.* New Haven: Yale University Press, 2000.

———. *Luke and Vergil: Imitations of Classical Greek Literature.* NTGL 2. Lanham MD: Rowman & Littlefield, 2014.

———. "Lydia and Her Sisters as Lukan Fictions." Pages 105–10 in *A Feminist Companion to the Acts of the Apostles.* Edited by Amy-Jill Levine. FCNTECW 9. London: T&T Clark, 2004.

The Lynching Tree and the Cross:
James Cone, Historical Narrative, and the
Ideology of Just Crucifixion (Luke 23:41)

Shelly Matthews

A key aspect of Judith Perkins's scholarly contribution, as she has mapped the intersection of ancient Greco-Roman fiction and early Christian narrative, has been her attention to the ideology of the texts she studies. Noting that the ancient romance novels are both written by and for the elite class, she has exposed how an ideology supportive of elite interests infuses this literature. With respect to the question of sustaining the elite powers of the city through marriage alliances, she demonstrates how the novels work to support that power through the celebration of the conjugal union of the young highborn protagonists. Because these protagonists are destined for the happy ending of blissful union, they remain chaste and unscathed as they travel the Mediterranean, in spite of the lust of their captors and the physical torments they face.[1] With respect to criminal justice, she points out that the elite are never pronounced guilty of high crimes, never subject to the scourge of crucifixion or other forms of violent execution. While a set of untoward circumstances might result in the threat of such violence, the favored elite protagonist always slips down from the cross, or out of his chains, unscathed.[2]

The reigning ideology, as Perkins notes, does not make explicit arguments on behalf of elite interests, but rather simply assumes them. The beauty and virtue of the elite are depicted as innate characteristics; pros-

---

1. See especially, Judith Perkins, *The Suffering Self: Pain and Narrative Representation in the Early Christian Era* (London: Routledge, 1995), 41–76.

2. See especially, Judith Perkins, *Roman Imperial Identities in the Early Christian Era*, RMCS (London: Routledge, 2009), 107–26.

perity, acclaim, and divine favor accrue to them naturally. The social and political functions of power that keep the benefits and resources of society in the hands of the elite are unacknowledged and sublimated. They remain hidden, under a "veil of power."[3] As Perkins observes, with respect to the failure of the ancient romance novels to see, much less to condemn, criminal activities of highborn protagonists:

> Within ideology, there are ideas that do not come to mind and contradictory views that aren't recognized as contradictory. In the ideological world of Second Sophistic productions, contradictions between the treatment of elite and non-elite in matters of justice and the judicial system go unrecognized and uncommented upon. The perspective that creates this misrecognition ("This is just the way things are") signals the presence of the ideological. Ideology allows social injustice to go unseen, even by—or especially by—its perpetrators.[4]

This essay takes up the question of elite perspectives on criminal justice, on misrecognition with respect to the unequal treatment of elite and non-elite, and on the normalizing effects of hegemonic ideology.[5] It turns these insights on ideology, which Perkins employs in her analysis of Greek, Roman, and noncanonical early Christian texts, onto a text from the New Testament canon that also pertains to the workings of the judicial system: the story of the thief on the cross who converses with Jesus in the Gospel of Luke (Luke 23:39–43). While the thief in Luke famously proclaims Jesus's innocence, he characterizes his own crucifixion as a matter of deserved justice. It will be demonstrated that the workings of Luke's ideology of just crucifixion have gone unseen by both ancient and modern biblical commentators and that this misrecognition has fed into an acceptance of social injustice across time.

---

3. For many in our disciplines, this phrase for the sublimated workings of ideology is known from the essay under that title by Richard Gordon. See Richard Gordon, "The Veil of Power: Emperors, Sacrificers and Benefactors," in *Pagan Priests: Religion and Power in the Ancient World*, ed. Mary Beard and John North (Ithaca, NY: Cornell University Press, 1990), 201–31. See also Perkins, *Suffering Self*, 54–59.

4. Perkins, *Roman Imperial Identities*, 112.

5. Though in the quotation above Perkins equates *ideology* and *hegemonic ideology*, it should be emphasized that the distinction is not between ideology and some unfiltered social reality, but rather between competing ideologies, or dominant and oppositional cultures. Resistance to a reigning ideology is possible, even if that resistance cannot fully escape from the sway of that ideology.

An important means of exposing an elite ideology as an ideology, rather than as an unbiased reflection of reality—just the way things are—is to challenge that ideology with a countercultural perspective, from someone who resists rather than accedes to the hegemonic system, and thus sees from another angle. Because this is so, and because his subject matter is richly comparable to the subject of this essay, I draw upon the black liberation theologian James Cone's recent scholarship on the entanglement of crucifixion and the American practice of lynching, *The Cross and the Lynching Tree*.[6] As a theologian, taking the long view on the perpetuation of racist violence in the US context, Cone proposes that contemplating the crucifixion of Jesus makes possible a fuller understanding of Christian identity, white supremacist violence, and the legacy of slavery in the *contemporary* US context.[7] As a historian who acknowledges that present social contexts and concerns inevitably frame our narratives of the past, I argue that the inverse relationship also holds: scholars of the ancient Roman Empire might consider modern lynching practices, as a means to understand more fully the workings of *ancient* crucifixion.

To be sure, in proposing that fruitful analogies are produced by understanding ancient crucifixion as a type of lynching, this essay does not seek to revive arguments, problematic on both historical and ethical grounds, that the death of Jesus owed to the machinations of a "Jewish lynch mob," before whom Pilate bowed, a helpless and reluctant governmental official. Minimizing Roman involvement in the crucifixion, while retelling the story of Jesus's death as the result of Jewish mob violence is not historically credible, even if such narrative framing is as old as the New Testament itself.[8] This essay acknowledges the historical and ethical importance of scholarship from recent decades that has pushed against this longest of lies that the Jews killed Jesus. Furthermore, it acknowledges the reasons for framing the scholarly question in recent decades in terms of an either/or binary, embedded in the historical and ethical concerns of the time, in

---

6. James H. Cone, *The Cross and the Lynching Tree* (Mary Knoll, NY: Orbis, 2011).

7. "Until we can see the cross and the lynching tree together, until we can identify Christ with a "recrucified" black body hanging from a lynching tree, there can be no genuine understanding of Christian identity in American, and no deliverance from the brutal legacy of slavery and white supremacy" (Cone, *Cross and Lynching Tree*, xv).

8. See here, especially the book of Acts. For discussion, Shelly Matthews, *Perfect Martyr: The Stoning of Stephen and the Construction of Christian Identity* (New York: Oxford University Press, 2010), 58–78.

order to affirm that Jesus's crucifixion was the outcome of a Roman juridical process *and not* the responsibility of a vicious (Jewish) lynch mob. Yet, this essay resists the notion that the question of how to frame the practice of Roman crucifixion must be rendered as a choice between these two options—*not* lynching *but* crucifixion.

Jesus was not killed by "the Jews" but by the Roman imperial system, under the jurisdiction of the Roman prefect, Pontius Pilate, in the occupied province of Judea.[9] But crucifixion within this Roman imperial system holds in common with modern lynching practices (at least) the following: (1) both processes involve extreme measures of sadism; (2) both ancient crucifixion and modern lynching function as forms of social terror; (3) both forms of torture have been administered, almost without exception, on the most vulnerable segments of society, what Cone might call "the death-bound-subject"[10]—slaves, freedmen, the racialized Other, the stateless, and the despised underclasses; and (4) especially for the despised underclasses, the lines between judicial, quasi-judicial, or extrajudicial proceedings are often blurred.

We turn now to the text that is of primary concern in this essay, from the canonical Gospel of Luke.

The Thieves alongside Jesus in Gospel Traditions

Each of the canonical gospels, as well as the Gospel of Peter, preserve stories that Jesus was crucified with two others, one to the left, one to the right. Our focus here is on the distinctive version of the story related in the Gospel of Luke, along with two variations that stand in closest textual relationship to it, from the Gospel of Mark and the Gospel of Peter.[11] Mark's version, which is a source for Luke, is characteristically stark:

---

9. For an important argument for shifting from specific persons, to the imperial system, in order to account for the death of Jesus, see Ellis Rivkin, "What Crucified Jesus," in *Jesus' Jewishness: Exploring the Place of Jesus in Early Judaism*, ed. James H. Charlesworth (New York: Crossroad, 1996), 226–57.

10. Abdul R. JanMohamed, *The Death-Bound-Subject: Richard Wright's Archeology of Death* (Durham, NC: Duke University Press, 2005), cited in Cone, *Cross and Lynching Tree*, 15.

11. The versions preserved in Matt 27:38, 44 and John 19:18 vary only slightly from the Markan narrative.

And with him they crucified two bandits, one on his right and one on his left.... Those who were crucified with him also taunted him. (Mark 15:27, 32b NRSV)

The Gospel of Peter, which derives from a source also available to Luke, includes details not found in the canonical tradition, along with some recognizable overlap with Luke:

Then they brought two evildoers, and they crucified the Lord up between them.... And one of those evildoers reproached them [the crucifiers], saying, "We have suffered in this way, on account of the evils that we have done, but this man, who has become the Savior of humans, how did he wrong you?" Annoyed by him, they called for his legs not to be broken, so that he might die tortured. (Gos. Pet. 1.4.13–14, my translation)[12]

Luke's version, sharing common features both with Mark and the Gospel of Peter, reads:

There were also others, two evildoers, who were carried off with him.... One of the evildoers hanging there blasphemed him, saying, "Are you not the Christ? Save yourself and us!" But the other rebuked him saying, "Do you not fear God, for you are under the same judgment? And we, on the one hand, justly, for we receive what is worthy of the things we have done [καὶ ἡμεῖς μὲν δικαίως, ἄξια γὰρ ὧν ἐπράξαμεν ἀπολαμβάνομεν], but he, on the other hand, has done nothing out of place." (Luke 23:32, 39–41, my translation)

One means of accounting for the agreement across these gospels that Jesus was crucified with two others, and for the multiply attested detail of the mocking, is to point to the process of "searching the scriptures" by which a written passion narrative for Jesus was first constructed. Allusions exist

---

12. For a useful summary of debate on the direction of influence between the Gospel of Luke and the Gospel of Peter, see Mark Glen Bilby, *As the Bandit Will I Confess You: Luke 23,39–43 in Early Christian Interpretation*, Cahiers de Biblia Patristica 13 (Strasbourg: University of Strasbourg, 2013), 39–43. I am persuaded by Bilby's argument that the constellation of agreement and disagreement with respect to terminology and narrative detail between these two texts points to a common source (whether oral or written), rather than direct textual dependence of one of these gospels upon the other. The most recent critical edition of the Gospel of Peter argues instead that Gospel of Peter depends on Luke. See Paul Foster, *The Gospel of Peter: Introduction, Critical Edition and Commentary*, TENTS 4 (Leiden: Brill, 2010), 142–45.

here to Ps 22:6–7 (LXX 21): "I am … a reproach of men and a scorn of the people. All that saw me mocked me"; and to Isa 53:12: "he was numbered among the lawless [ἐν τοῖς ἀνόμοις ἐλογίσθη]."[13] Further, the positioning of victims crucified on Jesus's left and right may signal an underlying parody of Jesus's kingship, with these men serving as a ghastly sort of king's retinue, as do the men in Philo's *Flaccus* who stand on either side of Carabas guarding him with spears when he is ridiculed as king (*Flacc.* 38).[14]

While both Mark and Matthew identify the two crucified with Jesus as bandits or insurrectionists—λῄσται—Luke, like the Gospel of Peter, instead names them criminals or evildoers—κακοῦργοι. This shift in nomenclature, away from the more seditiously marked term insurrectionist to a more generic term for evildoing, can be accounted for by the Lukan redactional tendency to temper any suggestion in his sources that the Jesus group posed a political threat to the Roman Empire. Depoliticization also explains the juxtaposition Luke creates between the bad thief, who suggests that the sign of messianic status would be the ability to save them all from the cross ("Are you not the Christ? Save yourself, and us!" Luke 23:39), and the good thief, who affirms the merits of crucifixion in this world. The former, wishing for a Messiah who might rescue from earthly tortures, is dismissed as a blasphemer, while the latter is pointed for solace to the ethereal realm of paradise, a place for an afterlife to be entered *only after* he suffers his merited death upon the cross.[15]

---

13. This phrase from Isaiah, also quoted at Luke 22:37, is part of the manuscript tradition of the Gospel of Mark (Mark 15:28), explicitly cited as an explanation for the crucifixion of Jesus between two thieves. See here also John Dominic Crossan, *Who Killed Jesus? Exposing the Roots of Anti-Semitism in the Gospel Story of the Death of Jesus* (San Francisco: HarperSanFrancisco, 1995), 133–37.

14. As suggested by Joel Marcus, "Crucifixion as Parodic Exaltation," *JBL* 125 (2006): 73–87, esp. 73–74. See also Douglas R. A. Hare, *Matthew*, IBC (Louisville: John Knox, 1993), 320, who suggests that in the Gospel of Matthew, the two may possibly serve as caricatures of James and John who had asked for places on Jesus's left and right. With regard to the structural similarities between ancient crucifixion and modern lynching practices carried out in the United States, consider how the lynching of Henry Smith in Paris, Texas, in 1893, also includes elements of mock coronation: "*The negro was placed upon a carnival float in mockery of a king upon his throne*, and, followed by an immense crowd, was escorted through the city so that all might see the most inhuman monster known in current history." Ida B. Wells: *The Light of Truth: Writings of an Anti-Lynching Crusader* (New York: Penguin Books, 2014), 243, my emphasis.

15. For one instance of commentary on this pericope celebrating the shift in Luke from political to spiritual salvation, see Luke Timothy Johnson, *The Gospel of Luke*,

Luke's redactional tendency toward depoliticization is also clear from comparison with the Gospel of Peter. Both of these gospels grant speech to the good thief pertaining to the crucifixion. But the following three narrative details indicate that Luke's Gospel assesses the imperial system of crucifixion more favorably. First, in the Gospel of Peter, in contrast to Luke, the one who speaks from the cross directly rebukes the men who are actually implementing crucifixion. Rather than rebuking the torturers, Luke's good thief repudiates a victim of the torture for his wish to be saved from the process. Second, while the thief who speaks in the Gospel of Peter does concede that the criminals are crucified as a consequence of doing bad things—τὰ κακὰ, Luke's thief goes beyond this simple concession by underscoring the meritorious nature of the execution they face, through use of the adverb "justly" (δικαίως) and the neuter plural ἄξια—that which is "meritorious" or "worthy"—in describing his execution. Finally, through one brief phrase in the Gospel of Peter, the brutality of crucifixion is acknowledged as pertaining not to Jesus alone, but also to the thief as well. In punishment for the speech of the thief and for the expressed purpose of causing him to suffer a more painful extended death, the crucifiers refrain from breaking his legs (Gos. Pet. 4.14).[16] As will be discussed further below, Luke and his interpreters have tended to focus on the injustice of the crucifixion as it pertains to Jesus alone, as a breach in an otherwise acceptable system of criminal punishment. But in this naked act of cruelty aimed at one crucified alongside Jesus, the Gospel of Peter allows a somewhat wider view of the sadism of crucifixion as a general practice.[17]

SP 3 (Collegeville MN: Liturgical Press, 1991): "The reader [of Luke] has ... learned that salvation does not consist in political liberation or in the perpetuation of life" (380–81).

16. On refraining from the breaking of legs as a means to increase the torment of crucifixion, see also Acts Andr. Mth. 51.1; 54.4.

17. I read Gos. Pet. 4.14 as anger addressed at the criminal for his speech in 4.13, causing the command for his torture to be prolonged. A number of scholars have suggested instead that 4.14 must refer to Jesus himself, but this seems to owe to the limits of imagination when reading historical narratives about Jesus and the suffering of others in the company of Jesus. Many scholars can imagine the crucifixion and its horrors as only relevant to Jesus himself. See Foster, *Gospel of Peter*, 306, for summary of this scholarship.

Luke's Distinctive Take on Crucifixion as a Just Practice:
Reception History

While the words of the good thief have been of intense interest to both
ancient and modern readers, these readers have considered the speech
primarily with respect to what is said *about Jesus*, or about the piety of the
good thief, *in relation to Jesus*.[18] With respect to their function in relation
to Jesus, it is clear that the words of the good thief serve the distinctively
Lukan agenda to emphasize Jesus's innocence, in the juridical sense, both
in the formal and informal trials.[19] The concern to underscore Jesus's innocence aligns this gospel with ancient literature pertaining to the deaths of
illustrious persons, which frequently fixates on the question of whether an
execution is just or unjust.[20] With respect to the piety of the good thief,
Mark Glen Bilby documents how the thief becomes a model penitent for
early Christian readers, one who "lends a face and a voice to sympathetic
hearers who identify with and vicariously participate in the confession of
wrongdoing."[21] None of these ancient interpreters of Luke call the practice
of crucifixion itself into question; indeed, the notion that the tortures of
crucifixion are a plight deserved by everyone is sometimes implicit, sometimes explicit, in the commentary.

---

18. Bilby, *As the Bandit I Will Confess You.*

19. See Heather M. Gorman, *Interweaving Innocence: A Rhetorical Analysis of
Luke's Passion Narrative (Lk 22:66–23:49)* (Cambridge: Clarke, 2016), 74–160, for
the following structure concerning the innocence claims: Declarations of Innocence:
(1) Pilate, Luke 23:4; (2) Herod and Pilate, Luke 23:6–16; (3) Pilate, Luke 23:22–25;
(4) Good Thief, Luke 23:40–43; (5) Cosmic signs—darkness and rending veil, Luke
23:44–46; (6) Centurion, Luke 23:47–49. I agree with Gorman that while for Luke
δικαίως might include the meaning "righteous," the term is best translated "innocent,"
in view of Luke's concern for juridical process (see *Interweaving Innocence*, 178–79).

20. I assume that Luke's education included exposure to *chreiai* pertaining to
Socrates. Though we cannot ascertain Luke's precise curriculum, a widespread *chreia*
attributed to Socrates, preserved in the progymnasmata of Theon and repeated by
Xenophon, Seneca, and Diogenes Laertius, merits consideration here. In response to
a student's lament that the Athenians have condemned him unjustly, Socrates asks,
laughingly, whether it is better to be condemned unjustly or justly. See Ronald F. Hock
and Edward N. O'Neil, *The Progymnasmata*, vol. 1 of *The Chreia in Ancient Rhetoric*,
TT 27 (Atlanta, GA: Scholars Press, 1986), 337. See also Plato, *Phaed.* 118A, and John
S. Kloppenborg, "*Exitus clari viri*: The Death of Jesus in Luke," *TJT* 8 (1992): 106–20,
esp. 113.

21. Bilby, *As the Bandit Will I Confess You*, 19.

Contemporary exegetes whose readings are theologically inflected tend to align with their ancient counterparts. Rather than questioning the horrific nature of the Roman state punishment, these readings also focus on the good thief's defense of Jesus, and his request to be remembered, as exemplary acts of repentance and conversion. Here may be included reflections on the existential choices facing "everyman" up until the hour of his death.[22] In searching for a modern interpreter who might comment on the cruelty of the torturous death inflicted on the two thieves, merely turning to scholarship written outside theological circles is no solution. Bart Ehrman, in his widely taught New Testament introduction, writing quite emphatically *not* as a theologian but as a (presumably objective) historian, notes simply of this scene that Jesus is engaging "in intelligent conversation" with the criminal beside him.[23] To my knowledge, the only Christian commentators in the US context taking notice of the cruelty of the torture inflicted upon the Lukan thieves do so in defense of death penalty laws in this country.[24]

In short, both the fact that there has been near universal assent that the thieves deserved to be crucified and that pious readers throughout the ages identify with the crucified, accepting the subject position of those who also deserve crucifixion, point to the powerful grip of a 2000-year-old ideology. Luke has directed readers to accept the punishment of crucifixion for those deemed evildoers as just the way things are. Luke's concession to the cruel force of the Roman Empire is largely unrecognized and uncommented upon.

---

22. The reflections of François Bovon on the good thief may be considered typical for this genre: "To acknowledge one's guilt and to fear God are, in the eyes of the writer of this episode, an act of repentance and the beginning of conversion. Such a move, such action, is possible—this is the implicit message—until the last hour of one's life." See his *Luke 3: A Commentary on the Gospel of Luke 19:28—24:53*, Hermeneia (Minneapolis: Fortress, 2012), 310; see also Johnson, *Gospel of Luke*, 78, where the good thief's rebuke is cast as "a call to authentic acceptance of his own destiny and a need for decision."

23. Bart D. Ehrman, *A Brief Introduction to the New Testament*, 2nd ed. (Oxford: Oxford University Press, 2004), 105. For his understanding of the distinction between "the Historian and the Believer," see 9–11.

24. See, for example, Joseph M. Bessette and Edward Feser, "Why the Church Cannot Reverse Past Teaching on Capital Punishment," *Catholic World Report*, June 7, 2017, https://tinyurl.com/SBL4217b. I thank Mark Glen Bilby for conversation concerning this issue and for alerting me to this link.

To challenge this ideology, we remind again that crucifixion is a type of lynching and argue that all such torturous executions are unjust. We focus not on Jesus's innocence, nor on the piety of the good thief in relation to Jesus, but squarely on the two named evil doers and their plight. Because the vast majority of persons subject to such executions come from precariously situated populations, we ask of these two labeled κακοῦργοι by Luke: Do these count as human? Do these lives count as lives? Are these lives grievable?[25] We ask further: In the ancient Roman imperial context, what range of deeds, tactics, and circumstances would result in one's actions falling under the umbrella category of κακία and thus bring one to the cross? Who in the ancient world would agree with Luke that the criminals hanging next to Jesus deserve to die; that their deeds, unlike the deeds of Jesus, merit crucifixion? From what ideological vantage point does a storyteller—and in this case an evangelist—put into the mouth of a victim of crucifixion, while he hangs from the cross, the affirmation that his torture owes to a meritorious judicial process? With what ancient extant literature might this affirmation of Jesus's innocence, constructed against the backdrop of the criminal's affirmation of just crucifixion, be compared? And finally, why have these questions escaped the attention of virtually every modern biblical scholar since the invention of the discipline?

The Cruelest of Punishments

Scholars working on the ancient practice of crucifixion, whether in the abstract or with the specific story of Jesus in mind, are in basic agreement concerning its ubiquitous, capricious, sadistic, and often extrajudicial nature in the Roman era. Crucifixion was famously known in the ancient Roman world as the slave's punishment. Aside from slaves, those subject to crucifixion, with few exceptions, included other types of nonpersons, including those deemed rebels, captive barbarians, robbers and thieves, devotees of foreign cults whose practices drew suspicion, and noncitizens otherwise deemed subversive. Fear of crucifixion among slaves is a widespread trope in Roman comedy, and indications of its pervasiveness as a

---

25. See Judith Butler, *Precarious Life: The Powers of Mourning and Violence* (London: Verso, 2004), 19–49, esp. 20. On the question of ancient crucifixion and rituals associated with grief, I take as verisimilitudinous the narrative detail from Petronius's *Satyricon* that the parents of a crucified thief steal back the body of their son in order to give him burial rites (*Satyr.* 112).

cultural specter surface also in dream interpretations of the period as well as in jokes across a variety of genres.[26]

With regard to the capriciousness of the practice applied to slaves, consider the following: in the satires of Juvenal, to underscore his portrait of the elite matron as shrew, he imagines that she would crucify a slave for no other reason than to assert her authority over both slave and husband (Juvenal, *Sat.* 6.219–224). Horace cites as a sign of a master's madness the possibility that he might crucify his slave for so small a slight as tasting his soup (Horace, *Sat.* 1.3.80). While the satirists' barbs here may be understood as disapproving of a cruelty when taken too far, the right of the slave owner to kill his slave is widely assumed across our historical sources.

In an inscription regarding the procedures to be followed by undertakers in the ancient Roman world, there are instructions for how a slave owner might make private arrangement to pay for the execution of his slave, for only a modest fee. There are inscriptions that allow, whenever a citizen is found murdered, for any slave who might be found in the region to be tortured and crucified.[27] According to Tacitus, Nero revived the Roman practice of executing every slave of the household, as vengeance for the murder of the master (*Ann.* 13.32.1). Tacitus further recounts an instance in which a slave does murder his master, the city prefect Pedanius Secundus. In revenge for this murder, hundreds of Secundus's house slaves, including women, children, and the elderly are crucified, with Nero

---

26. Martin Hengel's monograph on crucifixion has had broad influence and is extant in several languages and editions. For this essay, we have relied on Martin Hengel, *Crucifixion in the Ancient World and the Folly of the Message of the Cross* (Philadelphia: Fortress, 1977), and also Hengel, "*Mors turpissima crucis*: Die Kreuzigung in der antiken Welt und die 'Torheit' des 'Wortes vom Kreuz,'" in *Rechtfertigung: Festschrift für Ernst Käsemann*, ed. Johannes Friedrich et al. (Tübingen: Mohr Siebeck, 1976), 125–84. See also H. W. Kuhn, "Die Kreuzesstrafe während der frühen Kaiserzeit: Ihre Wirklichkeit und Wertung in der Umwelt des Urchristentums," *ANRW* 2.25.1:648–793. For attention to mime, farce, and other popular forms as sources for crucifixion, see Justin Meggitt, "Laughing and Dreaming at the Foot of the Cross: Context and Reception of a Religious Symbol," in *Modern Spiritualities: An Inquiry* (Amherst, NY: Prometheus Boosk, 1997), 63–70; L. L. Welborn, *Paul, The Fool of Christ: A Study of 1 Corinthians 1–4 in the Comic-Philosophical Tradition* (London: T&T Clark, 2005), 124–60.

27. John Granger Cook, "Envisioning Crucifixion: Light from Several Inscriptions and the Palatine Graffito," *NovT* 50 (2008): 262–85, esp. 265–66. These inscriptions discussed by Cook suggest that the episode in Chariton's *Chaer.* 4.2, in which all members of a sixteen-person chain gang are summarily crucified after some from among them have murdered their overseer, is verisimilitudinous.

lining up detachments to separate the victims from those protesting their innocence (*Ann.* 14.42–45). In this episode, the Roman senator Gaius Cassius argues before the assembled body of his peers that the benefits of the practice of mass crucifixion, especially in view of Rome's colonial reach, outweigh any collateral damage that might be done to innocent slave children or women.[28]

Unbounded opportunities for ratchetting up the sadism of executions by crucifixion are also a widely acknowledged feature of the practice. Executioners were apparently granted a measure of freedom and creativity in devising the cruelest and most spectacular forms of crucifixion they could imagine.[29] Seneca indicates as much in his description of crucifixion as an example of a tortuous fate from which death is an escape:

> I see instruments of torture [*cruces*], not indeed of a single kind, but differently contrived by different peoples; some hang their victims with head toward the ground, some impale their private parts, others stretch out their arms on a fork-shaped gibbet. (*Marc.* 20.3 [Basore, LCL])

Josephus reports that Titus allows his soldiers free reign to nail those captured in attempting to flee a besieged Jerusalem in as many postures as they could concoct, on as many crosses as they could raise (*B.J.* 5.449–451). Among the tortures inflicted to increase the suffering of the victims were floggings—sometimes with whips fortified with bone parts or lead—and clothing the victim with pitch to facilitate the torching of the victim.[30]

---

28. *Ann.* 14.44: "To our ancestors the temper of their slaves was always suspect, even when they were born on the same estate or under the same roof and drew in affection for their owners in their earliest breathe. But now that our households comprise nations—with customs the reverse of our own, with foreign cults or with none, you will never coerce such a medley of humanity except by terror" (Jackson, LCL).

29. Hermann Fulda, *Das Kreuz und die Kreuzigung: Eine antiquarische Untersuchung nebst Nachweis der vielen seit Lipsius verbreiteten Irrthümer; Zugleich vier Excurse über verwandte Gegenstände* (Breslau: Koebner, 1878), 61–62; Marcus, "Crucifixion as Parodic Exaltation," 81. On the sadistic theatrics of Roman execution with focus on the arena, see Kathleen Coleman, "Fatal Charades: Roman Executions Staged as Mythological Enactments," *JRS* 80 (1990): 44–73.

30. Cook, "Envisioning Crucifixion," 267–70. For a comparably sadistic lynching from the Jim Crow era, consider the account of the lynching of Lee Walker in Memphis Tennessee, in 1892, in Wells, *Light of Truth*, 136–51.

Because commentary on the good thief in Luke sometimes characterizes his speech as a defense of the death penalty,[31] it seems important
to remind that unlike the sanitized and heavily bureaucratized administration of the death penalty in the contemporary US context, most often
these nonpersons were sentenced to crucifixion summarily; without the
benefit of the opportunity to plead a case before an impartial judge, much
less a jury; without a lawyer; without any presumption of innocence until
proven guilty; without any concern to prove guilt beyond a reasonable
doubt; and—it goes without saying—without any concern that the penalty
be administered humanely.[32]

Furthermore, even if in some cases crucifixion was the outcome of trial
proceedings, it should be noted that in the Roman world, public trials were
part and parcel of the violent spectacle of torture and execution, rather
than some antiseptic space where the accused was protected from bodily
harm. The gospels hint as much with their references to Pilate's flogging
of Jesus (Matt 27:26; Mark 15:15; John 19:1; cf. Luke 23:16, 22). Seneca's
more expanded ruminations on the terrors of the judicial procedure
administrated by those in power make clear that the sadism of the process
permeated the courtroom as well as the execution site proper (Seneca, *Ep.*
14.2; Cyprian, *Don.* 10).[33]

These are but a few of the extant sources that can be marshalled
to illustrate the grim nature of crucifixion. As noted above, no controversy surrounds the idea, whether in the abstract or in relation to Jesus,
that crucifixion was an exceptionally cruel form of Roman punishment,
administered primarily upon slaves and other nonpersons. Why then are
Jesus's fellow sufferers on Golgotha outside of the circle of concern for
most readers? One clue in surveying the literature of ancient crucifixion is
that elite authors tend to signal their horror over crucifixion only when the
torture might pertain to one from their own ranks. To the analysis of this
phenomenon we now turn.

---

31. See, for example, Johnson, *Gospel of Luke*, 378.

32. To be sure, the contemporary practice of state execution in the United States
is racially biased, lacking in impartiality, and otherwise morally abhorrent; but those
who argue in its support do include the legal safeguards mentioned here among its
justifications.

33. Both of these sources are analyzed in Brent Shaw, "Judicial Nightmares and
Christian Memory," *JECS* 11 (2003): 533–63.

"To Crucify Him Is—What?" (Cicero, *Verrine Orations*): The Search for Analogues

We have already considered the speech of the good thief alongside its closest analogues in gospel tradition. Another body of literature to which the crucifixion of Jesus in Luke is often compared is the literature of martyrdom. Cases are made on both sides of the debate about whether or not Luke intends to sculpt Jesus as a martyr.[34] Particular moments in the Lukan passion narrative that seem martyr-like include the lengthy farewell discourse during the final meal (Luke 22:14–38) and Jesus's tranquility in the face of death.[35] But the speech of the good thief breaks the mold of the type of speech that is associated with traditions of martyrdom and noble death.

To be sure, the mouth is often the focus at the scene of the martyr's execution, as the last words of the dying, or the martyr's self-discipline in refraining from crying out, are a matter of great interest. Sometimes the martyr raises the voice defiantly to express contempt for executioner; sometimes to invoke divine vengeance (both of these responses are associated with the Maccabean tradition); sometimes the display of self-mastery includes enduring the tortures in silence. In a variation of the silent death, the graphic account of Diogenes Laertius tells that Anaxarchus dies in silence because he has bitten off his own tongue before the execution (*Vit. Phil.* 9.58–59); in another variation on the theme of self-mastery demonstrated by the mouth, Josephus tells of a crucified Jew of Jotapata, smiling down at his tormentors from the cross (*B.J.* 3.321;

---

34. See Greg Sterling, "*Mors philosophi*: The Death of Jesus in Luke," *HTR* 94 (2001): 383–402; Martin Dibelius, *From Tradition to Gospel* (New York: Scribner's Sons, 1965), 178–218, esp. 199–204; Hans-Werner Surkau, *Martyrien in jüdischer und frühchristlicher Zeit* (Göttingen: Vandenhoeck & Ruprecht, 1938), 98–100; Brian E. Beck, "'Imitatio Christi' and the Lucan Passion Narrative," in *Suffering and Martyrdom in the New Testament*, ed. William Horbury and Brian McNeil (Cambridge: Cambridge University Press, 1981), 28–47; Graham Stanton, *Jesus of Nazareth in New Testament Preaching*, SNTSMS 27 (Cambridge: Cambridge University Press, 1974), 32–36.

35. William S. Kurz, S.J., "Luke 22:14–38 and Greco-Roman and Biblical Farewell Addresses," *JBL* 104 (1985): 251–68; Sterling, "*Mors philosophi*"; Kloppenborg, "*Exitus clari viri.*" Kurz acknowledges resonance between Luke 22:14–38 and the farewell address in the tradition of Plato's *Phaedo*, while arguing that the biblical examples of the form are closer analogies.

cf. 2.153; 7.418).[36] However, sorting through this literature, it is difficult to find any analogue in which one who is coexecuted bemoans the martyr's unjust death, on the one hand, while affirming his own guilt and the merits of the judicial process, on the other.

Roman comedy turns up no better analogue than martyrdom literature for this type of speech. Plautus is known for his gallows humor and for the multitude of references to crucifixion offered up by the slaves that inhabit his stage. In Plautus, slaves fear the cross, they are threatened with the cross, they make jokes about the cross as an impending punishment they would rather avoid. But in a feature that has puzzled some scholars of Roman comedy, none of the slaves of Plautus are ever actually crucified and thus are given no opportunity to speak of their own crucifixion as just deserts.[37]

In searching for comparative material, we do better to turn from tropes pertaining to dying last words to a larger thematic: ancient elite authors who express outrage pertaining to the unjust crucifixion of a particular victim of high station, while otherwise remaining undisturbed by the practice.

A bilevel assessment of crucifixion—as unjust for the elite, while just for the underclasses—presents itself in the ancient Greek novels, a phenomenon that should be of no surprise to those with knowledge of Perkins's scholarship on class, ideology, and ancient fiction.[38] Recall the scene from Chariton's *Chaereas and Callirhoe*, where sixteen members of a chain gang are ordered to be crucified summarily as punishment for those among them who break chains and murder their overseer (*Chaer.* 4.2). The elite protagonist Chaereas, who is wrongly imprisoned with the chain gang in the first place, escapes unscathed. Xenophon's elite protagonist Habrocomes in *An Ephesian Tale* likewise is sentenced to death by crucifixion. His prayer from the cross, "if I Habrocomes, have done anything

---

36. Compare also Diogenes on Zeno biting the tyrant's ear and spitting out his own tongue before his exectuion (*Vit. Phil.* 9.26–27).

37. Welborn, *Paul, the Fool of Christ*, 145; G. E. Duckworth, *The Nature of Roman Comedy: A Study in Popular Entertainment* (Princeton: Princeton University Press, 1952), 253, 288, 290 (it should be noted that Duckworth defends Roman slavery as "civilized and humane," 288); Erich Segal, *Roman Laughter: The Comedy of Plautus* (Cambridge: Harvard University Press, 1968), 141–69.

38. See both Perkins, *Roman Imperial Identities*, and Perkins, *Suffering Self*, esp. 41–76.

wrong, may I perish miserably" (4.2 [Reardon]), is answered immediately through divine intervention and rescue. This unambiguous signal of the innocence, and thus of the lack of need for crucifixion in Habrocomes's case, conforms to the especially protected status granted to the elite across the Greek novel.[39]

Josephus also takes special umbrage when the victims of crucifixion are of high station. Among the multiple accounts of crucifixion in the *Bellum judaicum*, the one that strikes Josephus as unprecedented and unsurpassed in terms of Roman cruelty is the crucifixion administered by the procurator Florus, as he plunders the city of Jerusalem in the lead up to its destruction. In Josephus's telling, the novelty, and the superlative cruelty of this deed (τὸ καινὸν τῆς Ῥωμαίων ὠμότητος) lies in the fact that the victims nailed up at Florus's order were men of equestrian rank (*B.J.* 2.306–308).

Because of its importance to New Testament scholarship on ancient crucifixion, Marcus Tullius Cicero's second *Verrine Oration* merits particular consideration. In this speech written in 70 BCE and solicited as part of the prosecution of the former governor of Sicily, Gaius Verrus, one of the crimes for which Cicero rails against Verrus is that he crucified the Roman citizen Publius Gavius. Because Cicero's account of Verrus's crucifixion of Gavius underlines the horror of the penalty in starkest terms, it serves as a crucial data point in Martin Hengel's monograph on crucifixion, as well as for those who build upon, or position their scholarship against, Hengel's contribution.[40] Cicero qualifies Verrus's deed as an abominable cruelty (*nefaria crudelitate*, 2.159) and calls the penalty of crucifixion cruel and disgusting (*crudelissimi taeterrimique*, 2.166). Ultimately, he regards Verrus's crime as beyond description:

> To bind a Roman citizen is a crime, to flog him is an abomination, to slay him is almost an act of murder: to crucify him is—what? There is no fitting word that can possibly describe so horrible a deed [*verbo satis digno tam nefaria res appellari nullo modo potest*]. (2.170 [Greenwood])

---

39. For comparable discussion of the plight of the lowborn Theron in contrast with that of the highborn protagonist Chaereas in *Chaereas and Callirhoe*, see Perkins, *Roman Imperial Identities*, 110–12.

40. For a critical assessment of Hengel's use of Cicero with respect to the question of crucifixion as "summum supplicium," see Kuhn, "Kreuzesstrafe," 745–51.

Cicero's assessments serve to paint the backdrop in Hengel's argument concerning the scandal of Paul's message of Jesus's death on the cross. Still, it must be remembered that the abominable cruelty for Cicero is not crucifixion per se, but only that such a penalty would be executed upon a Roman citizen.[41]

In short, from the perspective of elite authors of the Roman period, as is especially laid bare in the ancient orator Cicero, the problem with crucifixion is not its ubiquitous, capricious, and sadistic administration upon slaves, barbarians, rebels, and the underclasses, but simply its misapplication. In the ideology of these bodies of literature, both just and unjust crucifixion exist. The words of the good thief demonstrate that Luke too adopts this "masterly point of view."[42] The κακοῦργοι deserve a tortuous death; the slave's punishment is unjust *only* as it applies to Jesus, who is king and not slave.[43]

The Staying Power of the Reigning Ideology

We turn now to consider why this ideology of just crucifixion has held such enduring sway in scholarly analysis of the words of the good thief. The ancient sources need not concern us at any length. They take no pity on the thieves because they follow Luke's rhetorical markers and accept

---

41. For Cicero the misapplication of the punishment is not merely a victimizing of one Publius Gavius, but a nailing to the cross of "the universal principle that Romans are free men" (170). The logic that a slave punishment executed upon a free man destroys freedom itself illustrates the integral relationship between freedom and slavery. As Sylvester Johnson notes, "freedom cannot be imagined as a metaphysical, celestial virtue. Freedom, rather, is an institution in the same sense that slavery is an institution. Freedom is literally constituted through the formation of negotiated statuses whose relative scale operates within a field of plural morphologies … and that becomes intelligible as one of multiple possible social sites along a continuum of degrees of obligation." Sylvester Johnson, *African American Religions, 1500–2000: Colonialism, Democracy, and Freedom* (Cambridge: Cambridge University Press, 2015), 167. Compare also Orlando Patterson, *Freedom in the Making of Western Culture* (New York: Basic Books, 1991).

42. Sandra Joshel and Lauren Hackworth Petersen, *The Material Life of Roman Slaves* (Cambridge: Cambridge University Press, 2014), 89.

43. To employ John Dominic Crossan's familiar way of making distinctions through emphasis in his historical Jesus work, we might say that for Luke, it is not that Jesus was *crucified*; but that *Jesus* was crucified. Compare John Dominic Crossan, *Jesus: A Revolutionary Biography* (San Francisco: HarperCollins, 1994), 27.

his point of view without question. But why have so few modern biblical scholars, equipped with historical-critical tools and the freedom to ask
any question of the text that occurs to them, neglected to challenge Luke's
framing? Two intertwined reasons are proposed here.

The first owes to the fact that in the dominant strand of Christian biblical scholarship, personal identification of the scholar with Jesus himself
overshadows analysis of the system of Roman imperial oppression. As
noted above, biblical scholarship on ancient crucifixion typically includes
reflection on the gruesomeness of the punishment, the arbitrary and ubiquitous nature of the practice—along with its primary application as the
slave's punishment. But in a crucial interpretive turn, the significance
of that gruesomeness is most often pared down to its implications specifically for—indeed exclusively for—Jesus of Nazareth, the hero of the story
with whom the scholar identifies. In as much as the scholar identifies with
Jesus, Jesus is set apart from the thousands of degraded subjects destined
for Roman crucifixion and acclaimed for his exceptional death.[44]

Another (related) reason for the staying power of the ideology of just
crucifixion is specifically linked to the social class and racial privilege of
the vast majority of those engaged in biblical scholarship. Scholarship on
ancient crucifixion comes largely from scholars trained *not* to reflect on
their social location as beneficiaries of empire, settler colonialism, and
racial privilege.[45] Consider again Hengel's classic and highly influential

---

44. Here I accept the analysis of Elisabeth Schüssler Fiorenza that mainstream
Jesus scholars both rely on the "Western definition of humanity as elite, white, educated masculinity" and construct Jesus in that image—even if that image is displaced
by projecting it onto the Other—the peasant, the revolutionary, the magician, the
ascetic, and so forth. See Elisabeth Schüssler Fiorenza, *Jesus and the Politics of Interpretation* (New York: Continuum, 2000), 9–13, 21. Feminist scholars such as Schüssler
Fiorenza have argued for "decentering Jesus," that is, shifting focus from Jesus as heroic
male to emancipatory movements centered around the vision of the *basileia* of God, in
which Jesus took part. In addition to Schüssler Fiorenza, *Jesus and the Politics*, see also
Melanie Johnson DeBaufre, *Jesus among Her Children: Q, Eschatology and the Construction of Christian Origins*, HTS 55 (Cambridge: Harvard University Press, 2005).

45. For comparable observations with respect to the correlation between the
economic situation of biblical scholars and their evaluation of the economic standing of Pauline Christians, see Steven J. Friesen, "Poverty in Pauline Studies: Beyond
the So-Called New Consensus," *JSNT* 26 (2004): 323–61. Consider especially Friesen's
conclusions (336): "We need to recognize the powerful influence the ideological battle
between Marxism and capitalism has had on Pauline scholarship during the twentieth
century. Perhaps what has passed in Pauline studies for 'mainstream interpretation' or

essay, *Crucifixion*, well known for its unflinching and expansive documentation of the horrors of this Roman imperial means of torture, as illustrative of this perspective. In the process of amassing a large body of sources to document the cruelty of crucifixion, Hengel pauses to ask how the rural population would have perceived the practice of crucifying robbers, rebels, and pirates in their midst. He answers his own question as follows:

> As a rule the rural population [*die Landbevölkerung*] were grateful when a governor took a hard line against the plague of robbers, which was widespread and from which they suffered severely. And since, under the *Pax Romana* of the first century, times were peaceful, law was relatively secure and the administration functioned well, crucifixion was an instrument to protect the populace against dangerous criminals and violent men, and accordingly brought contempt on those who suffered it. Because the robbers often drew their recruits from run-away slaves, abhorrence of the criminal was often combined here with disgust at the punishment meted out to slaves.... In the eyes of the average Roman citizen [*des römischen Durchschnittsuntertanen*] and even of the diaspora Jews the dangers from "robbers" (... II Corinthians 11.26) had a positive connection with the need for a magistrate to wield the sword who is mentioned in Romans 13.4. The sight of crucified robbers served as a deterrent and at the same time exacted some satisfaction for the victim.... Quintilian could therefore praise the crucifixion of criminals as a good work: in his view the crosses ought to be set up on the busiest roads.[46]

In short, Hengel's response to the question of capricious and brutal state torture is to imagine that rustics, average Romans, and Jews of the diaspora alike applauded their emperors for being tough on crime. Uncharacteristically for Hengel, this musing on the common people and their acceptance of crucifixion as a social good is supported by only a meager collection of primary sources. These sources include two references to letters of Paul, whom Hengel apparently regards as supporting crucifixion in necessary cases. I suggest that these remarks reflect cavalier thinking, representative

---

'majority opinion' or 'a consensus among scholars' regarding social setting should now be more precisely labeled as 'capitalist criticism,' a hitherto unacknowledged method in New Testament studies. After all, why should the burden of self-disclosure fall only on the shoulders of Marxist critics?"

46. Hengel, *Crucifixion*, 49–50 (for the German, see "*Mors Turpissima Crucis*," 156).

of our discipline, pertaining to those most vulnerable to the machinery of a repressive state.

A Countervoice

Finally, we consider an oppositional perspective, one that offers up a depiction of the good thief as a victim of an unjust lynching: the narrative of W. E. B. DuBois published as part of his *Darkwater* autobiography, entitled "Jesus Christ in Texas" and summarized here.[47]

In DuBois's short story, set in the age of Jim Crow, Jesus, without his true identity being recognized, visits the prospering city of Waco, Texas, and interacts with its ranking citizens, including the rector and a gathering organized by the wife of the colonel in their home. Jesus also encounters a black convict sentenced to forced labor in Waco in the construction of the expanding railroad. The story culminates in the convict being lynched by a mob, after he is falsely accused of making advances toward the wife of the farmer in whose barn he is lodging. As the wife peers out the window at the commotion surrounding the lynching, she sees the dying convict, and—much to her surprise—she also sees Jesus, crucified simultaneously. While they both hang dying, Jesus consoles the convict with the words: "Today you will be with me in Paradise" (Luke 23:43).

Crucially, while he quotes the words of the Lukan Jesus to the good thief and imagines Jesus being crucified alongside the good thief, DuBois does not accept the Lukan story line that this crucifixion/lynching is just. In DuBois's story, the thief is tortured and lynched on a ruse. The lynched thief is not the repentant thief, because the thief has done nothing worthy of repentance. Though DuBois, of course, is no biblical scholar, in this resistant reading of the Lukan crucifixion scene, he proves to be more perceptive than Hengel, and virtually all biblical scholars in the guild. DuBois sees clearly the injustice of this abominable cruelty and precisely who is most vulnerable to its implementation.

To conclude: distinctive among the gospel narratives, Luke introduces the notion that crucifixion is a just and meritorious fate for the victims hanging alongside of Jesus. This emphasis, explained by Luke's redactional concern to minimize the subversive nature of the Jesus movement, has

---

47. W. E. B. Dubois, *Darkwater: Voices from within the Veil* (New York: Harcourt, Brace, 1920), https://tinyurl.com/SBL4217c. For further discussion see Cone, *Cross and Lynching Tree*, 101–8.

remained largely unquestioned throughout the history of biblical interpretation, even while scholars decry the cruelty of crucifixion in the abstract. The staying power of Luke's ideology of just crucifixion is a function of the guild's conformity to hegemony. Dominant exegetical studies of this gospel are undertaken by those who project their own elite standing upon Jesus himself. This makes it possible to read the execution of Jesus as the problem of a just punishment applied unjustly once on Golgotha, in an exceptional case. Protected by class and racial privilege from the possibility of ever facing judicial, quasi-judicial and/or extrajudicial torture, it does not occur to the guild to see the crucifixion of those alongside of Jesus as anything but just the way things are.

In contrast, Cone and DuBois before him, well recognize the cruelty of lynching, the analogy between crucifixion and lynching, and the humanity of those most commonly subject to these tortures. From that recognition, Cone calls on his readers to connect the cross "to the ongoing suffering and oppression of human beings"; DuBois imagines sympathetically a thief who is crucified unjustly. These countercultural voices deserve a hearing in the disciplines of biblical studies and early Christian history, so that our historical narratives might do better justice to those who suffer most under the reigning ideology.

Bibliography

Beck, Brian E. "'Imitatio Christi' and the Lucan Passion Narrative." Pages 28–47 in *Suffering and Martyrdom in the New Testament*. Edited by William Horbury and Brian McNeil. Cambridge: Cambridge University Press, 1981.

Bessette, Joseph M., and Edward Feser. "Why the Church Cannot Reverse Past Teaching on Capital Punishment." *Catholic World Report*. June 7, 2017. https://tinyurl.com/SBL4217b.

Bilby, Mark Glen. *As the Bandit Will I Confess You: Luke 23,39–43 in Early Christian Interpretation*. Cahiers de Biblia Patristica 13. Strasbourg: University of Strasbourg Press, 2013.

Bovon, François. *Luke 3: A Commentary on the Gospel of Luke 19:28–24:53*. Hermeneia. Minneapolis: Fortress, 2012.

Butler, Judith. *Precarious Life: The Powers of Mourning and Violence*. London: Verso, 2004.

Cicero. *Against Verres, Part 2, Books 3–5*. Vol. 2 of *The Verrine Orations*. Translated by L. H. G. Greenwood. LCL. Cambridge: Harvard University Press, 1935.

Coleman, Kathleen. "Fatal Charades: Roman Executions Staged as Mythological Enactments." *JRS* 80 (1990): 44–73.

Cone, James H. *The Cross and the Lynching Tree*. Maryknoll, NY: Orbis Books, 2011.

Cook, John Granger. "Envisioning Crucifixion: Light from Several Inscriptions and the Palatine Graffito." *NovT* 50 (2008): 262–85.

Crossan, John Dominic. *Jesus: A Revolutionary Biography*. San Francisco: HarperCollins, 1994.

———. *Who Killed Jesus? Exposing the Roots of Anti-Semitism in the Gospel Story of the Death of Jesus*. San Francisco: HarperSanFrancisco, 1995.

DeBaufre, Melanie Johnson. *Jesus among Her Children: Q, Eschatology and the Construction of Christian Origins*. HTS 55. Cambridge: Harvard University Press, 2005.

Dibelius, Martin. *From Tradition to Gospel*. New York: Scribner's Sons, 1965.

Dubois, W. E. B. *Darkwater: Voices from within the Veil*. New York: Harcourt, Brace, 1920. https://tinyurl.com/SBL4217c.

Duckworth, G. E. *The Nature of Roman Comedy: A Study in Popular Entertainment*. Princeton: Princeton University Press, 1952.

Ehrman, Bart D. *A Brief Introduction to the New Testament*. 2nd ed. Oxford: Oxford University Press, 2004.

Foster, Paul. *The Gospel of Peter: Introduction, Critical Edition and Commentary*. TENTS 4. Leiden: Brill, 2010.

Friesen, Steve. "Poverty in Pauline Studies: Beyond the So-Called New Consensus." *JSNT* 26 (2004): 323–61.

Fulda, Hermann. *Das Kreuz und die Kreuzigung: Eine antiquarische Untersuchung nebst Nachweis der vielen seit Lipsius verbreiteten Irrthümer; Zugleich vier Excurse über verwandte Gegenstände*. Breslau: Koebner, 1878.

Gordon, Richard. "The Veil of Power: Emperors, Sacrificers and Benefactors." Pages 201–31 in *Pagan Priests: Religion and Power in the Ancient World*. Edited by Mary Beard and John North. Ithaca, NY: Cornell University Press, 1990.

Gorman, Heather M. *Interweaving Innocence: A Rhetorical Analysis of Luke's Passion Narrative (Lk 22:66–23:49)*. Cambridge: Clarke, 2016.

Hare, Douglas R. A. *Matthew*. IBC. Louisville: John Knox, 1993.

Hengel, Martin. *Crucifixion in the Ancient World and the Folly of the Message of the Cross.* Philadelphia: Fortress, 1977.

———. *"Mors turpissima crucis:* Die Kreuzigung in der antiken Welt und die 'Torheit' des 'Wortes vom Kreuz.'" Pages 125–84 in *Rechtfertigung: Festschrift für Ernst Käsemann.* Edited by Johannes Friedrich et al. Tübingen: Mohr Siebeck, 1976.

Hock, Ronald F., and Edward N. O'Neil. *The Progymnasmata.* Vol. 1 of *The Chreia in Ancient Rhetoric.* TT 27. Atlanta: Scholars Press, 1986.

JanMohamed, Abdul R. *The Death-Bound-Subject: Richard Wright's Archeology of Death.* Durham, NC: Duke University Press, 2005.

Johnson, Luke Timothy. *The Gospel of Luke.* SP 3. Collegeville, MN: Liturgical Press, 1991.

Johnson, Sylvester. *African American Religions, 1500–2000: Colonialism, Democracy, and Freedom.* Cambridge: Cambridge University Press, 2015.

Joshel, Sandra, and Lauren Hackworth Petersen. *The Material Life of Roman Slaves.* Cambridge: Cambridge University Press, 2014.

Kloppenborg, John S. *"Exitus clari viri:* The Death of Jesus in Luke." *TJT* 8 (1992): 106–20.

Kuhn, H. W. "Die Kreuzesstrafe während der frühen Kaiserzeit: Ihre Wirklichkeit und Wertung in der Umwelt des Urchristentums." *ANRW* 2.25.1:648–793.

Kurz, William S., SJ. "Luke 22:14–38 and Greco-Roman and Biblical Farewell Addresses." *JBL* 104 (1985): 251–68.

Marcus, Joel. "Crucifixion as Parodic Exaltation." *JBL* 125 (2006): 73–87.

Matthews, Shelly. *Perfect Martyr: The Stoning of Stephen and the Construction of Christian Identity.* New York: Oxford University Press, 2010.

Meggitt, Justin. "Laughing and Dreaming at the Foot of the Cross: Context and Reception of a Religious Symbol." Pages 63–70 in *Modern Spiritualties: An Inquiry.* Amherst, NY: Prometheus Books, 1997.

Patterson, Orlando. *Freedom in the Making of Western Culture.* New York: Basic Book, 1991.

Perkins, Judith. *Roman Imperial Identities in the Early Christian Era.* RMCS. London: Routledge, 2009.

———. *The Suffering Self: Pain and Narrative Representation in the Early Christian Era.* London: Routledge, 1995.

Reardon, B. P., ed. and trans. *Collected Ancient Greek Novels.* Berkeley: University of California Press, 2008.

Rivkin, Ellis. "What Crucified Jesus." Pages 226–57 in *Jesus' Jewishness: Exploring the Place of Jesus in Early Judaism*. Edited by James H. Charlesworth. New York: Crossroad, 1996.

Schüssler Fiorenza, Elisabeth. *Jesus and the Politics of Interpretation*. New York: Continuum, 2000.

Segal, Erich. *Roman Laughter: The Comedy of Plautus*. Cambridge: Harvard University Press, 1968.

Seneca. *De Consolatione ad Marciam; De Vita Beata; De Otio; De Tranquillitate Animi; De Brevitate Vitae; De Consolatione ad Polybium; De Consolatione ad Helviam*. Vol. 2 of *Moral Essays*. Translated by John W. Basore. LCL. Cambridge: Harvard University Press, 1932.

Shaw, Brent. "Judicial Nightmares and Christian Memory." *JECS* 11 (2003): 533–63.

Stanton, Graham. *Jesus of Nazareth in New Testament Preaching*. SNTSMS 27. Cambridge: Cambridge University Press, 1974.

Sterling, Greg. "*Mors philosophi*: The Death of Jesus in Luke." *HTR* 94 (2001): 383–402.

Surkau, Hans-Werner. *Martyrien in jüdischer und frühchristlicher Zeit*. Göttingen: Vandenhoeck & Ruprecht, 1938.

Tacitus. *Annals: Books 13–16*. Translated by John Jackson. LCL. Cambridge: Harvard University Press, 1937.

Welborn, L. L. *Paul, The Fool of Christ: A Study of 1 Corinthians 1–4 in the Comic-Philosophic Tradition*. London: T&T Clark, 2005.

Wells, Ida B. *The Light of Truth: Writings of an Anti-Lynching Crusader*. New York: Penguin Books, 2014.

The Spatial, Literary, and Linguistic Translations of the *Mandylion*

Ilaria L. E. Ramelli

Introduction: The *Mandylion* as Image Relic and Its Spatial, Literary, and Linguistic Translations

The *Mandylion* (μανδύλιον, "towel"), an image relic, was transported (allegedly) from Jerusalem to Edessa, thence to Constantinople, and possibly to the West.[1] The most famous of the ἀχειροποίηται εἰκόνες, images "not made by (human) hand," it functioned as a statement against iconoclasm in late antique Byzantium.[2] In the arrangement it had in Edessa, it featured Christ's head and beard, as its numerous reproductions indicate. I shall analyze the relic's transformations and translations, in both space and language.

The first part of this study will examine the development of the story, closely related to the *Mandylion*, of Addai and Abgar of Edessa (first century CE). This legend, I argue, arose from a historical nugget: the political correspondence between Abgar and Tiberius. I shall trace the legend's

---

It is a pleasure and a privilege to participate in this Festschrift for a great scholar. A previous version of this article was presented in 2016 at the Institute for Historical Research, School of Advanced Study of the University of London. I am grateful to the audience for the fruitful discussion, especially to Rosamond McKitterick.

1. Martin Illert, *Doctrina Addai* (Turnhout: Brepols, 2007). See my review of *Doctrina Addai*, by Martin Illert, *RBL* (2009), www.bookreviews.org/BookDetail .asp?TitleId=6797. See also Han J. W. Drijvers, "The Image of Edessa in Syriac Tradition," in *The Holy Face and the Paradox of Representation*, ed. Herbert L. Kessler and Gerhard Wolf (Bologna: Nuova Alfa Editoriale, 1998), 13–31; M. Guscin, *The Image of Edessa* (Leiden: Brill, 2009).

2. Vladimir Baranov, "The Iconophile Fathers," in *The Wiley-Blackwell Companion to Patristics*, ed. Ken Parry (Oxford: Wiley-Blackwell, 2015), 344–45.

stages and literary transformations, all influenced by political-ecclesiastical agendas. As I will show, the story probably first took shape around 200 CE in the entourage of Abgar the Great of Edessa, as a way to praise and defend him through his first-century namesake. The subsequent stages appear in Eusebius, whose account comes from three different sources, the Syriac *Doctrina Addai*, the Armenian history of Moses of Chorene, and the Syriac *Acta Maris*. Indeed, the legend related to the *Mandylion* underwent many linguistic translations, through Syriac, Greek, Armenian, and Latin.

The second part of this study will research the emergence and transformation of the *Mandylion* within the Addai legend. Eusebius does not mention the *Mandylion*, but the *Peregrinatio Egeriae* in the 380s arguably alludes to it. This is why Macarius of Magnesia describes Berenice/Veronica as Edessan. In the early fifth century, the *Doctrina Addai* identifies the Edessan image as a painted portrait, as the Armenian legend of Moses does thereafter. In Evagrius's writings, the portrait becomes an *acheiropoieta*, and its presence in the city is said to defend Edessa from a siege in 544 CE. After 544, the relic was transferred to the main church in Edessa. The *Acta Maris* in the seventh century reports that the *Mandylion* was still in Edessa and also characterizes the *Mandylion* as an *acheiropoieta*. In the same century, or possibly earlier, the *Acta Thaddaei* present the *Mandylion* as folded up four times. A Byzantine *narratio* and other sources related to the (spatial) translation of the *Mandylion* from Edessa to Constantinople (944 CE) are the first to associate the relic with Jesus's passion. Both Rainer Riesner and Karlheinz Dietz agree that the Edessan image is possibly Jesus's shroud (preserved by the Jerusalem Jewish-Christian community) and the Turin Shroud.[3]

From History to Legend: The Literary Transformations and Linguistic Translations of Addai and King Abgar

According to tradition, in the first century CE, a Christian disciple named Addai (often conflated with the disciple Thaddeus) evangelized Edessa and

---

3. Rainer Riesner, "Von Jerusalem nach Edessa?," in *Das Christusbild*, ed. Karlheinz Dietz et al. (Würzburg: Echter, 2016), 360–92; Karlheinz Dietz, "Abgars Christusbild als Ganzkörperbild," in Dietz, *Das Christusbild*, 393–447. Contrast Averil Cameron, *Continuity and Change in Sixth-Century Byzantium* (London: Variorum Reprints, 1981), ch. 6, against the identification of the *Mandylion* with the Turin Shroud; see also Cameron, "The History of the Image of Edessa," *Okeanos* 7 (1983): 80–94.

the Mesopotamian region of Osrhoene, converting King Abgar Ukkama to Christianity. Religious discourses and agendas over the centuries shaped the development of the Addai narrative through various literary genres (epistles and epistolary novels, history, hagiography, biography, acts of apostles, and historical novels) and translations into different languages.[4] The historical points of departure were likely the letters exchanged in the 30s CE, for political reasons, between Abgar and the Roman emperor Tiberius. These letters originally had little to do with Abgar's conversion to the Jesus movement but were later incorporated into the Syriac apostolic novel *Doctrina Addai*, as well as the Armenian version of the legend in Moses and some Syriac *Transitus Mariae*.

The first extant account of the legend, in Eusebius, reports a fictional Abgar-Jesus correspondence, but not the Abgar-Tiberius letters. This indicates that the source of the Abgar-Tiberius letters differs from that of the pseudepigraphic Abgar-Jesus letters and is ancient, since, as I have argued elsewhere,[5] the Abgar-Tiberius letters include historical details that fit the political panorama of the mid-30s, when the emperor was maneuvering against the Parthians, shortly after Jesus's death and Abgar's reestablishment after a usurpation (31 CE). Abgar needed the emperor's support against his opponents, and Tiberius needed the faithfulness of vassal kings close to the Parthian border, such as Abgar. The Abgar-Tiberius letters reflect this situation, including exact historical details such as the use of the Caucasian Iberians by Tiberius against the Parthians in the mid-30s. For political reasons, not as a consequence of a conversion, Abgar wrote to Tiberius about Jesus's execution by Pilate and Caiaphas's party. Abgar intended to take advantage of the Jesus affair to cast his adversaries Herod and Pilate in a bad light before the emperor.[6]

The story of Abgar Ukkama's conversion to Christianity arose under Abgar the Great (177/9–212/4), by which time there was a Christian church in Edessa (Chronicum Edessenum 1). Other sources indicate that

---

4. Ilaria Ramelli, "The Addai-Abgar Narrative: Its Development through Literary Genres and Religious Agendas," in *Early Christian and Jewish Narrative: The Role of Religion in Shaping Narrative Forms*, ed. Ramelli and Judith Perkins (Tübingen: Mohr Siebeck, 2015), 205–45.

5. Ilaria Ramelli, *Possible Historical Traces in the Doctrina Addai?* (Piscataway, NJ: Gorgias, 2009).

6. As demonstrated in Ilaria Ramelli, "The Possible Origin of the Abgar-Addai Legend," *Hug* 16 (2013): 325–41.

Christianity had spread in Osrhoene by then, and the education of Abgar the Great's son was entrusted to Christian intellectuals, Africanus and Bardaisan.[7] The evidence of the letters in which Abgar Ukkama denounces the unjust killing of Jesus suggests that the legend of Abgar Ukkama's and his kingdom's conversion was shaped under Abgar the Great, who perhaps became a Christian, as Bardaisan indicates in the *Liber legum regionum*.[8]

This legend extolled Abgar the Great by eulogizing Abgar Ukkama. Bardaisan, a Syriac Christian philosopher, theologian, historian, polymath, and friend of the Abgar the Great, could have had access to the royal archive that contained the letters of the Edessan kings. He or other courtiers may have read the Abgar-Tiberius correspondence on Jesus and the situation in Palestine in the mid-30s and from them created the legend of Abgar Ukkama's conversion. Bardaisan's history probably included an account of the first evangelization of Edessa in order to celebrate Abgar the Great through his homonymous predecessor. From Bardaisan's history, or another Edessan history, this legend passed on to Eusebius's *Historia ecclesiastica*, where it was joined to the forged Abgar-Jesus letters that surface again in the Doctrina Addai, the Armenian legend of Moses, and elsewhere. Riesner expressly accepts my hypothesis that the Abgar legend took shape in the Severan age and was spread by Bardaisan or his school.[9]

The first layer of the legend, incorporated by Eusebius, included the conversion of Abgar Ukkama to Christianity thanks to Addai's miracles— absent from the earlier Abgar-Tiberius letters. As I have demonstrated elsewhere, Eusebius's narrative consists of three layers.[10] Eusebius's most

---

7. Ilaria Ramelli, "Dal Mandilion di Edessa alla Sindone: Alcune note sulle testimonianze antiche," '*Ilu* 4 (1999): 173–93.

8. See Ramelli, "Dal Mandilion di Edessa," and Ramelli, *Bardaisan of Edessa: A Reassessment of the Evidence and a New Interpretation* (Piscataway, NJ: Gorgias, 2009).

9. Riesner, "Von Jerusalem," 379, 381.

10. Ilaria Ramelli, "The Biography of Addai: Its Development between Fictionality and Historicity," *Phrasis* 51 (2010): 83–105; Ramelli, "Addai-Abgar Narrative," *passim*. Andrea Nicolotti, *From the Mandylion of Edessa to the Shroud of Turin* (Leiden: Brill, 2014), 8, thinks that Eusebius had only one source, Syriac, or a "fraudulent Greek translation of a supposed original Syriac." So does Andrew Palmer, "Edessan Images of Christ," in Dietz, *Das Christusbild*, 231, but I demonstrated that Eusebius had at least two sources, one very celebratory of Abgar and probably stemming from Abgar the Great's entourage, possibly Bardaisan, and the other, common to the Doctrina, containing the Abgar-Jesus pseudepigraphic correspondence.

recent layer is his own final summary of the Addai legend. The middle layer contains the Jesus-Abgar letters and the Addai narrative. The most ancient layer (*Hist. eccl.* 1.13.1–4), without letters, speeches, or dialogues, narrates the key events of the Abgar legend. This last layer reveals an extremely encomiastic tone, and the evident intention is to exalt the ancient king of Edessa; it must go back to an Edessan source, maybe Bardaisan.[11] This section focuses on Abgar Ukkama as a great monarch, his illness, his learning of Jesus's miracles, and Jesus's promise to heal him, which resulted in Abgar's and the Edessans' conversion to Christianity through Addai.

This first outline of the legend may have developed from the Abgar-Tiberius correspondence about Jesus and Palestine in 35–37 CE. This story was intended to celebrate Abgar the Great and create a precedent for his benevolence toward Christianity, which stirred tensions, as suggested by Cassius Dio's report about Abgar the Great's forced abolition of a pagan ritual mutilation: according to Dio, the abolition was under the official pretext of Romanization; according to Bardaisan, it was a result of Abgar the Great's conversion.[12] If Bardaisan told the Addai story, he intended to celebrate his friend Abgar the Great and the spread of Christianity in Osrhoene (as he also does in the *Liber legum regionum*). This celebration was magnificent, since Abgar Ukkama is described in Eusebius's first source as the first Christian monarch and hyperbolically as a great dynast who reigned over whole peoples, whereas Eusebius's second source much more modestly calls him a toparch.

That Bardaisan or his entourage elaborated the Addai legend is further suggested by the following: in the fourth century, orthodoxy established itself at the expense of heresies in Edessa. Bardaisan was misrepresented as a heretic, and Addai was appropriated by Syrian orthodoxy, as expressed in the Doctrina Addai (early fifth century). Addai's theological speeches and doctrinal teachings there highlight his orthodoxy. This insistence on Addai's orthodoxy is understandable if the (by then) heretic Bardaisan or his circle first developed the Addai legend. Eusebius, however, did not

---

11. Eusebius would have read Bardaisan's works translated into Greek. That Bardaisan wrote a history of the Near East where the Addai story was found is attested by Moses of Chorene (*Hist. Arm.* 2.66), a favorable and informed source on Bardaisan. Moses was acquainted with Bardaisan's history and used it for the events of Ukkama's time.

12. Ilaria Ramelli, ed., *Bardaisan on Free Will, Fate, and Human Nature* (Tübingen: Mohr Siebeck, forthcoming).

deem Bardaisan heretical; he quoted Bardaisan's arguments as authoritative and therefore did not stress Addai's orthodoxy.

The Doctrina Addai expanded the Edessan lore used by Eusebius,
adding long doctrinal speeches and narrative expansions (such as a
reworking of Helena's *inventio crucis*), which served the religious agenda
of the Edessan church.[13] The Doctrina Addai proposed "a paradigm of
normative Edessan Christianity, supported by the local ecclesiastical and
historical lore, which [the author] hoped would play an authoritative role
in the largely Christological controversies of his own days."[14] This narrative promoted the current bishop's program for the Edessan "Church of the
Empire."[15] The newly established Syriac orthodoxy sought to reappropri-
ate Edessa's apostle, who was first celebrated by heretics such as Bardaisan's
entourage. This is why Addai in the Doctrina Addai pronounces lengthy
doctrinal homilies shining with orthodoxy that are absent from Eusebius
and his two sources.

The Doctrina Addai also contains the first direct reference to the *Mandylion*. It narrates that Abgar Ukkama sent two Edessan nobles and his
archivist, Hannan, on a diplomatic mission to the Roman official in Eleu-
theropolis. On their way back, they passed by Jerusalem and learned of
Jesus's miracles. Abgar, informed, sent a letter to Jesus, inviting him to
come to Edessa and heal him. Jesus promised in a letter that a disciple
would soon arrive at Edessa. Abgar's archivist painted Jesus's portrait,
which Abgar then enshrined in one of his palaces. After Jesus's resurrection, Thomas, one of the Twelve, sent to Edessa one of the seventy-two,
Addai, who worked miracles and healed and converted Abgar with all of
his people.

The Acta Maris, another Syriac apostolic novel with historical nug-
gets and fictional material finalized in the late sixth–seventh century,[16]

---

13. See Han J. W. Drijvers, "The Protonike Legend, the Doctrina Addai, and
Bishop Rabbula," *VC* 51 (1997): 288–315; Alexander Mirkovic, *Prelude to Constantine:
The Abgar Tradition in Early Christianity* (Frankfurt: Lang, 2004).

14. Sidney Griffith, "The Doctrina Addai as a Paradigm of Christian Thought in
Edessa in the Fifth Century," *Hug* 6.2 (2003): 3.

15. Griffith, "*Doctrina Addai*," 46; Philip Wood, *Christian Political Thought in
Greater Syria* (Oxford: Oxford University Press, 2010), 82–116.

16. Ilaria Ramelli, *Atti di Mar Mari* (Brescia: Paideia, 2008); reviewed by Sebastian Brock, review of *Atti di Mar Mari*, by Ilaria Ramelli, *Ancient Narrative* 7 (2008):
123–30, https://tinyurl.com/SBL4217d; and by Judith Perkins, review of *Atti di Mar
Mari*, by Ilaria Ramelli, *Aevum* 83 (2009): 269–71.

connects the Addai legend to Mari, the apostle of Mesopotamia. Political-ecclesiastical reasons shaped this narrative, which supplied evidence for the apostolic origins of the church in Seleucia-Ctesiphon, thereby justifying the hegemonic plans of the eastern Syriac patriarch of Seleucia-Ctesiphon. As we shall see, the *Mandylion* here underwent a transformation into an *acheiropoieta*.

Moses of Chorene's *History of Armenia* 2.36 relates a different development of the legend shaped by different motivations. Both Eusebius and the Armenian version of the Doctrina Addai probably were among Moses's sources, but Moses introduces Abgar Ukkama as an Armenian king—something still reflected in the Chronicle of 1234[17]—and offers an Armenian etymology of his name, to trace back to him the origin of Christianity in Armenia (Moses incorporates many territories in his idea of Armenia). To increase the prestige of Armenia, Moses suggested that already in the first century an Armenian kingdom adopted Christianity as its state religion. The *Mandylion* is said by Moses to have been in Edessa still in his day. Subsequent sources report its transfer to Constantinople.

Spatial and Literary Translations of the *Mandylion*

Eusebius does not mention Jesus's portrait, perhaps due to his aversion to representations of Christ, as indicated by his statement that Christ images are a "pagan habit" (ἐθνικὴ συνήθεια, *Hist. eccl.* 7.18.4) and his *Letter to Constantia*.[18] Likewise, he omits Helena's *inventio crucis*, being suspicious of relics concerning Christ's earthly life. As Frances Young states, "Political and logical reasons have been proposed to explain Eusebius's silence—there is plenty of evidence that elsewhere he suppressed material that did not suit his purpose."[19] However, Eusebius's sources, including his Severan-age Edessan source, may have mentioned the image. Bardaisan in his history also could have mentioned Christ's Edessan image, being

---

17. CSCO 81.109.

18. PG 20:1545–49. See Stephen Gero, "Eusebius' Letter to Constantia Reconsidered," *JTS* 32 (1981): 460–70; Knut Schäferdiek, "Untersuchungen zu Verfassenschaft und Situation der Epistula ad Constantiam," *ZKG* 91 (1980): 177–86; C. Sode and P. Speck, "Ikonoklasmus vor der Zeit?," *Jahrbuch der Österreichischen Byzantinistik* 54 (2004): 113–34.

19. Frances Young, "Prelude," in *The Cambridge History of Christianity* (Cambridge: Cambridge University Press, 2006), 1:4–5.

interested in images of Christ; he even describes one, a statue of the cosmic Christ, in *De India*.[20]

Egeria alludes to the *Mandylion* but does not report seeing the relic on her pilgrimage to Edessa (381–384 CE), presumably because it was inaccessible to the public or had been hidden, as later reports recount. Rather, Egeria quotes the Edessan bishop as stating, "Here is King Abgar, who, *before seeing the Lord*, believed that he was truly the Son of God" (*Peregr. Eg.* 19.6: Ecce rex Aggarus, qui antequam videret Dominum credidit ei, quia esset vere filius Dei).[21] The bishop clearly believes that Abgar had never seen Jesus, only his image. His statement is in keeping with the legend that Abgar Ukkama believed in Jesus's divinity before seeing his image, strictly on the basis of his envoys' reports about Jesus's miracles. Andrea Nicolotti remarks that in the *Peregrinatio* "there is still no mention of any images."[22] The mention is implicit, though. Abgar believed, not "without seeing" Jesus (which is reminiscent of John 20:29, as in Eusebius, *Hist. eccl.* 1.13.10), but "*before* seeing" him, clearly in his image, which according to tradition was brought to Abgar by Ananias or Thaddeus. Because of the association of Christ's image with Edessa already in the 380s, as suggested by the *Peregrinatio*, Macarius of Magnesia described Berenice/Veronica, linked with Christ's image,[23] as an Edessan (*Apocriticus* 1).

In Egeria's day, as in the time of the Doctrina Addai (early fifth century), the image was shut away. In the late sixth–seventh century, in the time of the Acta Maris, the relic was in Edessa's Great Church, accessible to the public and venerated. Its transfer there occurred after the 544 siege (below). The Doctrina Addai identifies the Edessan image as a portrait painted before Jesus's passion by Hannan-Ananias, Abgar's archivist and emissary. The relic was brought to Edessa and kept in one of the royal palaces (Doctr. Add. 13). Around 410, Daniel of Galash saw the relic in Edessa, as attested in his biography attributed to Jacob of Sarugh.[24] Moses

---

20. See Ramelli, *Bardaisan of Edessa*, 107–24; Ramelli, *Bardaisan on Free Will, Fate, and Human Nature*.

21. Unless otherwise noted, all translations are mine.

22. Nicolotti, *From the Mandylion of Edessa to the Shroud of Turin*, 9; Palmer, "Edessan Images of Christ," 234.

23. In Acta Pilati 7 (second/early third century), Berenike/Veronica heals Tiberius with Jesus's portrait. On the connection between Veronica and Haemorrhoissa see Emma Sidgwick, *From Flow to Face* (Leuven: Peeters, 2015).

24. The Syriac, unpublished, in Nicolotti, *From the Mandylion of Edessa to the Shroud of Turin*, 20.

of Chorene also narrates the story of this image and adds that it was still in Edessa in his days—or in those of his source (*Hist. Arm.* 2.32).

Around 593, the church historian Evagrius mentions an *image* of Christ, no longer a painting, but "divinely fashioned" (θεότευκτος, *Hist. eccl.* 4.27). According to Evagrius, the image defended Edessa against the Persians' siege (544): "They brought out the image produced by God, not made by human hands. Christ-God had sent it to Abgar, because Abgar desired [ἐπόθει] to see him." This explanation illuminates the *Peregrinatio*'s remark that Abgar believed "before seeing Christ," in his image. The same explanation occurs in *Hadriani Epistola ad Carolum*:[25] "The Redeemer of the human race replied to a certain king of the city of Edessa, who strongly wished to see him in his body: 'If you desire to see my face physically, hereby I am sending you the image of my countenance transferred onto a linen; thanks to this, you can quench the heath of your desire'" (Redemptor humani generis … cuidam regi Edessenae civitatis, *desideranti corporaliter Illum cernere* … respondisse quod si faciem meam corporaliter cernere *cupis*, en tibi vultus mei speciem transformatam in linteo dirigo, per quam et *desiderii tui fervorem* refrigeres). Here *desideranti* (compare *cupis; desiderii tui fervorem*) corresponds to Evagrius's ἐπόθει. Abgar's desire to see Jesus was fulfilled by the image, as Egeria also implied.

After the siege, Justinian devoted a chapel in Edessa's Hagia Sophia Great Church to the image, which was kept there from then on. Prior to this it had been stored away, which explains why Egeria did not see it even though the bishop knew of its existence. The *Narratio de imagine Edessena*, attributed to Constantine VII Porphyrogenitus, recounts that a bishop of Edessa, sensing danger, had the image relic walled in, a κέραμος (tile) placed on it, and the external surface of the wall smoothed (15–17). The image remained long hidden, but it was discovered in 544; the *Narratio* cites Evagrius's report (17–19). The κέραμος bore an imprint of the image, which in the day of the *Narratio* was still in Edessa: the *Keramion*, allegedly a copy of the *Mandylion* on a tile.

A period of invisibility of the *Mandylion* is reflected also in the *Doctrina Addai*, which recounts that the image relic was first venerated in Edessa under Abgar Ukkama, who placed it in one of the royal palaces. When a successor reverted to paganism and wanted to destroy the relic,

---

25. Domenico Mansi, *Sacrorum Conciliorum nova et amplissima collectio* (Florence, 1759), 13.768B.

the bishop stored it in a safe place. Moses of Chorene, too, speaks of the apostasy of a successor of Abgar (*Hist. Arm.* 2.34–35), and Procopius describes Abgar's successor as ἀνοσιώτατος ἁπάντων ἀνθρώπων ("the most impious of all humans," *De bello Persico* 2.12), like the *Menologion*, revised by Symeon Metaphrastes (below). An eighth-century Melkite colophon from Edessa confirms that in the seventh century a "house of the Lord's image" existed in Edessa.[26] The ἀχειροποίητος [εἰκών] ἡ ἐν Ἐδέσσῃ τῇ πόλει is also mentioned in Stephen Deacon's *Life of Saint Stephen the Younger*, martyred in 766.[27] Before then, Stephen saw the relic in Edessa, where it was publicly visible after 544. It is here understood as an *acheiropoieta* image, as in Evagrius and the Acta Maris.

Acta Maris 3 (sixth–seventh century) narrates how Abgar Ukkama, after receiving Jesus's letter, sent painters to Jerusalem, but they could not reproduce Jesus's appearance.[28] Jesus then pressed a cloth[29] on his face and gave them his portrait. This was put in the church of Edessa and remained there "until today." The same assertion is in Moses of Chorene. Jesus's portrait in the Doctrina Addai becomes an *acheiropoieta* in these Acta; its location in the Edessan church reflects the *Mandylion's* historical location after 544.

Unlike Eusebius, the Doctrina Addai, and Moses of Chorene, the Acts of Thaddaeus (seventh century, possibly going back to the third–fourth century[30]) represents Abgar Ukkama as healed by Christ's image brought by Ananias before Thaddaeus's arrival, specifically by the impression of Christ's figure on a cloth (Acta Thadd. 2–4). Jesus, after washing (νιψάμενος), wiped himself and impressed his appearance[31] (ἀπεμάξατο τὴν ὄψιν αὐτοῦ) on a σινδών, so his image was imprinted there (ἐντυπωθείσης τῆς εἰκῶνος). The linen was "fourfold, quadruple / four times double"

---

26. See Robert Thomson, "An Eighth-Century Melkite Colophon from Edessa," *JTS* 13 (1962): 249–58.

27. *Vita Sancti Stephani Iunioris*, PG 100:1085A.

28. Ilaria Ramelli, "La *Doctrina Addai* e gli *Acta Maris*," *AION* 65 (2005): 75–102; Ramelli, "The Narrative Continuity between the *Teaching of Addai* and the *Acts of Mari*," *OLA* 189 (2009): 411–50.

29. Syriac *seddona*, from σινδών.

30. So Palmer, "Edessan Images of Christ," 222 and *passim*.

31. Dietz ("Abgars Christusbild als Ganzkörperbild," 413) agrees with this translation, confirmed by Andrew of Crete, *Veneration of Sacred Images* 3 (PG 97.1304A), against Nicolotti's rendering, "face" (*From the Mandylion of Edessa to the Shroud of Turin*, 29–34).

(τετράδιπλον). By the time of these Acta it was known that the Edessan image was on a fabric "folded up in the middle four times," so that only Jesus's face was visible. In the *Synaxarion*, ῥάκος τετράδιπλον occurs within a narrative that parallels that of Acts of Thaddaeus. Ananias was unable to portray Jesus, who "asked to wash himself and, once this had happened, a cloth folded up four times / a fourfold cloth [ῥάκος τετράδιπλον] was given to him. After washing, he dried his immaculate, divine appearance in it. His divine shape and figure remained impressed [ἐντυπωθείσης] on the linen [ἐν τῇ σινδόνι], which Jesus then gave to Ananias." Jesus's image has no relation to the passion at this time, but it is no longer the Doctrina Addai's painting.[32] The expression ῥάκος τετράδιπλον returns in George Cedrenus's *Historiarum compendium* (eleventh–twelfth century).[33] Given the impossibility of painting his portrait, Jesus washed himself and gave to Abgar Ukkama's emissary "a cloth folded up four times, on which he wiped dry and took an impression [ἀπεμάξατο] of his incorruptible, divine appearance. And, look, immediately the reproduction [ἀπεικόνισμα] of his form was impressed [ἐνετυπώθη] on the linen [ἐν τῇ σινδόνι], which he gave to Ananias."

For John of Damascus, too, around 728–731, the image was an *acheiropoieta* still preserved in Edessa. He called it ἱμάτιον and ῥάκος, on which Jesus impressed his χαρακτήρ, resulting in an ἀπεικόνισμα, which Jesus sent to Abgar Ukkama, who "strongly desired" to see him (ποθοῦντι; see Evagrius, *Hist. eccl.*; Egeria, *Peregrinatio Egeriae*).[34] Also in the eighth century, the *Admonitio senis*, attributed to George of Cyprus, specified that the Edessan *acheiropoieta* was an ἄχραντος εἰκών obtained by the impression of Jesus's face on a cloth ἄνευ ὕλης καὶ χρωμάτων, "without material colors."

Andrew of Crete, before 740, in his anti-iconoclastic *Veneration of Sacred Images*,[35] calls the Edessan image Christ's εἰκών on a cloth (ῥάκος)

---

32. The Epistula trium patriarcharum 7, containing the proceedings of an 836 Jerusalem synod, describes the Edessan image as "the imprint [ἐκμαγεῖον] of Jesus's own shape on a σουδάριον" and repeats that the image is a result of the impression of liquids, having been obtained when Jesus dried his face: ὁ χαρακτὴρ τῆς ἁγίας μορφῆς αὐτοῦ was imprinted on that σουδάριον, τὰ χαρακτηριστικὰ αὐτοῦ πάντα ἰδιώματα ὡς ἐν χρώμασι τισί, but without colors.

33. George Cedrenus, *Historiarum compendium*, ed. Immanuel Bekker (Bonn: Weberi, 1838–1839), 1:309.17.

34. John of Damascus, *De fide orthodoxa* 89 (PG 94:1173); John of Damascus, *De imaginibus* 1.320A (PG 94:1261B).

35. Andrew of Crete, *Veneration of Sacred Images* 1 (PG 97:1301D).

"the imprint [ἐκμαγεῖον] of the features of his body [τοῦ σωματικοῦ αὐτοῦ χαρακτῆρος]" (1). Albeit without colors, the image was "in no way inferior to the painting made with colors." Andrew, like the *Admonitio*, speaks of an image without colors, but his use of the determinative article in "*the* painting," instead of "*a* painting," suggests that he also knew a painting representing Christ, as in the Doctrina Addai tradition, and was contrasting it with an *acheiropoieta*. A letter attributed to Pope Gregory II (715–731) written to Emperor Leo III the Isaurian also describes the Edessan image as *acheiropoieta* (αὐτίγραφον ἀχειροτεύκτως μορφῶσας). In the documents concerning the Second Council of Nicaea,[36] which authorized icon veneration, Leo Anagnostes from Constantinople was quoted as seeing the image in Edessa τὴν ἱερὰν τὴν ἀχειροποίητον εἰκόνα, "the sacred image not made by human hands, honored and venerated by believers" (in the year 787). The public veneration of the image in Edessa is also attested by Smera.

In tenth-century Codex Vossianus Latinus Q69,[37] an eighth/ninth-century account reports that an imprint of Christ's whole body was left on a canvas, still kept in a church in Edessa. The text quotes Smera from Constantinople. Abgar wanted to see Jesus, who promised to send him "a linen, in which you will be able to see not only the figure of my face, but also that of the whole of my body, standing, divinely transposed (onto the linen)" (linteum, in quo non solum faciei mee figuram, sed *totius corporis mei figuram* cernere poteris statum divinitus transformatum). Jesus "lay down on a linen white like snow, with the whole of his body" (supra quodam linteum ad instar nivis candidatum toto se corpore stravit). Thus, on the linen there remained impressed both "the glorious figure of the face of the Lord and the noblest one of his whole body, standing" (dominice faciei figura gloriosa et *totius corporis* nobilissimus status). The *Mandylion* reproduced Jesus's face and body. "This linen, which still now remains uncorrupted, even if it is so ancient, is kept in Mesopotamia, in the Syriac region, in the city of Edessa, in the main church" (Linteus adhuc vetustate temporis permanens incorruptus, in Mesopotamia Syrie apud Edissam civitatem in domo maioris ecclesie habetur repositus). On some feasts, all year round, the linen was extracted from its golden box and seen by every-

---

36. Mansi, *Sacrorum Conciliorum collectio*, 13.192C.

37. Manuscript 5696, fol. 35. Critical edition by Dietz ("Abgars Christusbild als Ganzkörperbild," 421–39), from which (col. 1) I quote.

one.[38] Smera confirms that the *Mandylion* was folded up but was unfolded every year and represented a full figure.

This is repeated in Gervase of Tilbury's *Otia imperialia* 111, from some *Gesta Salvatoris*. Here Jesus says to Abgar Ukkama: "Look, I send you a linen, in which the figure of my face and that of the whole of my body, standing, is found" (en tibi dirigo lintheum in quo faciei mee figura et *tocius mei corporis* status continetur). Indeed, "A tradition from the archives of an ancient authority has that the Lord lay down on a most white linen, and, thanks to the divine power, on the linen there has remained impressed the most beautiful image not only of the Lord's face, but also of his whole body" (Traditur autem ex archivis auctoritatis antique quod Dominus super lintheum candidissimum *toto corpore* se prostreverit, et ita virtute divina non tantum faciei, sed etiam *tocius corporis* dominici speciosissima effigies lintheo impressa sit). Gervase wrote when the image was no longer in Edessa.[39]

The image is called μανδύλιον from the ninth–tenth century onward, the diminutive of μανδύας/μανδύης or μανδύα/μανδύη, a word attested, for example, in the LXX, Cassius Dio (*Hist. Rom.* 57.13), the Suda, and Pollux (*Onom.* 7.60) with the meaning "woollen cloak, mantel," properly a Persian piece of clothing (the noun is Persian).[40] The diminutive μανδήλιον/μανδύλιον is analogous to μαντίλιον/μαντήλιον (Latin *mantilium*).[41] A Syriac/Arabic influence can be detected in μανδύλιον (*mandil*, "towel, handkerchief"; Syriac *mandili*). In 843, after the end of iconoclasm, Byzantine emperors repeatedly tried to obtain the *Mandylion*, as reported in the *Synaxarion*, ascribed to Symeon Metaphrastes (tenth century). In 944, the general John Kourkouas, on behalf of Romanos I Lecapenus (920–944), besieged Edessa—which had been under Arab control since 637, during which time veneration of the *Mandylion* was not impeded—and obtained the *Mandylion*. The image was thus solemnly transported to Constanti-

---

38. "Cum hympnis et salmis ac specialibus canticis de scrinio producitur aureo atque adoratur ab omni populo cum magna honoris reverentia."

39. From his source he adds, "Hec Domini ymago in lintheo aput Edissam, que caput est Mesopotamidis Sirie, sine aliquo corruptionis vestigio in maiori ecclesia reservata, in precipuis festivitatibus Domini Salvatoris de aureo scrinio producitur et … adoratur."

40. Aelius Dionysius, apud Eustathius, *Ad Odysseam* 1854.32 ; Photius, *Lexicon*, s.v. Μανδύης.

41. E.g., Theophanes Continuatus 432.12; *Horologion* August 16.

nople, to the Blachernae church, and then, on August 16, to the imperial palace, where it was enthroned.[42] Its arrival is described in the *Narratio* attributed to Constantine VII Porphyrogenitus (a successor of Romanos who moved the *Mandylion* inside the imperial palace into the Pharos chapel of the Theotokos).[43] The Greek title calls the *Mandylion* ἀχειροποίητος θεία εἰκών. The translation was celebrated annually on August 16.

I have argued elsewhere that the *Narratio* includes details unknown from other sources, details that are probably historical,[44] such as the friendship between Abgar Ukkama and the prefect of Egypt. Here an alternative explanation of the origin of the *Mandylion* emerges, similar to Macarius's association of Edessa with the image of the suffering Christ. According to *Narratio* 11–13 (second redaction),[45] the image of Christ was impressed on a cloth through his blood in Gethsemane. It was taken "when Christ was about to enter his voluntary passion" (ἐν τῷ μέλλειν τὸν Χριστὸν ἐπὶ τὸ ἑκούσιον πάθος ἐλθεῖν), while "he was seen in agony and praying" (ἀγωνιῶν ὡρᾶτο καὶ προσευχόμενος), and "his sweat in various points[46] was distilling like big blood drops/clots" (τοὺς ἰδρῶτας αὐτοῦ ὡσεὶ θρόμβους σταλάσσειν αἵματος). Jesus "took from one of his disciples this slice of fabric that can be seen now" (τὸ νῦν βλεπόμενον τοῦτο τεμάχιον τοῦ ὑφάσματος) and "dried away the drops of sweat everywhere[47] in it" (τὰς τῶν ἰδρώτων λιβάδας ἐν αὐτῷ ἀπομάξασθαι). "Immediately, this imprint [ἐκτύπωσιν] that can be seen of that divine appearance/form remained impressed [ἐντυπωθῆναι]." Later this image, coming from the impression of bloody liquids, was brought to Edessa, not by Abgar Ukkama's emissary-painter before Jesus's death, but by Thaddeus/Addai after Jesus's resurrection. Abgar, ill, took the fabric from the apostle and "reverently placed it around his own head, eyes, and lips, nor did he deprive the other parts of his body of such a touching"

---

42. S. Engberg, "Romanos Lekapenos and the Mandylion," in *Byzance et les reliques du Christ*, ed. J. Durand and B. Flusin (Paris: Centre d'histoire et civilisation de France, 2004), 121–42.

43. *Narratio de imagine Edessena* (PG 113:421–54).

44. Ilaria Ramelli, "Edessa e i Romani tra Augusto e i Severi," *Aevum* 73 (1999): 107–43; Ramelli, "Abgar Ukkama e Abgar il Grande alla luce di recenti apporti storiografici," *Aevum* 78 (2004): 103–8.

45. PG 113:434A–35A. This text underwent several redactions: the first, by Constantine, may be lost; one revision coincides with the *Synaxarion* of Constantinople, and another ended up into the *Menologion*, revised by Symeon around 1000.

46. Literally, "his sweats."

47. Literally, "the drops of his sweats."

(οὐδὲ τ' ἄλλα τῶν τοῦ σώματος μερῶν στερήσας τῆς τοιαύτης προσψαύσεως): "all limbs" (τὰ μέλη πάντα) were healed. This story associates the *Mandylion* with Christ's passion, speaks of bloody sweat, and intimates that the image included Jesus's full body.

Likewise a passage of the Byzantine *Menaion* preserved in an Athos manuscript[48] recounts that Abgar Ukkama, receiving Christ's image from Thaddeus, saw "the whole human form of the image" (τὸ τῆς εἰκόνος ὅλον ἀνθρωπόμορφον) and was startled, because he recognized God in "flesh and blood and intellectual soul." The *Narratio* also explains that in Constantinople the image was laid to sit on the throne, possibly unfolded.[49] Likewise, a miniature in an illuminated codex containing John Skylitzes's Σύνοψις Ἱστοριῶν[50] shows Romanos receiving from his *cubicularius* Theophanes and embracing, on August 15, 944, τὸ ἅγιον μανδύλιον (so the caption), here represented not as a small piece of imprinted and enshrined cloth but as Christ's tridimensional head on top of a long piece of reddish cloth, within a hardly visible white frame from which both the head and the cloth seem to emerge. This could suggest that in Constantinople the *Mandylion*, previously folded up, may have been unfolded. However, the copyist might have misunderstood details of an earlier model.

Gregory the Referendary (who received petitions and directed the chancery), of the great church of Constantinople, composed a sermon on the translation of the *Mandylion* (preserved in a Vatican Library manuscript).[51] Gregory knew that Eusebius made no mention of the image, so he went to Edessa and investigated (*Hom.* 9). He found Syriac documents that he translated into Greek. This may have been the Doctrina Addai, but Gregory's account of the formation of the image differs: the Doctrina Addai mentions a painting, Gregory the impression of Jesus's bloody sweat, like the *Narratio*, which links the Edessan image to Christ's passion. In Gregory's *Hom.* 10–13, the image, brought to Abgar not by Ananias but by Thaddeus, is not painted with colors but made of light and shadows, because Jesus "impressed on the cloth his image, during the agony that led to his voluntary passion [πρὸς τὸ ἑκούσιον πάθος αὐτοῦ ἀγωνιῶν]": Jesus "took this cloth [ὀθόνη] and dried against it the drops of

---

48. Athos, MS Iveron 1684, fol. 85r.

49. *Narratio de imagine Edessena* 30 (PG 113:452C).

50. Madrid, Biblioteca Nacional de España, MS Graecus Vitr. 26-2, fol. 131r. See Vasiliki Tsamakda, *The Illustrated Chronicle of Skylitzes* (Leiden: Brill, 2002).

51. Codex Vaticanus Graecus 511, fols. 143–50.

his sweat, like big blood drops/clots shed by his face during the agony [ἀγωνιῶντος ὡσεὶ θρόμβους αἵματος ἱδρῶτας]." In *Hom.* 26–27, Gregory repeats that the image remained imprinted (ἐντετύπωται) from Jesus's "sweat shed during his agony, like drops of blood" (ἐναγωνίοις ἱδρῶσι τοῖς ὡσεὶ θρόμβοις κατασταλάξασιν αἵματος). The body by which these bloody drops were shed, on the cross "became adorned by the blood drops [ῥανίσι] from its own side." This linked the Edessan image to the passion. When Jesus descended from Gethsemane, he gave that imprinted cloth, ἀχειροποίητος εἰκών (*Hom.* 14), to Thomas, who gave it to Thaddaeus. In the Edessan tradition, Thaddaeus was sent by Thomas. When the Edessan image was enthroned, after its transfer to Constantinople, the emperor put the imperial crown on top of the "light of the face" of Christ (*Hom.* 28). This version differs from that of the Doctrina Addai, which featured a painting representing a nonsuffering Jesus.

The transfer of the *Mandylion* to Constantinople was incorporated into Constantinople's *Synaxarion* and *Menologion*, later revised by Symeon Metaphrastes. There the Edessan image relic is called ἀχειρότευκτος (constructed without [human] hands) and ῥάκος τετράδιπλον, Θεοῦ θέα θαῦμα (a cloth folded up four times/a fourfold cloth, a marvel of God to see). The *Menologion* before its revision by Symeon contains a lengthy description of the Lenten liturgy dedicated to the image still in Edessa, between 544 and 944—although this may reflect the Byzantine liturgy celebrated in Constantinople. The large box in which the image was stored was hidden by panels, removed only during Lent; even then, "it was not permitted to anyone to come close [προσεγγίσαι], nor even to approach the holy shape with one's lips *or eyes* [οὐδὲ χείλεσιν ἢ ὄμμασιν προσψαῦσαι]." Only the bishop, once a year, could open the box and see the linen.

An eleventh-century document, the description of Constantinople by the Anonymus Tarraconensis, confirms that the "the linen is always closed in a golden box and (obstinately) locked very diligently" (linteum semper sit clausum aureo vase et obfirmatum diligentissime). Unlike other relics in the imperial palace, this one was never shown to anyone, not even to the emperor, and its box was never opened.[52] The author provides an etiology: when once it was opened, a terrible earthquake struck, which was placated

---

52. "This linen, on which there is the figure of the face of our Redeemer, is shown to no one, is opened for no one, not even the emperor of Constantinopolis himself" (Istud linteum in quo continetur nostri Redemptoris vultus figuratus nulli demonstratur, nulli aperitur, nec ipsi Constantinopolitano imperatori).

only when the image was sealed in its box. It is therefore impossible to ascertain whether that box, seen in Constantinople by Robert de Clary (below), still contained the linen.[53]

Early in the tenth century, Al-Masudi identified the *Mandylion* with the cloth with which Jesus dried himself after baptism (*Meadows of Gold* 29). Given that baptism was by immersion of the whole body, this version suggests that the *Mandylion* included Christ's whole body, as in Smera; as in other testimonies, it was formed by the impression of liquids, not blood, nor was it a painting. Odericus Vitalis, in *Church History* 9.11, around 1130, also described the Edessan image as impressed on a linen (pretiosum linteum) and a result of the imprint of liquids, in particular sweat: "with which Jesus wiped away the sweat of his face; in it, the image of the same Savior shines out wondrously represented: to those who watch, it shows the aspect and size of the body of the Lord" (quo faciei suae sudorem extersit, in quo eiusdem Salvatoris imago mirabiliter depicta refulget; quae dominici corporis speciem et quantitatem intuentibus exhibit). The reference to "the stature/size/greatness of the Lord's body" also suggests that the *Mandylion* reproduced Jesus's whole body.

The tenth-century *Chronographia* (52), ascribed to Symeon Magister, reports that, on the *Mandylion*'s arrival at Constantinople, Constantine and Stephen, Emperor Romanos's sons, could see only the vague shape of a face (μὴ βλέπειν τι ἢ πρόσωπον μόνον), without distinguishing its features, whereas Romanos's son-in-law, Constantine Porphyrogenitus, could distinguish eyes and ears (βλέπειν ὀφθαλμοὺς καὶ ὦτα) by divine grace— the grace that placed him on the throne. The same detail emerges from *Vita Sancti Pauli Iunioris* 37, around 970: a copy was taken of the Edessan image by laying a linen on it; the εἰκών impressed on the linen was clearly (καθαρῶς) visible *only* to the saint. When the image was presented to the saint, it was unfolded (ὑφαπλωθέν). This intimates, again, that the Edessan image was a long linen folded up.

Early in the thirteenth century, Nicolas Mesarites—the supervisor of the imperial relic treasure in the Pharos chapel—compiled a list of the

---

53. Robert de Clary, *Li estoires de chiaus qui conquisent Coustantinoble = La conquête de Constantinople* 83, reports that he saw two golden vessels in the Pharos chapel, one containing the Keramion, "a tile" (*une tuile*), and one the *Mandylion*, "a cloth" (*une touaile*), but did not see their contents. He saw another linen in which the full figure of Christ's dead body was imprinted: this was often lifted up and shown to the public (below).

relics of the imperial chapel in Constantinople. A shroud mentioned by him[54] was kept in that chapel until the arrival of the crusaders in 1204. Mesarites described it as Christ's linen burial shrouds (ἐντάφιοι σινδόνες … ἀπὸ λίνου), "still smelling of myrrh" (ἔτι πνέουσαι μύρα) and uncorrupted, because they had wrapped up Christ's "dead body, naked, embalmed with myrrh, uncircumscribed/incomprehensible/indeterminate/indefinite/not enveloped/not wrapped" (ἀπερίληπτον[55] νεκρὸν γυμνὸν ἐσμυρνημένον). The same object, or an *imago pietatis*,[56] was seen by the French crusader Robert de Clary. In *Li estoires de chiaus qui conquisent Coustantinoble* (= *La conquête de Constantinople*), de Clary reports that he saw in Constantinople in 1204 a shroud on which was the figure of Jesus's body: "there was another church which was called My Lady Saint Mary of Blachernae, where the sheets [*li sydoines*] in which Our Lord had been wrapped were kept, which every Friday rose up straight, so that one could clearly see the figure [*le figure*] of Our Lord on it." It cannot be ruled out that this was the unfolded *Mandylion*.

Conclusion: The Significance of This Contribution for Further Study

I have indicated how the spatial, literary, and linguistic translations (especially Greek, Syriac, Latin, and Armenian) of the *Mandylion* are intertwined. I have examined the evolution of the Abgar story, arguing that it developed from a historical nugget: the political correspondence between Abgar Ukkama and Tiberius. I traced the literary transformations of the legend, influenced by political-ecclesiastical agendas. The story probably first took shape in the entourage of Abgar the Great as a way to praise him through his first-century namesake. The subsequent stages are in Eusebius—whose account, I have argued, comes from three sources—the Doctrina Addai, the Armenian history of Moses of Chorene, and the Acta Maris. Literary transformations took shape together with linguistic translations.

I investigated the emergence and transformation of the *Mandylion* within the Addai legend, arguing that Eusebius's first source (Bardaisan?)

---

54. Nicolas Mesarites, *Seditio Ioannis Comneni* 13.

55. Ἀπερίληπτος means "uncircumscribed, incomprehensible," "indeterminate, indefinite," or "not embraced/enveloped/wrapped."

56. See H. Belting, *Il culto delle immagini* (Rome: Carocci, 2008), 319–21; Filippo Burgarella, "Dy Mandylion au Linceul de Turin," *Nouvelles de l'Association Carmignac* 71 (2016): 3–4.

may have mentioned it and that the *Peregrinatio* first alludes to it. This is why Macarius described Berenice/Veronica as Edessan. The *Doctrina* identifies the *Mandylion* as a painted portrait, as does Moses of Chorene. In Evagrius, the portrait becomes an *acheiropoieta* and defends Edessa from the 544 siege. Then it was transferred to the main church in Edessa, and the Acta Maris in the seventh century reports that it was still there and also characterizes it as *acheiropoieta*. In the seventh century, possibly earlier, the Acts of Thaddaeus present it as folded up four times. The Byzantine *Narratio* and other sources related to the translation of the *Mandylion* to Constantinople first associate it with Jesus's passion.

I thus individuated the transformations of the *Mandylion* from a painted portrait to an *acheiropoieta* representing Jesus alive and well to an impression of liquids, water, sweat, or blood, the last revealing a connection with Jesus's agony and passion. The dimensions also change, from just Jesus's face to his entire body; hence the emergence of the clarification that the *Mandylion* was a larger fabric folded up. All these transformations, which parallel the spatial, literary, and linguistic translations of the *Mandylion*, may reflect improved examinations of the relic, before and after its unfolding, and call for rigorous comparisons with other ancient *acheiropoietai* representing Christ.

Bibliography

Baranov, Vladimir. "The Iconophile Fathers." Pages 338–51 in *The Wiley-Blackwell Companion to Patristics*. Edited by Ken Parry. Oxford: Wiley-Blackwell, 2015.

Belting, H. *Il culto delle immagini*. Rome: Carocci, 2008.

Brock, Sebastian. Review of *Atti di Mar Mari*, by Ilaria Ramelli. *Ancient Narrative* 7 (2008): 123–30. https://tinyurl.com/SBL4217d.

Burgarella, Filippo. "Dy Mandylion au Linceul de Turin." *Nouvelles de l'Association Carmignac* 71 (2016): 3–4.

Cameron, Averil. *Continuity and Change in Sixth-Century Byzantium*. London: Variorum Reprints, 1981.

———. "The History of the Image of Edessa." *Okeanos* 7 (1983): 80–94.

Cedrenus, George. *Historiarum compendium*. Vol. 1. Edited by Immanuel Bekker. Bonn: Weberi, 1838–1839.

Dietz, Karlheinz. "Abgars Christusbild als Ganzkörperbild." Pages 393–447 in *Das Christusbild*. Edited by Karlheinz Dietz et al. Würzburg: Echter, 2016.

Drijvers, Han J. W. "The Image of Edessa in Syriac Tradition." Pages 13–31 in *The Holy Face and the Paradox of Representation*. Edited by Herbert L. Kessler and Gerhard Wolf. Bologna: Nuova Alfa Editoriale, 1998.

——. "The Protonike Legend, the *Doctrina Addai*, and Bishop Rabbula." *VC* 51 (1997): 288–315.

Engberg, S. "Romanos Lekapenos and the Mandylion." Pages 121–42 in *Byzance et les reliques du Christ*. Edited by J. Durand and B. Flusin. Paris: Centre d'histoire et civilisation de France, 2004.

Gero, Stephen. "Eusebius' Letter to Constantia Reconsidered." *JTS* 32 (1981): 460–70.

Griffith, Sidney. "The *Doctrina Addai* as a Paradigm of Christian Thought in Edessa in the Fifth Century." *Hug* 6.2 (2003): 1–46.

Guscin, M. *The Image of Edessa*. Leiden: Brill, 2009.

Illert, Martin. *Doctrina Addai*. Turnhout: Brepols, 2007.

Mansi, Domenico. *Sacrorum Conciliorum nova et amplissima collection*. Florence, 1759.

Mirkovic, Alexander. *Prelude to Constantine: The Abgar Tradition in Early Christianity*. Frankfurt: Lang, 2004.

Nicolotti, Andrea. *From the Mandylion of Edessa to the Shroud of Turin*. Leiden: Brill, 2014.

Palmer, Andrew. "Edessan Images of Christ." Pages 222–76 in *Das Christusbild*. Edited by Karlheinz Dietz et al. Würzburg: Echter, 2016.

Perkins, Judith. Review of *Atti di Mar Mari*, by Ilaria Ramelli. *Aevum* 83 (2009): 269–71.

Ramelli, Ilaria. "Abgar Ukkama e Abgar il Grande alla luce di recenti apporti storiografici." *Aevum* 78 (2004): 103–8.

——. "The Addai-Abgar Narrative: Its Development through Literary Genres and Religious Agendas." Pages 205–45 in *Early Christian and Jewish Narrative: The Role of Religion in Shaping Narrative Forms*. Edited by Ramelli and Judith Perkins. Tübingen: Mohr Siebeck, 2015.

——. *Atti di Mar Mari*. Brescia: Paideia, 2008.

——. *Bardaisan of Edessa: A Reassessment of the Evidence and a New Interpretation*. Piscataway, NJ: Gorgias, 2009.

——, ed. *Bardaisan on Free Will, Fate, and Human Nature*. Tübingen: Mohr Siebeck, 2018.

——. "The Biography of Addai: Its Development between Fictionality and Historicity." *Phrasis* 51 (2010): 83–105.

——. "Dal Mandilion di Edessa alla Sindone: Alcune note sulle testimonianze antiche." '*Ilu* 4 (1999): 173–93.

———. "Edessa e i Romani tra Augusto e i Severi." *Aevum* 73 (1999): 107–43.

———. "La *Doctrina Addai* e gli *Acta Maris*." *AION* 65 (2005): 75–102.

———. "The Narrative Continuity between the *Teaching of Addai* and the *Acts of Mari*." *OLA* 189 (2009): 411–50.

———. *Possible Historical Traces in the Doctrina Addai?* Piscataway, NJ: Gorgias, 2009.

———. "The Possible Origin of the Abgar-Addai Legend." *Hug* 16 (2013): 325–41.

———. Review of *Doctrina Addai*, by Martin Illert. *RBL* (2009), www.bookreviews.org/BookDetail.asp?TitleId=6797.

Riesner, Rainer. "Von Jerusalem nach Edessa?" Pages 360–92 in *Das Christusbild*. Edited by Karlheinz Dietz et al. Würzburg: Echter, 2016.

Schäferdiek, Knut. "Untersuchungen zu Verfassenschaft und Situation der Epistula ad Constantiam." *ZKG* 91 (1980): 177–86.

Sidgwick, Emma. *From Flow to Face*. Leuven: Peeters, 2015.

Sode, C., and P. Speck. "Ikonoklasmus vor der Zeit?" *Jahrbuch der Österreichischen Byzantinistik* 54 (2004): 113–34.

Thomson, Robert. "An Eighth-Century Melkite Colophon from Edessa." *JTS* 13 (1962): 249–58.

Tsamakda, Vasiliki. *The Illustrated Chronicle of Skylitzes*. Leiden: Brill, 2002.

Wood, Philip. *Christian Political Thought in Greater Syria*. Oxford: Oxford University Press, 2010.

Young, Frances. "Prelude." Pages 1–34 in vol. 1 of in *The Cambridge History of Christianity*. Cambridge: Cambridge University Press, 2006.

Drunk in Love: Who's Afraid of a Spiritual Marriage?

Jeannie Sellick

In one of the opening scenes of the Acts of Thomas, a newlywed couple receives an unexpected guest on their wedding night.[1] When the groom enters the bridal chamber to consummate his new union, he finds not only his bride but also Jesus. Cloaked as the titular apostolic hero, Jesus (referred to as "the Lord" throughout this passage) embarks on a speech to persuade the couple to "abandon this filthy intercourse" and instead wait to receive the "incorruptible and true marriage" (Acts Thom. 12).[2] His tactics work, and the couple "refrained from their filthy passion and so remained throughout the night in that place" (12). Jesus successfully transforms the bridal chamber from a site of bodily pleasure into a schoolhouse of chastity,[3] the marriage bed into a place of continence, and a corporeal marriage into a spiritual one.

The next morning it is time for the bride's parents to be surprised. They see "the bride with her face unveiled and the bridegroom very cheerful." Apparently baffled by this, her mother questions her daughter's

---

This paper draws on themes discussed in a 2014 study on the spiritualization of the family unit in late antiquity. See Jeannie Sellick, "Ordered Love: Reshaping Familial Relations in the Age of Asceticism" (unpublished paper, 2014). For my discussion of spiritual marriage and the *subintroductae*, see pages 7–12.

1. The following section deals with conclusions drawn in my own work, "One's Proper Kin: The Elevation of the Spiritual Family in the Apocryphal Acts" (unpublished paper, 2015), 17–19. The following story from the Acts of Thomas is also used in that paper as evidence of the elevation of the spiritual in the Acts.

2. All translations of the Acts of Thomas are adapted from Han J. W. Drijvers's translation, "The Acts of the Holy Apostle Thomas," in *NTApoc* 2:339–411.

3. See Andrew S. Jacobs's discussion of Plutarch's "ethical schoolhouse" in "A Family Affair: Marriage, Class, and Ethics in the Apocryphal Acts of the Apostles," *JECS* 7 (1999): 105–38.

unashamed demeanor, asking why she behaves "as if you lived a long time with your own husband?" For his part, her father asks whether "great love for her husband" is why she does not veil herself (Acts Thom. 13). While the bride confirms his suspicion of love, it is not for her temporal husband, but for her newly betrothed—the Lord, Jesus. As to her openness she claims, "that I do not veil myself is because the mirror of shame has been taken from me; and I am no longer ashamed or abashed because the world of shame and bashfulness has been removed far from me" (14). What makes this example particularly remarkable for a spiritual marriage is the lack of anxiety both partners feel about remaining together. Though we are treated to but a glimpse, in the afterglow of their spiritualized marriage, the author highlights the ease between the couple as the bride sits unveiled and unashamed. After their conversion the couple adopts a spiritual child, converts the bride's father, and eventually joins Thomas in India (16). The author of the Acts of Thomas harbors no anxiety about the physical closeness between a celibate man and woman.

Though frequently overlooked, this episode in the Acts of Thomas provides an early depiction of a tantalizing yet condemned practice: spiritual marriage. While the Acts of Thomas provides the most striking depiction, it is far from the only example of this phenomenon in the apocryphal acts. Part of the reason the apocryphal acts have found themselves excluded from conversations about spiritual marriage is the lack of scholarly consensus as to the historical reality behind the texts. On one side exists scholarship that argues these stories provide a glimpse of real communities and social practices.[4] On the other end of the spectrum, some posit that any social reality behind these acts remains tenuous at best.[5] For the matter at hand, I would like to try another way of understanding the apocryphal acts, which sidesteps the issue of historical reality.

In her essay "Fictional Narratives and Social Critiques," Judith Perkins argues that the apocryphal acts can be useful in helping us understand how certain groups of early Christians may have grappled with their

---

4. Notably, Stevan L. Davies, *The Revolt of the Widows: The Social World of the Apocryphal Acts* (Carbondale: Southern Illinois University Press, 1980), esp. ch. 4; Virginia Burrus, *Chastity as Autonomy: Women in the Stories of the Apocryphal Acts* (Lewiston, NY: Mellen, 1987); Dennis R. MacDonald, *The Legend and the Apostle: The Battle for Paul in Story and Canon* (Philadelphia: Westminster, 1983).

5. Kate Cooper, *The Virgin and the Bride: Idealized Womanhood in Late Antiquity* (Cambridge: Harvard University Press: 1996), esp. ch. 3.

identities. Perkins maintains that the fact the acts were later rejected as heretical "should not subvert their valuable testimony for the kinds of self-understandings, beliefs, and attitudes motivating Christians in an earlier period."[6] The apocryphal acts as a collective unit, Perkins says, "offer an opportunity to view how Christians understood and positioned themselves vis-à-vis and in dialogue with other members of a complex and highly mobile society."[7] Although the acts themselves are pieces of literary fiction, they can help shed light on the ways in which some early Christians understood Scripture and attempted to shape their lives according to that understanding.

Despite the apocryphal acts later being deemed heretical by some, Perkins argues that they continued to provide a treasure trove for "engaging Christian imaginations."[8] It is this idea of the potential of the acts to engage the Christian imagination that I would like to explore here—particularly with regard to the issue of spiritual marriage in late antiquity. Were situations like that of the bride and groom from Thomas common in the later Christian world? If so, what drove these couples to engage in spiritual marriage? Why did the practice of male and female virgins living together in this union become so controversial that it was condemned at no less than six church councils in the fourth century alone?[9]

Spiritual Marriage in Later Antiquity

While several church fathers give us some insight into spiritual marriage, there is no better evidence for the practice than a series of invective treatises from the fourth century by John Chrysostom. In one particularly choice condemnation, Chrysostom rails, "This 'virginity in the company of men' is more severely slandered among all than prostitution. Having lost its own proper place, it has rolled headlong down into the abyss of

---

6. Judith Perkins, "Fictional Narratives and Social Critique," in *Late Ancient Christianity: A People's History of Christianity*, ed. Virginia Burrus and Rebecca Lyman (Minneapolis: Fortress, 2005), 47.

7. Perkins, "Fictional Narratives," 48.

8. Perkins "Fictional Narratives," 47.

9. Elizabeth A. Clark, "John Chrysostom and the *Subintroductae*," *CH* 46 (June 1977): 171–85. See 172–73 for a discussion of the condemnation of spiritual marriage in the fourth century by church councils.

harlotry!" (*Fem. reg.* 4).[10] At first glance, this statement appears shock-ing. What could possibly cause John Chrysostom, one of the foremost architects of female virginity, to slander it so? The women at the heart of Chrysostom's invective were no ordinary virgins. His attack is aimed at an elusive group of women known as the *subintroductae*. Sometimes referred to as *apagetae*, these early Christian women were engaged in the practice of *syneisaktism*—the most controversial manifestation of spiri-tual marriage. This practice consisted of male and female ascetics who, though they had taken vows of chastity, lived together as if married. They shared the same house, ate, drank, and spoke with one another all while remaining celibate. While John Chrysostom is far from the only patris-tic author to condemn the practice of *syneisaktism*, two of his treatises provide the most thorough treatment of the phenomenon. While the two works, *Contra eos qui apud se habent subintroductas virgines* and *Quod regulares feminae viris cohabitare non debeant*,[11] list many reasons for the impropriety of spiritual marriage, there is one unique issue that under-girds his critiques: friendship.

Although the *subintroductae* and Chrysostom's treatises have received relatively little treatment in scholarship, the majority of studies concerning the early Christian phenomenon of spiritual marriage acknowledge that couples engaged in this practice may have acted out of a desire for a new kind of intersexual relationship. Hans Achelis's 1902 work *Virgines Sub-introductae* was a study dedicated to understanding these live-in virgins. While he admitted his uncertainty, Achelis suggested that these virgin cou-ples may have been acting out of an interest in "Platonic love."[12] Modern scholars have also picked up on Achelis's hypothesis. In a short article on

---

10. All translations of John Chrysostom are adapted from Elizabeth A. Clark, *Jerome, Chrysostom, and Friends* (Lewiston, NY: Mellen, 1979).

11. *Contra eos qui apud se habent subintroductas virgines* is in PG 47:495–532. The most up-to-date critical edition is Jean Dumortier, *Saint Jean Chrysostome: Les cohabitations suspectes* (Paris: Les Belles Lettres, 1955). The most recent English trans-lation of this text comes from Clark, *Jerome, Chrysostom, and Friends*, 164–206. In this study I follow Dumortier's edition and numbering system. *Quod regulares feminae viris cohabitare non debeant* is in PG 47:495–532. The critical edition is Dumortier, *Saint Jean Chrysostome*. The most recent English translation of this text comes from Clark, *Jerome, Chrysostom, and Friends*, 209–46. In this study I follow Dumortier's edition and numbering system.

12. Hans Achelis, *Virgines Subintroductae: Ein Beitrag zum VIII Kapitel des I. Korintherbriefs* (Leipzig: Hinrichs, 1902), 72–74.

the treatises, Elizabeth Clark elaborates on Achelis's suggestion. She notes that spiritual marriage could provide a unique degree of spiritual intimacy that had previously been unavailable between men and women.[13] In a more recent work on Chrysostom's treatises, Blake Leyerle also describes the potential spiritual marriage held for friendship. Her work persuasively illustrates that by portraying spiritual marriage as a theatrical production—and the virgin couples as its buffoonish players—Chrysostom reveals that the couples' "holiness is an elaborate and deceptive façade."[14]

While each of these works provides passing commentary on the dynamics of friendship in spiritual marriage, it is Rosemary Rader who provides the most comprehensive study on early Christian friendship to date. In her monograph *Breaking Boundaries* she argues that nascent Christianity opened up new avenues through which men and women could interact. In her discussion of *syneisaktism*, she asserts that in spiritual marriage the husband-wife corollary of the ancient society could be transformed into a unique space for men and women to pursue friendship.[15] Though intriguing, Rader's discussion of the dynamics of *syneisaktism* and friendship is tantalizingly brief and only mentions Chrysostom's treatises in passing.

My work here builds on the studies of Clark, Leyerle, and Radar. In reexamining Chrysostom's two treatises, I would like to bring into focus his underlying critique of intersexual friendship. By focusing on his critiques, my goal in this study is twofold: The first is to investigate the core issue Chrysostom sees in this kind of relationship. I will show that although he does concede spiritually married couples can aspire toward a kind of *philia*, the fruits of their friendship are damaging and misdirected. A celibate closeness between men and women skews their God-given gender roles. Additionally, for the women, this closeness carries with it the charge of a kind of infidelity toward Christ. My second goal is to allow Chrysostom's critiques to serve as a lens through which to gain some historical perspective on these couples. Throughout my analysis, I will attempt to peel back Chrysostom's rhetoric so that we might catch a glimpse of how these couples may have understood their own newfound friendship.

---

13. Clark, "John Chrysostom and the *Subintroductae*," 183.

14. Blake Leyerle, *Theatrical Shows and Ascetic Lives: John Chrysostom's Attack on Spiritual Marriage* (Berkeley: University of California Press, 2001), 9.

15. Rosemary Radar, *Breaking Boundaries: Male/Female Friendship in Early Christian Communities* (New York: Paulist Press, 1983), esp. 62–71. For her discussion of Chrysostom's work see 67.

The Reality behind the Rhetoric:
Spiritual Marriage in and out of the Apocryphal Acts

In order to understand why John Chrysostom's treatises are our best source
for exploring the issue of intersex friendship, it is important to have a brief
overview of the history of spiritual marriage in early Christianity. Aside
from the episode in the Acts of Thomas, other apocryphal acts also contain
narratives in which married couples adopt the celibate life together. While
many of the acts emphasize stories of married couples being driven apart
by the apostle's message,[16] this only happens in cases in which one member
(the husband) refuses to convert. But as David Konstan has noted, the Acts
of John in particular accentuates the spiritualization of the conjugal couple
rather than its dissolution.[17] The apostolic hero converts at least two married couples: Lycomedes and Cleopatra (Acts of John 19), and Drusiana
and Andronicus.[18] Like in the Acts of Thomas, after each of these couples
is converted the husband and wife are not separated but rather are able to
remain together in close physical (and spiritual) proximity. But the roots
of spiritual marriage may go even deeper than the apocryphal acts.

    Some scholars have argued that the birth of Christian *syneisaktism* can
be found in 1 Cor 7:36–38.[19] Early church fathers typically understood this
passage as a father's question about whether to marry off his virgin daughter, and some modern scholars even followed suit.[20] But as Dale Martin
has suggested, this unlikely reading may have been colored by the church

---

16. Most famously, Thecla and Thamyris from the Acts of Thecla and Maximilla
and Aegeates in the Acts of Andrew.

17. David Konstan, "Acts of Love: A Narrative Pattern in the Apocryphal Acts,"
JECS 6 (1998): 25.

18. Translated by Knut Schäferdiek in *NTApoc* 2:152–209. The latter episode is
included in a section reconstructed by Schäferdiek; see *NTApoc* 2:178–79.

19. This theory began with Eduard Grafe, "Geistliche Verlöbnisse bei Paulus,"
Theologische Arbeiten aus dem rheinischen wissenschaftlichen Prediger-Verein 3 (1899):
57–69. See also Achelis, *Virgines Subintroducate*, 59. For a fuller discussion of this
debate see Clark, "John Chrysostom and the *Subintroductae*," 173–75, and Roland
Sebolt, "Spiritual Marriage in the Early Church: A Suggested Interpretation of 1 Corinthians 7:36–38," *Concordia Theological Monthly* 30 (1959): 103–19.

20. Notably, Archibald Robertson and Alfred Plummer, *A Critical and Exegetical
Commentary on the First Epistle of St. Paul to the Corinthians* (Edinburgh: T&T Clark,
1929). They reject the reading of spiritual marriage on the grounds that Paul would
never endorse "so perilous an arrangement" (159).

fathers' anxiety about any interpretation that would have allowed for spiritual marriage.[21] Achelis was the first major scholar to popularize a spiritual marriage view of 1 Cor 7; he even argued that Paul may have endorsed the practice.[22] Despite Achelis's impassioned arguments, the evidence for this being an example of spiritual marriage is inconclusive at best.[23]

Aside from Chrysostom, evidence of spiritual marriage can be found in many patristic sources. Cyprian of Carthage addresses the question of spiritual marriage in a letter to one of his priests. Apparently, there were women who "confessed that they had slept with men, yet declare that they are chaste" (*Ep.* 61.1).[24] Cyprian is outraged at this practice and condemns it as a scandal. While he suggests that repentant (and not pregnant) virgins can be allowed back into the church, those who "obstinately persevere, and do not mutually separate themselves, let them know that, with this their immodest obstinacy, they can never be admitted by us into the Church, lest they should begin to set an example to others to go to ruin by their crimes" (61.4). An anonymous letter from the fifth century known as the Pseudo-Titus Epistle levels similar charges against celibate couples.[25] The author is baffled by virgins who, though they are "already betrothed to Christ," are "united with carnal men."[26] While these couples "give an appearance of humility and chastity" they violate "earthly flesh" through intercourse.[27]

No author more clearly articulates his disgust than Jerome. In his work *Libellus de virginitate servanda*, more commonly known as *Letter 22*, Jerome similarly mocks the chastity of the *subintroductae*. He condemns these "one-man harlots" and their partners, writing that "a brother deserts his unmarried sister, a virgin despises her bachelor brother, and (although they pretend to be devoted to the same aim) they seek spiritual solace among strangers—to have carnal intercourse at home" (14.2).[28] In

---

21. Dale B. Martin, *The Corinthian Body* (New Haven: Yale University Press, 1996), 221.

22. Achelis, *Virgines Subintroducate*, 21–29.

23. See Martin, *Corinthian Body*, 219–28.

24. Translations of this epistle follow R. E. Wallis, *ANF* 5:357.

25. The exact circumstances of this letter are unknown, but Aurelio de Santos Otero has argued that it may have come from fifth-century Priscillianist circles. See Otero, "Pseudo-Titus Epistle," in *NTApoc* 2:53–74.

26. Otero, "Pseudo-Titus Epistle," *NTApoc* 2:55.

27. Otero, "Pseudo-Titus Epistle," *NTApoc* 2:63.

28. Translations of this epistle follow Charles Christopher Mierow, *The Letters of St. Jerome*, ACW 33 (New York: Newman, 1963), 146.

Jerome's mind there is no question about the couples' chastity, as the virgins' "swelling wombs" betray them (13.1). The driving force behind each of these authors' condemnations is an underlying mistrust in the claims these couples make to celibacy. Although each of these accounts provides an enticing glimpse at practice, John Chrysostom's two treatises are the fullest and most fruitful for discussing the dynamics of friendship in spiritual marriage.

The "Handmaid of Virtue": Friendship in Antiquity

While almost every patristic author rejects spiritual marriage on the grounds of false celibacy, this charge does *not* figure prominently in Chrysostom's treatises.[29] What makes Chrysostom's attacks so unique is his willingness to challenge spiritual marriage in its ideal form. On the whole he concedes the charge of sexual immorality and instead dismantles the practice using a different set of critiques. For Chrysostom, there are innumerable reasons to condemn the practice: the insatiable lust it causes the male and female virgins, the lust it inspires in weaker Christians, and its ripeness for non-Christian slander. Yet at the heart of his critique lies the problematic friendship it engenders between men and women. In both treatises, he specifically characterizes their relationship as one built on *philia*. Chrysostom implores the men to end this toxic relationship; he appeals, "How can we help ourselves if we are not even conscious of our intoxication with this friendship [τῇ φιλίᾳ μεθύοντες]?" (*Subintr.* 11.20–21).

Chrysostom's critique of this particular form of friendship is clearly rooted in widely held ancient notions. The fullest treatment of ancient friendship is found in Aristotle's *Nicomachean Ethics*. In books 8 and 9, Aristotle defines and discusses the ideal friendship. For Aristotle, there are three modes of friendship: those based on utility, pleasure, and virtue. Those in relationships founded on utility "do not love each other in their own right, but rather in so far as something good comes to them from the other" (*Eth. nic.* 8.3.11–13).[30] This is a base form of friendship, however; when either party outlives their usefulness, their relationship will also dry up. The second form, pleasure, is a relationship usually connected with the

---

29. Clark, "John Chrysostom and the *Subintroductae*," 176.

30. Translations of the *Nicomachean Ethics* follow Michael Pakaluk, *Aristotle Nicomachean Ethics, Books VIII and IX* (Oxford: Clarendon, 1998).

young. Aristotle describes the players in these pleasure relationships: "They love quick-witted people, not because the latter have a certain character, but rather because they are pleasant to them.... Those who love on account of pleasure, love on account of what is pleasant to themselves—and not in so far as the beloved is <what he is>, but rather in so far as he is useful or pleasant" (*Eth. nic.* 8.14–18). To Aristotle this form of friendship is equally base and merely imitates the highest form of friendship: that based on the mutual pursuit of virtue. He writes, "The friendship of good people alike in virtue is complete, since they similarly wish good things to each other and they are good in their own right" (*Eth. nic.* 8.4.7–9). Furthermore, this type of friendship cannot be fleeting or immediate, but takes time, trust, and love. While friendship of utility or pleasure may sometimes look like that of virtue, it is merely a cheap imitations of the highest form. Central to this highest form of friendship is the idea that friendship is equality. While he does leave some space for friendships of disparity,[31] the highest form is exclusively available to men of comparable status and intellectual value (8.7). Close friends aim at living their lives in close proximity, eating, drinking, playing games, and philosophizing together (9.12.1–7).

Cicero's *De amicitia* defines friendship in similar terms. He reiterates Aristotle's understanding that true friendship springs not from a "calculation of how much profit friendship is likely to afford" but from "an inclination of the soul joined with a feeling of love" (*Amic.* 8.27).[32] Proper friendship exists between two men "whose habits and character are congenial ... because in him we seem to behold, as it were, a sort of lamp of uprightness and virtue" (8.27). True friendship should bring honor and virtue to both parties. Cicero claims that it is the duty of a friend "to strive with all his might to arouse a friend's prostrate soul and lead it to a livelier hope and into a better train of thought" (16.59). When looking for a friend, one should choose someone who is "frank, sociable, and sympathetic—that is, one who is likely to be influenced by the same motives as yourself" (18.65).

Women are almost entirely absent from these discussions of ancient friendship. This should hardly come as a shock, given that women were excluded from most forms of public life in ancient Greece and Republican Rome. Marriage was the primary arena in which men and women

---

31. For example, those between a ruler/subject, father/son, husband/wife, etc.

32. Translations of *De amicitia* follow Cicero, *On Old Age, On Friendship, On Divination*, trans. W. A. Falconer, LCL (Cambridge: Harvard University Press, 1923).

of antiquity had space to interact with one another. In his discussion of unequal friendship, Aristotle does provide some acknowledgment of the friendship between a husband and wife. But because this relationship is based on inequality, Aristotle notes that "affections too must be proportionate" (*Eth. nic.* 8.7.24–25). Thus, the "inferior" partner must supply the "superior" with a greater degree of love than that received in return.

With these interlocking definitions of friendship in mind, it is a little surprising that Chrysostom would even be willing to apply *philia* to spiritual marriage. Is it possible that his use of the characterization comes directly from the mouths of the *subintroductae* and their partners? It is perhaps not a stretch to imagine that they would have actively understood their marriage in this way. They likely would have seen their relationship as something that transcended the boundaries of the typical conjugal marriage and opened up a new space previously closed off to men and women. Yet Chrysostom wields his concession artfully. Although he applies the term, he shows that their friendship is not one of virtue but something base. Their spiritual marriage births not virtue but licentiousness. Through his treatises to the virgin couples, Chrysostom shows both men and women that their friendship destroys gender boundaries. Furthermore, he illustrates, particularly to the *subintroductae*, that their *philia* has been woefully misplaced in human partners.

Be Not Servants of (Wo)men

One of the primary ways in which Chrysostom paints this friendship as disadvantageous is by arguing that it skews the natural gender roles of men and women. In his appeal directed toward the male partners of the *subintroductae*, Chrysostom claims that (spiritual) married life transforms soldiers of Christ into slaves of women. According to Chrysostom, they spend all their time going from the perfumery to the linen store to the silversmiths to pick up items for their live-in virgin (*Subintr.* 9). Their servitude is made all the worse by the fact that it is on public display. At church, "the men both receive [the women] at the doors, and strutting as if they have been transformed into eunuchs [εὐνούχων γινόμενοι σοβοῦσιν], when everyone is looking, they guide them in with enormous pride" (10.38–42). Christ, he insists, meant for men to be soldiers and athletes equipped with "spiritual weapons" that become wasted when used to help women with effeminate tasks. He continues to appeal to men's sense of *andreia* ("manliness" or "bravery"). He asks,

If when a soldier has donned his helmet, his shin-guards, his armor; after he has taken up his sword, his shield, his bows, arrows and quiver; when the trumpet shrilly resounds, summoning everyone; when the enemy, grasping mightily, is ready to raze the city to the ground; if you then saw a man who did not hasten to his position but entered a house and sat down with his armor amidst the women, would you not run him through the middle with a sword without uttering a word? (11.1–11)

Not only do these men become slaves, but they also develop a distinctly effeminate character. When men spend their lives with female virgins, "the habits and speech of women are stamped upon [their] souls" (10.78–79: ἤθη καὶ ῥήματα γυναικεῖα εἰς τὴν ἑαυτῶν ἐναποματτόμενοι ψυχήν). Aside from being transformed into servants, close proximity to women also endows men with womanly traits. The friendship between men and women is above all damaging because "unspeakable evil streams into [their] souls." What is this unspeakable evil? It is "all the corrupting feminine customs" that women "stamp onto the souls of these men" (11.32–34: καὶ ἁπλῶς πάντα τὰ γυναικεῖα ἤθη τὰ διεφθαρμένα φέρουσαι εἰς τὰς τούτων ἐναπομάττονται ψυχάς). By sitting, drinking, talking, and eating with women, men somehow become "softer than wax." And this, according to Chrysostom, is unforgivable in the eyes of God.

As if those arguments are not enough, Chrysostom also claims that women lack respect for the men who submit to their "tyranny." When the gender roles are reversed, women become disdainful of the soft men who serve them. Revealing his apparent understanding of female psychology,[33] Chrysostom writes:

Ask those very women: whom do they praise and approve more—those who serve or those who rule over them; those who are subordinate, who do and suffer everything for their favor, or those who put up with nothing of this kind, but are ashamed even of their dreadful commands? If they wish to speak truthfully, they will surely admit the latter. Rather, there is no need for an answer, since the facts speak for themselves. (11.79–88)

If these men have been rendered "softer than wax," then their female counterparts become far too masculine.

In his treatise addressed directly to the *subintroductae*, Chrysostom continues his characterization of these women as tyrants. He asks the

---

33. Clark, "John Chrysostom and the *Subintroductae*," 182.

women whether they "think their overpowering men is laudable" (*Fem. reg.* 7.62–63). However, he is quick to rid them of this false assumption. Their domination humiliates not only the slavish men but also themselves. He writes, "For it is not the woman who enslaves men, but rather the one who respects them that is esteemed and distinguished by all" (7.69–71: Οὐδὲ γὰρ ἡ δουλουμένη τοὺς ἄνδρας γυνή, ἀλλ᾽ ἡ αἰδουμένη αὕτη πᾶσίν ἐστιν αἰδέσιμός τε καὶ ἐπίσημος). He reminds women of both Eve's punishment that "your husband shall rule over you" (Gen 3:16) and Paul's proclamation that "the man is the head of his wife" (1 Cor 11:3). He chastises them for disobeying the apostle, writing, "It is a great disgrace when the upper assumes the position of the lower so that the head is below, the body is above. If this is disgraceful in marriage, how much more so is it in this union [συζυγίας]" (*Fem. reg.* 7.76–79: Ὥστε ἀσχημοσύνη μεγάλη, ὅταν τὰ ἄνω κάτω γίνηται, κάτω μὲν ἡ κεφαλή, τὸ σῶμα δὲ ἄνω. Εἰ δὲ ἐπὶ γάμου τοῦτο αἰσχρὸν, πολλῷ μᾶλλον ἐπὶ ταύτης τῆς συζυγίας). By adopting the position of the head, Chrysostom argues that these women have subverted God's very law.[34] Sex acts as a container not only for lust but for proper gender roles. Once sexual intimacy and procreation are removed from the equation, the natural gender of men and women becomes completely unhinged and imbalanced.

Although he likely exaggerates, is there any way we could imagine some truth behind Chrysostom's accusations of gender subversion? If we look back to *De amicitia*, Cicero does provide some advice for friendships of inequality. While he emphasizes that the best friendships are based on equality of character, Cicero does not discount friendships of mixed status. In the case of friendships between a superior and inferior it is critical that the two create grounds for equality. The onus is particularly on the superior to "enhance the dignity of all his friends" so that they can stand on equal ground (*Amic.* 19.69–70). It is possible that the spiritual couples were attempting to form some kind of equal footing. As Leyerle has noted, not only has gender been reversed by these women's behavior, but the very walls that represent her feminine enclosure have been removed.[35] By actively sharing in one another's experiences both in and outside the home, these couples subvert the spatial barriers between male and female. While it is impossible to say with certainty, Chrysostom's gender attacks

---

34. Clark, "John Chrysostom and the *Subintroductae*," 183.
35. Leyerle, *Theatrical Shows*, 175–76.

may provide a glimpse into ways in which these couples were actively trying to create space for virtuous friendship.

Adulteresses of Christ

Chrysostom saw the friendship between these ascetics as both damaging and, particularly for the *subintroductae*, entirely inappropriate. Not only was a virgin rendered domineering and manly, but her friendship with a man would transform her into an adulteress. By the fourth century, the idea that female virgins were formally betrothed to Christ had begun to take shape.[36] Upon taking their vows of continence, virgins were viewed as actual brides of Christ. Thus, a bride's marriage to a fleshly man could be read as an affront to her heavenly bridegroom. By no means is this charge unique to Chrysostom's invective. The charge of adultery is present in most works condemning the practice of spiritual marriage. Cyprian compares Christ to a cuckolded husband and raises the question: "What shall Christ our Lord and Judge think, when He sees His virgin, dedicated to Him and destined for His holiness, lying with another?" (*Ep.* 61.3). Pseudo-Titus claims that through associating with a man, these women have "cast off Christ" and "separated from him."[37] Jerome states that in the afterlife, the *subintroductae* will be convicted of "adultery against Christ" (*Ep. 22*, 13.2). In a similar vein, Chrysostom claims that the virgins have "trampled upon the contract [they] made with God" (*Fem. reg.* 7). This alone is not surprising. Yet again it is the interweaving of friendship into this charge that makes Chrysostom's work remarkable.

Although Chrysostom characterizes spiritual marriage as friendship in both treatises, the term *philia* appears more than twice as many times in his address to the female virgins. Not only is her relationship with her spiritual companion described in terms of *philia*, but her relationship with her heavenly bridegroom is described in similar terms. Chrysostom presents the example of an ideal virgin. He asks the *subintroductae* to imagine a beautiful girl who denied her many suitors because she "chose to wait and

---

36. For more on the intricacies of the bride of Christ metaphor, see Karl Shuve, *The Song of Songs and Fashioning Identity in Early Christianity* (Oxford: Oxford University Press, 2016); Dyan Elliott, *The Bride of Christ Goes to Hell: Metaphor and Embodiment in the Lives of Pious Women, 200–1500* (Philadelphia: University of Pennsylvania Press, 2001).

37. Otero, "Pseudo-Titus Epistle," 55.

suffer all things whatsoever rather than betray her friendship with Christ and destroy the bloom of her chastity" (*Fem. reg.* 8.17–19: ἀλλ' εἵλετο πᾶν ὁτιοῦν ὑπομεῖναι καὶ παθεῖν, ἢ τὴν τοῦ Χριστοῦ προδοῦναι φιλίαν, καὶ τὸ τῆς σωφροσύνης ἄνθος ἀφανίσαι). This woman would be thrice blessed. But since through their spiritual marriage the *subintroductae* have shown a "friendship with the world," they have spoiled themselves for Christ. Even if she has not engaged sexually, her closeness with a man has destroyed her virginity for Christ. He asserts: "When she learns to discuss things frankly with a man, and to sit by him, to look at him in the face, to laugh in his presence, and to disgrace herself in many other ways yet does not think this terrible, the veil of virginity is snatched away, the flower trampled underfoot" (11.26–31: Ὅταν γὰρ μετὰ παρρησίας μάθῃ διαλέγεσθαι ἀνδρὶ, καὶ συγκαθέζεσθαι, καὶ ἀντιβλέπειν, καὶ γελᾶν παρόντος, καὶ πολλὰ ἕτερα ἀσχημονεῖν, καὶ μηδὲν ἡγῆται τοῦτο εἶναι δεινὸν, ἀναιρεῖται τὸ καταπέτασμα τῆς παρθενίας, καὶ πατεῖται τὸ ἄνθος).

This apparent paucity of friendship similarly fits with the older concepts of Aristotle and Cicero. Both men agree that *philia* is not in unlimited supply. There is a scarcity that accompanies true friendship. "To be friends with many people in a complete friendship is not possible, just as it is not possible to be in love with many people at the same time. For it is like an excess, and that sort of thing occurs naturally in relation to one person" (Aristotle, *Eth. nic.* 8.6.12–13.9). Cicero similarly notes the limits, writing, "this thing called friendship has been so narrowed that the bonds of affection always united two persons only, or, at most, a few" (*Amic.* 5.315). It is this same scarcity that seems to underlie Chrysostom's accusation. He charges that there are many crimes these virgins have committed; but their greatest crime is that "above all else they have dishonored the name of the Bridegroom" (*Fem. reg.* 9). Virgins' spiritual intimacy with another man presumably sours the virgin's ability to achieve the same friendship with Christ. In his final appeal, Chrysostom reminds these women what is at stake. Should they opt for a celibate life with a partner, the *subintroductae* will deny themselves not only a heavenly bridegroom but "a lover more ardent than any man" (12).

Conclusions

While intersex friendship is hardly the only issue with spiritual marriage, for John Chrysostom, it is one that looms large. Although he may be willing to concede the availability and desire for male-female friendship within the confines of spiritual marriage, he thinks the side effects are too grave a risk. The physical and emotional intimacy between celibate couples destabilizes traditional, so-called God-given gender roles. Additionally, these close relationships between male and female virgins jeopardize their status as brides of Christ. Therefore, these relationships can never achieve the highest state of virtuous *philia*.

Yet behind his critiques against the celibate couples, we can catch a glimpse of how these couples may have viewed their relationships. We could imagine that by destabilizing the God-given gender roles, these couples could have been striving for a form of friendship that can only exist between equals. Whether consciously or not, by breaking down the equalizing that occurs in these relationships, Chrysostom breaks down the very potential of true intersex friendship. We can speculate that in the eyes of these virgins, this form of intersexual intimacy was something uniquely available to Christians—men and women who could strive to "live like angels" on earth. But in Chrysostom's eyes, this form of friendship completely undermined the tenets of Christianity.

At the close of her essay on the *subintroductae*, Clark humors the idea that underlying the practice of spiritual marriage may have been the couples' understanding of Scripture.[38] Borrowing from Wayne Meeks, she suggests that their understanding of male and female may have been part of a "realized eschatology."[39] While this is a compelling hypothesis, could it also be plausible that these couples drew inspiration from stories like that in the Acts of Thomas? Although we have no evidence that these couples were explicitly modeling their lives after the apocryphal acts, we do know that some mixed-gender ascetics did read these texts.[40] Regardless of whether the *subintroductae* and their partners were inspired directly by the apocryphal acts, the self-understandings, beliefs, and attitudes enshrined in these stories could continue to engage the imaginations of Christians throughout late antiquity.

---

38. Clark, "John Chrysostom and the *Subintroductae*," 184.

39. Clark, "John Chrysostom and the *Subintroductae*," 184, quoting Wayne A. Meeks, "The Image of the Androgyne: Some Uses of a Symbol in Earliest Christianity," *HR* 13 (1973–1974): 202.

40. For example, Priscillian and his followers. For a discussion of Priscillian's use of apocryphal texts see Virginia Burrus, *The Making of a Heretic: Gender, Authority, and the Priscillianist Controversy* (Berkeley: University of California Press, 1995).

Bibliography

Achelis, Hans. *Virgines Subintroductae: Ein Beitrag zum VIII Kapitel des I. Korintherbriefs.* Leipzig: Hinrichs, 1902.

Burrus, Virginia. *Chastity as Autonomy: Women in the Stories of the Apocryphal Acts.* Lewiston, NY: Mellen, 1987.

———. *The Making of a Heretic: Gender, Authority, and the Priscillianist Controversy.* Berkeley: University of California Press, 1995.

Cicero. *On Old Age, On Friendship, On Divination.* Translated by W. A. Falconer. LCL. Cambridge: Harvard University Press, 1923.

Clark, Elizabeth A. *Jerome, Chrysostom, and Friends.* Lewiston, NY: Mellen, 1979.

———. "John Chrysostom and the *Subintroductae.*" *CH* 46 (June 1977): 171–85.

Cooper, Kate. *The Virgin and the Bride: Idealized Womanhood in Late Antiquity.* Cambridge: Harvard University Press: 1996.

Davies, Stevan L. *The Revolt of the Widows: The Social World of the Apocryphal Acts.* Carbondale: Southern Illinois University Press, 1980.

Drijvers, Han J. W. "The Acts of the Holy Apostle Thomas." *NTApoc* 2:339–411.

Dumortier, Jean. *Saint Jean Chrysostome: Les cohabitations suspectes.* Paris: Les Belles Lettres, 1955.

Elliott, Dyan. *The Bride of Christ Goes to Hell: Metaphor and Embodiment in the Lives of Pious Women, 200–1500.* Philadelphia: University of Pennsylvania Press, 2001.

Grafe, Eduard. "Geistliche Verlöbnisse bei Paulus." *Theologische Arbeiten aus dem rheinischen wissenschaftlichen Prediger-Verein* 3 (1899): 57–69.

Jacobs, Andrew S. "A Family Affair: Marriage, Class, and Ethics in the Apocryphal Acts of the Apostles." *JECS* 7 (1999): 105–38.

Konstan, David. "Acts of Love: A Narrative Pattern in the Apocryphal Acts." *JECS* 6 (1998): 15–36.

Leyerle, Blake. *Theatrical Shows and Ascetic Lives: John Chrysostom's Attack on Spiritual Marriage.* Berkeley: University of California Press, 2001.

MacDonald, Dennis R. *The Legend and the Apostle: The Battle for Paul in Story and Canon.* Philadelphia: Westminster, 1983.

Martin, Dale B. *The Corinthian Body.* New Haven: Yale University Press, 1996.

Meeks, Wayne A. "The Image of the Androgyne: Some Uses of a Symbol in Earliest Christianity." *HR* 13 (1973–1974): 165–208.

Mierow, Charles Christopher. *The Letters of St. Jerome.* ACW 33. New York: Newman, 1963.

Otero, Aurelio de Santos, trans. "Pseudo-Titus Epistle." *NTApoc* 2:53–74.

Pakaluk, Michael. *Aristotle Nicomachean Ethics, Books VIII and IX.* Oxford: Clarendon, 1998.

Perkins, Judith. "Fictional Narratives and Social Critique." Pages 46–69 in vol. 2 of *Late Ancient Christianity: A People's History of Christianity.* Edited by Virginia Burrus and Rebecca Lyman. Minneapolis: Fortress, 2005.

Rader, Rosemary. *Breaking Boundaries: Male/Female Friendship in Early Christian Communities.* New York: Paulist Press, 1983.

Robertson, Archibald, and Alfred Plummer. *A Critical and Exegetical Commentary on the First Epistle of St. Paul to the Corinthians.* Edinburgh: T&T Clark, 1929.

Schäferdiek, Knut, trans. "Acts of John." *NTApoc* 2:152–209.

Sebolt, Roland. "Spiritual Marriage in the Early Church: A Suggested Interpretation of 1 Corinthians 7:36–38." *Concordia Theological Monthly* 30 (1959): 103–19.

Sellick, Jeannie. "One's Proper Kin: The Elevation of the Spiritual Family in the Apocryphal Acts." Unpublished paper, 2015.

———. "Ordered Love: Reshaping Familial Relations in the Age of Asceticism." Unpublished paper, 2014.

Shuve, Karl. *The Song of Songs and Fashioning Identity in Early Christianity.* Oxford: Oxford University Press, 2016.

Wallis, R. E., trans. Chrysostom. *Epistle 61. ANF* 5:357.

Suffering Thomas: Doubt, Pain, and Punishment in the Acts of Thomas and His Wonderworking Skin

Janet E. Spittler

In her important and influential monograph, *The Suffering Self: Pain and Narrative Representation in the Early Christian Era*, Judith Perkins writes:

> Traditionally, injuring other people, killing them, provided a method of establishing dominance, of establishing in explicit terms a winner and a loser. Bruises, wounds, broken bodies, provided unassailable, palpable evidence of realized power. But Christian discourse reverses this equation and thus redefines some of the most basic signifiers in any culture—the body, pain, and death.[1]

In the following brief contribution honoring the scholar who first recognized the central role of suffering not just in narratives of Jesus's death but as a representational strategy essential to the growth of the Christian institution, I introduce a relatively unknown narrative in which the extreme suffering of the apostle Thomas is the pivotal moment. I wouldn't quite say, "When I think of pain and torture, I think of Judith Perkins," but when translating this narrative for the first time and encountering its description of Thomas's flaying, I immediately pulled Judith's book from my shelf.

Text and Context

The Acts of Thomas and His Wonderworking Skin is extant in at least seven Greek manuscripts.[2] It has been edited twice: first by M. R. James

---

1. Judith Perkins, *The Suffering Self: Pain and Narrative Representation in the Early Christian Era* (London: Routledge, 1995), 115.

2. M. Geerard, *Clavis Apocryphorum Novi Testamenti*, Corpus Christianorum, Series Apocryphorum (Turnhout: Brepols, 1992).

in 1897 from a single British Museum manuscript, then by Donato Tamilia in 1903 from three manuscripts, including the one edited by James.
The following year, Augusto Mancini, who had stumbled on another witness in the university library at Messina, published an article in which he
collates the variant readings of the Messina text against Tamilia's edition,
also suggesting a few minor corrections of Tamilia's editorial work.[3] The
textual tradition is a little bit complex, with at least two witnesses (the M
text edited by James, and the Messina text discovered by Mancini) interpolating in idiosyncratic ways material from the longer Acts of Thomas.
Moreover, while the texts edited by James and Tamilia clearly narrate the
"same" story, the editions differ substantially in virtually every sentence. In
what follows, passing citations and quotations will be from a forthcoming
translation of Tamilia's text;[4] in more detailed discussions, however, I will
present both James's and Tamilia's texts.

In this essay I will deal exclusively with the Greek text, but it is important to note that the text is extant in Coptic fragments,[5] as well as in Arabic,
Ethiopic, and Church Slavonic. The Arabic and Ethiopic translations are
a part of the collection of texts generally referred to as the "Contendings
of the Apostles," available in English translations by Agnes Smith Lewis,
Solomon Malan, and E. A. Wallis Budge, respectively.[6] There are many

---

3. M. R. James, *Apocrypha Anecdota 2*, TS 5.1 (Cambridge: Cambridge University Press, 1897), 27–45; Donato Tamilia, "Acta Thomae apocrypha," *Rendiconti della
Reale Accademia dei Lincei, Classe di scienze morali, storiche e filologiche* 5 (1903):
387–408; Augusto Mancini, "Per la critica degli *Acta apocrypha Thomae*," *Atti dell
Reale Accademia della scienze di Torino* 39 (1904): 743–58; at least four other manuscripts are known but not yet edited. Previous scholarship has called this text Acta
Thomae minora or Acta Thomae abbreviata, both of which give the impression that
this is an abbreviated version of the better-known Acts of Thomas—which is simply
not the case. For an introduction and English translation, see Janet Spittler and Jonathan Holste, "The Acts of Thomas and His Wonderworking Skin," in *New Testament
Apocrypha: More Noncanonical Scriptures*, ed. Tony Burke and Brent Landau, vol. 2
(Grand Rapids: Eerdmans, forthcoming).

4. Spittler and Holste, "Acts of Thomas and His Wonderworking Skin."

5. Paul-Hubert Poirier, *La version copte de la Prédication et du Martyre du Thomas*,
Subsidia Hagiographica 67 (Brussels: Société des Bollandistes, 1984).

6. Agnes Smith Lewis, *Acta mythologica apostolorum/The Mythological Acts of the
Apostles*, HSem 3–4 (London: 1904), Arabic text, 1:67–78; English translation, 2:80–
93; Solomon Caesar Malan, *The Conflicts of the Holy Apostles: An Apocryphal Book of
the Early Eastern Church* (London: Nutt, 1871), translation of the Ethiopic text, 187–
214; E. A. W. Budge, *The Contendings of the Apostles; Being the Histories of the Lives*

reasons to think that the Acts of Thomas and His Wonderworking Skin originated—or at the very least circulated—in fourth- or early fifth-century Egypt. This essay will not treat this evidence directly, but in short: the Acts of Thomas and His Wonderworking Skin has multiple elements in common with the Acts of Peter and Andrew, the Acts of Andrew and Matthias in the City of the Cannibals, and other texts sometimes referred to as the "Egyptian cycle" of apocryphal acts, which seem to have been popular in fourth- and fifth-century Egypt and likely were composed in that milieu.[7]

A Different Acts of Thomas

The Acts of Thomas and His Wonderworking Skin begins in much the same way as the better-known Acts of Thomas, with the division of the world into missionary territories for each of the apostles. Just as in Acts of Thomas, India falls by lot to Thomas, a result that the apostle protests; like in Acts of Thomas, Thomas is ultimately sold into slavery to an agent of the Indian king Condiphorus, who immediately tasks him with building a palace. At this point in the narrative, however, similarities with the Acts of Thomas end. In the Acts of Thomas and His Wonderworking Skin, the apostle is transferred to the custody of a governor called Leucius; when Leucius departs for war, Thomas attempts to convert his wife, Arsenoë.[8]

---

and Martyrdoms and Deaths of the Twelve Apostles and Evangelists; The Ethiopic Texts Now First Ed. from Manuscripts in the British Museum (London: Frowde, 1899–1901), Ethiopic text, 1:265–86; and English translation, 2:319–345.

7. On this point, see Joseph Flamion, Les Actes Apocryphes de l'Apôtre André: Les Actes d'André et de Mathias, de Pierre et d'André et les textes apparentés (Leuven: Bureaux du Recueil, 1911), 310–24; Aurelio de Santos Otero, "Later Acts of the Apostles," in NTApoc 2:426–82; see esp. 457–58. Contra Flamion, see Dennis R. MacDonald, The Acts of Andrew and the Acts of Andrew and Matthias in the City of the Cannibals (Atlanta: Scholars Press, 1990), 6–47.

8. As M. R. James notes, "Leucius is a name which it is always interesting to find connected with Apocryphal Acts" (Apocrypha Anecdota, xliii). What connection there might be—if any—between this Leucius, governor of India, and the Leucius or Leucius Charinus frequently associated with authorship of the apocryphal acts is a topic for further research and/or speculation. Note that the name Arsenoë appears alongside multiple heroines of the apocryphal acts in the Psalms of Heracleides from the Manichaean Psalm-Book. See C. R. C. Allberry, A Manichaean Psalm-Book Part II (Stuttgart: Kohlhammer, 1938), 192, 194. Richard Bauckham has argued persuasively that the Arsenoë from the psalm is not to be identified with the Arsenoë in the

When the apostle turns her idols to dust, driving away the unclean spirits within them, Arsenoë gives away all of her riches and is baptized along with her entire household. When Leucius returns, a story familiar from multiple apocryphal acts unfolds: Arsenoë rebuffs his amorous advances and urges him to abandon all earthly desires; Leucius is enraged and immediately identifies Thomas as the source of his wife's new attitudes. The torture Leucius devises, however, is particularly cruel: he sends for all the leather cutters of the city and commands them to flay Thomas, keeping him alive for further torment.

The leather cutters are at first reluctant to flay the "just man, who healed the sick without payment" (Acts Thom. Skin 6.28), but Thomas encourages them to do as they are commanded. When Arsenoë hears that Thomas has been flayed, she throws herself from the roof of her home and dies. Leucius, now even more enraged, proceeds to torture the apostle, pouring salt and aged vinegar onto his skinless flesh.

At this point, Thomas calls out to Jesus for help; Jesus appears and verbally comforts Thomas, commanding him to "be a man," "rise," and perform "miracles on account of my name in this city and strengthen them in my faith," then to "go out into the city Kentêra" to save the souls of those living there (6.20, 24–25).[9] After Jesus is taken up into heaven, Thomas does indeed get up, going first to the body of Arsenoë. He "cast[s] his skin over" and commands her to rise from the dead; she does, immediately casting herself at his feet. When Leucius sees his wife returned to life, he too casts himself at the apostle's feet, begging for his forgiveness. Thomas responds that "God does not do evil things to those believing in his holy name, rather he forgives their sins" (6.34). He then baptizes Leucius and appoints him priest, also designating other members of his household as readers and deacons. Then, "after picking up his skin," Thomas departs "into the city Kentêra, where the Lord God commanded him" (6.36).

Acts of Thomas and His Wonderworking Skin, inasmuch as the Arsenoë from the psalm is consistently (also in the First Apocalypse of James and one of the Manichaean fragments from Turfan) listed as one of four women disciples (including also Mary, Martha, and Salome) of Jesus. See Richard Bauckham, "Salome the Sister of Jesus, Salome the Disciple of Jesus, and the Secret Gospel of Mark," NovT 33 (1991): 245–75.

9. The Greek translated here as "be a man" is ἀνδρίζου, which could also be rendered "be brave"; I have chosen to retain the gendered notion of bravery. On this phrase, see Martyrdom of Polycarp 9.

Immediately on entering Kentēra, Thomas meets an old man in a state of total neglect (filthy, in torn clothes). When the apostle asks why he has allowed himself to fall into such a state, the man relates how he lost all six of his sons:[10] he had arranged for his eldest son to marry the daughter of the governor, but shortly before the wedding the son had a vision of Christ, during which he commanded him not to take a wife. The old man reported the vision to the governor, who was so enraged that he murdered not just the eldest son but also his five younger brothers. With all his sons dead—and left with enormous debt from the wedding that never took place—the old man spends his days weeping at their tomb. After listening to the old man, Thomas identifies himself as the apostle of that very Christ and promises to raise his sons. Now followed by a large crowd from the city, Thomas and the old man go to their tomb. Thomas then hands his skin to some bystanders, commanding them to lay it on the place where the sons are buried. When they do, the six sons are raised along with nine other people who had been buried in that location before them.

The crowd is impressed. They decide, however, to go to the high priest at the "temple of the idols" (8.5) and report to him what has happened. There follows a brief showdown between the priest and the apostle: the priest convinces the crowd that Thomas is a magician—like the others from Galilee whom he has heard of—and commands them to stone him; bending down to pick up stones, however, they find that they cannot straighten their backs again. They beg Thomas: "Do not deal with us according to our unbelief [μὴ ποιήσεις ἡμῖν κατὰ τὴν ἀπιστίαν ἡμῶν]!" (8.22). Thomas sees their faith and prays to Christ on their behalf, asking that he suspend the priest in midair; immediately, an angel descends and lifts the priest into the air by his hair, at which point the priest himself repents. Thomas then baptizes everyone, overturns all the idols in the temple, turns the temple into a church, and makes the priest a bishop and the sons of the old man clerics.

The narrative then closes with the notice that, after three years, the Lord appears to Thomas once again and tells him to "be a man." This time, however, Jesus takes his skin and wraps it around his body, saying "be glued on your body, just as before" (9.2). He then takes Thomas up onto a cloud, which delivers him to a group of disciples already gathered with

---

10. This section is a rather complicated story within a story within a story: what the old man relates to Thomas includes what his son had related to him about an encounter with the risen Jesus.

Paul and Mary, "and each began to narrate the things which had happened to them" (9.6).

Thomas in Pain

Clearly, there are many interesting elements in this very different Thomas narrative, but perhaps most notable is the scene that describes Thomas's torture and suffering. The flaying itself is not narrated at length—"then they took and flayed him" or "they took his skin with much pain" is the very brief report in Tamilia's and James's texts, respectively. After the flaying, however, his torture by the governor Leucius is described in somewhat more detail:

> *Tamilia:* But Leucius said to Thomas ... "You don't think that my tortures have finished with you, do you?" And he said to his attendants, "Bring to me three-year-old vinegar and salt and sprinkle it on the whole body of the sorcerer." And they did the things commanded to them. (Acts Thom. Skin 6.6–8)

> *James:* But Leucius said, "Don't think that I will refrain from the tortures I am about to inflict on you because of these magic tricks of yours." The saint said, "Do not neglect to do as much as you wish." Then he issued a command, saying "Bring to me three-year-old vinegar and salt and throw it upon his body." Then they did as he commanded them.

Thomas then cries out to Jesus with a vivid description of his pain, begging for help and for rescue:

> *Tamilia:* Lord Jesus Christ, my God, be my help in this hour, for this torture has entered my guts and the marrow of my bones [ὅτι εἰσῆλθεν ἡ βάσανος αὕτη εἰς τὰ σπλάγχνα μου καὶ εἰς τὰ μέσα τῶν ὀστέων μου]. Listen to me, Master, and have compassion upon your slave, and take from me this torture [λάβε ἐξ ἐμοῦ τὴν βάσανον ταύτην]. Remember that I am a stranger. For no one is my help if not you, my Savior. You are the one who sent me here, in order for me to convert them to the knowledge of God. And you see, Master, what sorts of tortures this lawless man has brought on me, and you have not taken vengeance on him. (Acts Thom. Skin 6.8–13)

> *James:* Lord Jesus Christ, help me in this hour, for this torture now extends even into my entrails [ὅτι εἰσῆλθεν ἡ βάσανος αὕτη μέχρι καὶ τῶν ἐγκάτων μου]. Listen to me, Lord, and have mercy upon your slave and deliver me from this pain [ἀπάλλαξόν με τῆς ὀδύνης ταύτης], for I am suf-

fering these things on your account, so that I might bring these people around to your knowledge. For you see what sorts of tortures this lawless man inflicts upon me. But I beg you make everything come to naught by your mighty hand.

Thomas's cry is in stark contrast to the majority of martyrdom accounts, in which an impassive response to torture is the rule. As Stephanie Cobb has argued—building on Perkins's work—the tortured victim's experience of pain is generally *not* the narrative focus of martyrdom narratives.[11] That is, while the often quite vivid description of torture might cause the reader (or hearer) to cringe, the martyr generally does not express the sensation of pain. This passage is quite striking in comparison, with Thomas's descriptive language—including explicit references to his experience of the pain—and his plea to Jesus to make it stop.

The scene is not, however, totally unique among apocryphal acts. A comparable scene, which depicts a suffering apostle complaining of the torture and questioning the Lord, occurs in the Acts of Andrew and Matthias. There, Andrew is similarly tortured: a rope is placed around his neck, and he is dragged through the city until his flesh is torn (with a result not unlike flaying) until he weeps and cries out. When he is dragged for the second time, he calls out to the Lord: "Where are your words? 'A hair of your heads shall not perish' [Luke 21:18], but look—my flesh is torn from me!" A response to Andrew's complaint and objection comes in the form of a disembodied voice quoting a later verse from Luke 21: "And a voice said in Hebrew, 'My words shall not pass away [Luke 21:33]: look behind you.' And he saw great fruit-bearing trees growing up where his flesh and blood had fallen" (Acts Andr. Mth. 28 [James]). As we will see in a moment, the apostle in Acts of Thomas and His Wonderworking Skin also quotes Jesus's words back to him during his torment—another line from Luke 21, in fact—and Jesus likewise responds with another Gospel quotation. These similarities likely reflect a common milieu: as noted above, the Acts of Thomas and His Wonderworking Skin seems to be at home, alongside the Acts of Andrew and Matthias, among a group of apocryphal acts originating in fourth- or fifth-century Egypt.[12]

---

11. L. Stephanie Cobb, *Divine Deliverance: Pain and Painlessness in Early Christian Martyr Texts* (Oakland: University of California Press, 2016), *passim*.

12. The similarities noted here may well reflect a common milieu; see note 7 above.

Doubt and Suffering

Even more unusual than Thomas's complaint and expression of pain are the following lines, in which he attempts both to understand the torture as punishment inflicted in some sense *by Jesus* and to defend himself as not, in fact, deserving such punishment—even as he is willing to suffer it:

> *Tamilia:* If perhaps, Master, you are angry with me [ἔχεις μῆνιν κατ᾽ ἐμοῦ], I am prepared to endure all the tortures, rejoicing. Remember me, Master [μνήσθητί μου, δέσποτα], when you appeared to your disciples risen from the dead and I was not there with them. And, turning, they said to me, "We have seen the Lord" [John 20:25]. And since, Master, you said to us "Many will come to you in my name" [Mark 13:6 // Matt 24:5 // Luke 21:8], on account of this I said to my fellow disciples, "Unless I see in his hands the mark of the nails, et cetera, I will not believe" [John 20:25]. Look, they took my skin from me! Show yourself to me Lord, in order to help me. For I know, Master, that you are not far from me.

> *James:* And do not remember against us our earlier iniquities, for at your resurrection I did not believe [καὶ μὴ μνησθῇς ἡμῶν ἀνομιῶν ἀρχαίων, ὅτι ἐν τῇ ἀναστάσει τῇ σῇ ἠπίστασα]. For I said, when you had come into the midst of the disciples, "If I do not see the stamp of the nails in his hands and put my hand in his side, I will not believe" [John 20:25]. But, look, on account of this [ἕνεκα τούτου] now the skin of my flesh has been taken away from me and he wishes to inflict a great many other things upon me. But I know, master, that you are not far from me; indeed, make me strong on account of your holy name, the blessed one forever, amen.

In both versions of this fascinating little speech, Thomas either implies or explicitly states that his current torture is a result not simply of the wickedness of his persecutor, but of Jesus's anger with him. Moreover, he suggests a reason for that anger, reminding Jesus (and, of course, the reader) of his initial doubt when his fellow disciples reported to him their experience of his resurrection. Finally, and perhaps most interestingly, in Tamilia's text Thomas offers Jesus (and, again, also the reader) an excuse for his behavior: citing Jesus's synoptic warning that "many will come to you in my name" (Mark 13:6 // Matt 24:5 // Luke 21:8), Thomas argues that he was right to doubt the other disciples' report.

Reflection on Thomas's doubt abounds in Christian literature, from the earliest period straight through to the present. Such reflection takes, moreover, a wide variety of forms, including exegetical reasoning, graphic representations, and narrative retellings—though it is notable that explicit reflection on John 20:24–25 is absent from the best-known apocryphal works associated with Thomas, the Gospel of Thomas and the Acts of Thomas. In the Acts of Thomas, Thomas does quote from the doubting episode twice, but the quotation is of his declaration of faith in John 20:28 as opposed to the distrustful assertions that preceded it (Acts Thom. 10). The Gospel of Thomas never engages directly with the doubting episode; if there are allusions, they are subtle.

Patristic exegesis—while diverse in its treatment of Thomas[13]—also tends to emphasize Jesus's kindness and Thomas's eventual faith. John Chrysostom, for example, in his discussion in *Homily 87 on John*, writes:

> When you look at the disbelieving disciple, consider the Lord's love of humankind. He shows himself with his wounds for the sake of a single person. He appears so that he might also save this one person, even though Thomas is more thick-witted than the other disciples. This was why Thomas wanted proof for his dull sense-perception, and yet he would not believe with his eyes. Indeed, he did not just say "Unless I see" (20:25), but "Unless I touch," so that what he sees might not prove to be his imagination.[14]

Other exegetes put more effort into defending Thomas's actions, ultimately landing on explanations of his doubt that are more or less compatible with the explanation Thomas offers for himself in Acts of Thomas and His Wonderworking Skin. Peter Chrysologus, for example, writes:

> Brothers and sisters, his piety asked these things, his devotion examined them, so that future impiety itself might not doubt that the Lord had risen. Thomas cured not only his own uncertain heart, but the uncertain hearts of all; and because he was about to proclaim these things to the gentiles, this vigorous seeker made a thorough investigation about how

---

13. On this point, see Glen W. Most, *Doubting Thomas* (Cambridge: Harvard University Press, 2005), 122–54; see also Benjamin Schließer, "To Touch or Not to Touch? Doubting and Touching in John 20:24–29," *Early Christianity* 8 (2017): 69–93. A selection of patristic sources, from which I have drawn, can be found in Bryan A. Stewart and Michael A. Thomas, *John: Interpreted by Early Christian and Medieval Commentators*, The Church's Bible (Grand Rapids: Eerdmans, 2018), 580–88.

14. PG 59:473; translation adapted from Stewart and Thomas.

he might add to the mystery of such great faith. (*Sermon* 84.8 [Stewart and Thomas])[15]

This is a slightly different tack from that taken in Acts of Thomas and His Wonderworking Skin: here, too, Chrysologus presents Thomas's doubt as justified, but it is the result (curing the uncertainty of Christians who would come after) rather than the immediate cause of the doubt that makes it acceptable, even beneficial.

A particularly interesting example of patristic exegesis is Romanos the Melodist's hymn on doubting Thomas, which combines narrative expansion with interpretation. Taking an adaptation of Thomas's declaration in John 20:28 as a refrain ("You are our Lord and God"), Romanos retells the episode largely from Thomas's perspective, freely modifying and adding details. All eighteen strophes of the hymn are fascinating; here I will quote just the sections most relevant to Romanos's interpretation of Thomas's motives in expressing doubt:

> What happened? How and for what possible reason did the apostle lack faith?
> Let us ask, if it seems right, let us ask the son of Zebedee;
> For John clearly recorded the words of Didymus
>   In the Bible, in his Gospel.
> The wise man reports: After the Resurrection of Christ,
>   The other disciples said to Thomas:
>   "O friend, we have seen the Lord here."
> But Thomas at once said to them:
>   "Those who have seen Christ do not conceal it, but they cry out:
>   'You are our Lord and God.'
> Announce to all the people what you have seen and heard.
>   Do not, disciples, conceal the light under a bushel.
> What you say in darkness, proclaim aloud in the light.
>   With confidence take a stand openly.
> Right now you are in a concealed place and you take courage;
>   You say fine things when the doors are closed;
>   You cry out in a loud voice, 'We have seen the Creator';
> Let it be clear to all; let all Creation learn of it;
>   Let mortals be taught to cry out to the Risen One,
>   'You are our Lord and God.'
> How can I trust in you when you utter incredible words?

---

15. CCSL 24A:521–22.

For if the Redeemer had come, He would have asked for me,
    a member of His household;
If the day had shone, it would not seem past the right time;
    If indeed the Shepherd had appeared, He would have called his
    sheep;
Formerly He asked: 'Where did you bury Lazarus?'
    Now He did not say, 'Where have you sent Thomas?'
    Would he have deceived the one who wished to die with Him?
I remain incredulous until I see;
    Whenever I see and touch, I shall say,
    'You are our Lord and God.'"[16]

In Romanos's version of the episode, Thomas's reaction to the other disciples' announcement of the Lord's return is greatly expanded. He raises two primary objections: first, if the Lord had truly appeared, surely the disciples should have proclaimed it immediately to the world, rather than remaining in the room with closed doors; second, if the Lord had truly returned, surely he would have asked for Thomas. In the following strophe, Jesus immediately appears; three strophes are dedicated to Thomas's internal dialogue, consisting of both regret and rationalization of his initial reaction. Jesus's speech, also much expanded, confronts Thomas directly:

Sleeping a short sleep in the tomb, after three days I arose.
    I lay in the tomb for you and those like you;
And you, in place of gratitude, gave me lack of faith.
    For I heard what you said to your brothers.

Thomas's response is defensive:

Do not blame me, Savior, for I always trust You;
    But I find it hard to trust Peter and the others,
    For I know that, though they were not deceived,
    Still in a time of trouble they were afraid to say to You,
    "You are our Lord and God."

This defense is not exactly what we have seen in the Acts of Thomas and His Wonderworking Skin, but in both statements Thomas argues that

---

16. Romanos the Melodist, *On Doubting Thomas*, strophes 4–6, translation adapted from Marjorie Carpenter, *On the Person of Christ*, vol. 1 of *Kontakia of Romanos, Byzantine Melodist* (Columbia: University of Missouri Press, 1970), 330–31.

his doubt was reasonable based on previous experiences narrated in the canonical gospels.

While, as noted above, the most famous apocryphal texts associated with Thomas do not engage directly with the doubting Thomas episode, several narratives in which he is a more minor character do.[17] The most extensive of these is the Coptic Book of Bartholomew, a complicated text that relates, among other things, Jesus's resurrection appearances.[18] In a long excursus, this text offers an elaborate explanation for Thomas's absence during Jesus's first appearance to the disciples in John 20:19–23: "But Thomas, the one who is called Didymos, was not there when the Lord came, but had gone to his city, because news had been brought to him, saying, 'Your son has died.'"[19] The text goes on to narrate Thomas's resurrection of his son Siophanes, followed by Siophanes's narration to Thomas of his soul's journey, guided by the angel Michael, to heaven—a journey that included a tour of the twelve thrones reserved for Jesus's disciples. When news of Siophanes's resurrection spread, a great multitude from the city came to belief in Jesus; Thomas baptized twelve thousand—seemingly an excellent excuse for his absence—before being swept up into a cloud and returned to the Mount of Olives, where the other disciples have just been visited by the risen Jesus. Peter informs Thomas of what has happened, and Thomas responds as follows:

> Well then, after you arose from the [dead], my Lord, you revealed yourself to the disciples. But as for me, you separated me [from] my brothers. [If] you want to reveal yourself to me [...] that I gave, so that I can see you before you depart to [your Father]. Even though he [i.e., Siophanes?] lives in the name of my Lord, [Jesus] Christ, if I do not lay my finger on the wounds from the nails, and if I do not place my hand on the wounds from the spear, I will not believe [John 20:25] that he has risen from the dead. For I do not believe that he will arise [if] he has not revealed

---

17. See discussion by Most, *Doubting Thomas*, 108–15; note in particular the selection from the Epistle of the Apostles (quoted by Most), in which Thomas's doubt is attributed to all the disciples, several of which, including Thomas, touch and otherwise exam the physicality of the risen Jesus.

18. On this text, see Alin Suciu, "The Book of Bartholomew: A Coptic Apostolic Memoir," *Apocrypha* 26 (2015): 211–37; Christian H. Bull and Alexandros Tsakos, "The Book of Bartholomew (Book of the Resurrection of Jesus Christ): A New Translation and Introduction," in Burke and Landau, *New Testament Apocrypha*, vol. 2.

19. Translations of this text come from Bull and Tsakos, "Book of Bartholomew."

himself to me, and he will cause me pain, for he said to us, "I will not separate you from each other, but you shall have the same inheritance in my kingdom."

Much like in Romanos's hymn, here Thomas's doubt is explained in part as disbelief that Jesus would show himself to the other disciples but not to him. Of particular note with comparison to the Acts of Thomas and His Wonderworking Skin is the identification of a specific saying of the preresurrection Jesus that the present circumstance seems to contradict; while the wording of the quotation of Jesus found here does not correspond to any canonical saying, the idea is represented in Mark 10:35–45 and parallels as well as John 14.

Also much like in Romanos's hymn, when Jesus appears again, Thomas immediately affirms his belief while admitting to his expression of doubt: "I believe, my Lord and my God, that you are the Father, you are the Son, and you are <the> Holy Spirit. And you arose from the dead and that you raised everyone through your holy resurrection [John 20:28]. Yet this is what I told my brothers, the apostles: 'Unless I see that he has risen, I will not believe" (John 20:25). Jesus's response to Thomas in the Book of Bartholomew is interesting inasmuch as it picks up themes also included in the scene from the Acts of Thomas and His Wonderworking Skin:

Amen! I say to you, Thomas, little man, that I am with you everywhere you will preach my name, as is my good Father, and you will not enter a single town or a single village [Matt 10:11] where I am <not> following you, as is my good Father and the Holy Spirit. For whatever you will plant, my Father blesses it, I myself will make it grow, and the Holy Spirit will be its head.

Here Jesus confirms the notion that Thomas pronounces in Acts of Thomas and His Wonderworking Skin, that is, that Jesus is always with him on his missionary journeys.

Suffering and the "Second Christ"

The Acts of Thomas and His Wonderworking Skin continues with the Lord's response to Thomas's plea, as he appears and speaks to him. Notably, the various recensions of the text have substantial differences at this point:

Tamilia: Be a man and be strong, Thomas my elect, in all your troubles. For truly I say to you, as many troubles as you are about to bear on account of my name at the hands of human beings, are they not worth it for the kiss with which I am about to greet you when you sit upon the twelve thrones in my kingdom? [see Matt 19:28]. I called you "twin" [Acts Thom. 1] since you are a second Christ, Thomas. For your reward is great before my father in heaven. Rise. Demonstrate miracles on account of my name in this city and strengthen them in my faith. And after these things, depart from it and go out into the city Kentêra, so that you might save their souls through my blood, poured out for the salvation of the race of humans.

James: Be a man and be strong, Thomas my elect, in all your troubles. For truly I say to you that I will be with you in all that you are about to suffer. And now get up, for your reward is great before my father who is in heaven. Remember what I told you about—that "in my name you will cast out demons, lift up snakes, and should you drink poison it will not harm you. Place your hands upon the sick and they will be well" [Mark 16:18]. Do these things in my name, Thomas, and don't be afraid. From the time when you, then, baptize Leucius, go into the city Kentêra—this is to your east—so that you might preach to them my gospel and ransom them from the deceptive devil. For on account of them I emptied my blood on the cross.

As noted above, the response to Thomas's complaint and questioning includes, in both versions, a citation of a gospel. In Tamilia's text, there is an oblique but clear reference to the discussion of rewards for Jesus's followers in the Matthean version of the pericope of the rich young man (Matt 19:16–30), in which the reward for Jesus's followers is a seat on one of twelve thrones. In James's text we find instead "your reward is great before my father who is in heaven [ὁ μισθός σου πολύς ἐστιν ἔμπροσθεν τοῦ πατρός μου τοῦ ἐν οὐρανοῖς]," a reference to, if not precise quotation of, the last of the Beatitudes (Matt 5:12 // Luke 6:23). This reference to the Beatitudes, where the context is explicitly persecution, may on the face of it seem more fitting to Thomas's situation than the saying from the pericope of the rich young man, where the sacrifice to be rewarded is social and financial; it seems likely that the association of martyrs with enthronement is what drew the author/editor of Tamilia's text to Matthew 19:28.[20] The point, in any case is the same in both versions: those followers who suffer and make sacrifices for Jesus will be rewarded in heaven, in the age

---

20. On thrones and the "enthronement" of martyrs, see Candida R. Moss, *The Other Christs: Imitating Jesus in Ancient Christian Ideologies of Martyrdom* (Oxford: Oxford University Press, 2010), 150–55.

to come. James's text continues with a quotation of the longer ending of Mark; here, the emphasis seems to be on Thomas's power to endure, to survive and emerge unharmed from the seemingly deadly torture he is currently suffering. This emphasis is also evident in Thomas's own speech in James's text, when he asks the Lord to "make me strong [ἐνίσχυσόν με]," a phrase not present in Tamilia's text. Ultimately, both versions are quite similar to the exchange between Andrew and Jesus in the Acts of Andrew and Matthias: they function as a reminder and—inasmuch as the delivery of the message is miraculous in itself (a voice from the heavens in the Acts of Andrew and Matthias, and a vision of the risen Jesus in Acts of Thomas and His Wonderworking Skin)—a reassurance of Jesus's promise to his disciples.

But how does the risen Jesus respond to Thomas's suggestion that his initial doubt concerning the resurrection caused Jesus to be angry with him and ultimately brought on his punishment by flaying? Jesus does not refute Thomas's suggestion directly. That said, I would argue that, particularly in Tamilia's text, he offers an alternate explanation for his suffering when he reminds Thomas that he is his "twin," a "second Christ." Tamilia's text provides us with a refreshingly straightforward explanation of why Thomas is called the "twin" ("I called you 'twin' since you are a second Christ"), but is frustratingly less straightforward in defining what it means to be a "second Christ." It becomes clear, however, in what Jesus commands Thomas to do and, indeed, what he actually does throughout the remainder of the narrative.

In Tamilia's text Jesus commands Thomas to go to the city Kentēra in order to "save their souls through my blood, poured out for the salvation of the race of humans"; in James's text, Jesus similarly commands him to go, noting that it was "on account of them" (i.e., the Kentērans specifically) that he poured out his blood on the cross. In each version, then, Jesus's response to Thomas emphasizes his own physical suffering for the sake of saving others. This is, I think, what it means to be "Christ" in Acts of Thomas and His Wonderworking Skin, and this is what it means for Thomas to be a "second Christ": he suffers for the sake of saving others. Early Christian literature offers multiple models for how one might further explicate the notion of suffering for the sake of others: one model is provided by Origen in Exhortation to Martyrdom, where he uses expiatory sacrifice as his frame, arguing that more pain corresponds with greater efficacy; another model is found in the Martyrdom of Perpetua, where the heroine's willingness to suffer seems to accrue to her dead brother, whose suffering is thereby ameliorated.[21] Fascinatingly, Acts of Thomas and His Wonderworking Skin takes an entirely different tack, depicting the notion of suffering for the salvation of others in an extraordinarily literal and material way: Thomas must suffer in order to save others, because his own flayed skin is the tool with which he saves them. As noted above in the summary of Acts of Thomas and His Wonderworking Skin's contents, Thomas picks up his flayed skin and lays it on Arsenoë to raise her from the dead, an act that leads to the conversion of Leucius and the establishment of a church in their community; he then goes on to Kentēra, as commanded by Jesus, where the laying on of his skin raises fifteen more people from the dead, resulting in the conversion of the entire city and the establishment of another church.

Conclusion

This essay is, I hope, a decent illustration of a fundamental lesson that I learned from Judith Perkins, first by reading her scholarship and later through conversation: early Christian narratives, like the Greek romance novels and popular biographies and historiographies that are their closest extant literary relatives, are surely entertaining, but they are not only so. To the contrary: for their ancient authors, editors, and readers, these narratives were the sites of significant theological reflection and identity formation; these texts respond to the most significant issues raised in early Christian thought, often with as much or more sophistication—certainly

---

21. On the relationship of Perpetua's suffering and/or pain to her dead brother Dinocrates's salvation, see Cobb in conversation with Perkins in *Divine Deliverance*, 96. Perkins argues that the scene describing Perpetua's visions of her dead brother Dinocrates reveal an understanding of correspondence between the suffering of the martyr and the salvation brought to others: Perpetua "believes her suffering in prison has earned her favor and influence with the deity" (Perkins, *Suffering Self*, 108). Cobb notes that the text is not explicit in naming Perpetua's *suffering* as bringing about Dinocrates's salvation; she writes: "The active agent ... is the Spirit, not Perpetua, and it is the Spirit who works for the good of Dinocrates. Thus whatever suffering Perpetua endures in prison is not explicitly linked to her salvation or that of her brother" (Cobb, *Divine Deliverance*, 96). Cobb's attention to detail and insistence on precise, close reading is very helpful, frequently bringing Perkins's observations into even clearer focus. In this instance, however, I agree with Perkins's original interpretation of Perpetua's actions—including, but not limited to, suffering—as the ultimate cause of Dinocrates's salvation.

with more creativity—than the treatises and homilies of patristic authors. In Acts of Thomas and His Wonderworking Skin, we have seen this above all in the text's grappling with the doubting Thomas episode, wherein our author thinks along lines similar to what we find in patristic sources but resolves the questions narratively. For contemporary scholars, these narratives offer new insights into an incredibly broad swath of early Christian thought, practice, self-fashioning, and self-understanding. Careful attention to these narratives—to how they work and to the sorts of work they do—has already and will continue to increase our knowledge of Christianity's first centuries.

Bibliography

Allberry, C. R. C. *A Manichaean Psalm-Book Part II*. Stuttgart: Kohlhammer, 1938.

Bauckham, Richard. "Salome the Sister of Jesus, Salome the Disciple of Jesus, and the Secret Gospel of Mark." *NovT* 33 (1991): 245–75.

Budge, E. A. W. *The Contendings of the Apostles; Being the Histories of the Lives and Martyrdoms and Deaths of the Twelve Apostles and Evangelists; The Ethiopic Texts Now First Ed. from Manuscripts in the British Museum*. London: Frowde, 1899–1901.

Bull, Christian H., and Alexandros Tsakos. "The Book of Bartholomew (Book of the Resurrection of Jesus Christ): A New Translation and Introduction." In *New Testament Apocrypha: More Noncanonical Scriptures*. Edited by Tony Burke and Brent Landau. Vol. 2. Grand Rapids: Eerdmans, forthcoming.

Carpenter, Marjorie. *On the Person of Christ*. Vol. 1 of *Kontakia of Romanos, Byzantine Melodist*. Columbia: University of Missouri Press, 1970.

Cobb, L. Stephanie. *Divine Deliverance: Pain and Painlessness in Early Christian Martyr Texts*. Oakland: University of California Press, 2016.

Flamion, Joseph. *Les Actes Apocryphes de l'Apôtre André: Les Actes d'André et de Mathias, de Pierre et d'André et les textes apparentés*. Leuven: Bureaux du Recueil, 1911.

Geerard, M. *Clavis Apocryphorum Novi Testamenti*. Corpus Christianorum, Series Apocryphorum. Turnhout: Brepols, 1992.

James, M. R. *Apocrypha Anecdota 2*. TS 5.1. Cambridge: Cambridge University Press, 1897.

Lewis, Agnes Smith. *Acta mythologica apostolorum/The Mythological Acts of the Apostles*. HSem 3–4. London: 1904.

MacDonald, Dennis R. *The Acts of Andrew and the Acts of Andrew and Matthias in the City of the Cannibals.* Atlanta: Scholars Press, 1990.

Malan, Solomon Caesar. *The Conflicts of the Holy Apostles: An Apocryphal Book of the Early Eastern Church.* London: Nutt, 1871.

Mancini, Augusto. "Per la critica degli *Acta apocrypha Thomae.*" *Atti dell Reale Accademia della scienze di Torino* 39 (1904): 743–58.

Moss, Candida R. *The Other Christs: Imitating Jesus in Ancient Christian Ideologies of Martyrdom.* Oxford: Oxford University Press, 2010.

Most, Glen W. *Doubting Thomas.* Cambridge: Harvard University Press, 2005.

Otero, Aurelio de Santos. "Later Acts of the Apostles." *NTApoc* 2:426–82.

Perkins, Judith. *The Suffering Self: Pain and Narrative Representation in the Early Christian Era.* London: Routledge, 1995.

Poirier, Paul-Hubert. *La version copte de la Prédication et du Martyre du Thomas.* Subsidia Hagiographica 67. Brussels: Société des Bollandistes, 1984.

Schließer, Benjamin. "To Touch or Not to Touch? Doubting and Touching in John 20:24–29." *Early Christianity* 8 (2017): 69–93.

Spittler, Janet, and Jonathan Holste. "The Acts of Thomas and His Wonderworking Skin." In *New Testament Apocrypha: More Noncanonical Scriptures.* Edited by Tony Burke and Brent Landau. Vol. 2. Grand Rapids: Eerdmans, forthcoming.

Stewart, Bryan A., and Michael A. Thomas. *John: Interpreted by Early Christian and Medieval Commentators.* The Church's Bible. Grand Rapids: Eerdmans, 2018.

Suciu, Alin. "The Book of Bartholomew: A Coptic Apostolic Memoir." *Apocrypha* 26 (2015): 211–37.

Tamilia, Donato. "Acta Thomae apocrypha." *Rendiconti della Reale Accademia dei Lincei, Classe di scienze morali, storiche e filologiche* 5 (1903): 387–408.

Bibliography of Judith Perkins, 1974–2018

- "Valerius Flaccus: Synonyms and Style." PhD diss., University of Toronto, 1972.
- "An Aspect of Latin Comparison Construction." *TAPA* 104 (1974): 261–77.
- "An Aspect of the Style of Valerius Flaccus." *Phoenix* 28 (1974): 290–313.
- "Literary Criticism and Latin Poetry." Review of *Quality and Pleasure in Latin Poetry*, edited by Tony Woodman and David West. *Arion: A Journal of Humanities and the Classics* 3 (1976): 114–22.
- "Literary History: H. G. Gadamer, T. S. Eliot and Virgil." *Arethusa* 14 (1981): 241–49.
- "Rote Learning or Real Learning? Teaching a Course in Etymology." With Marleen Flory. *CJ* 79 (1984): 340–46.
- "The Apocryphal Acts of the Apostles and Early Christian Martyrdom." *Arethusa* 18 (1985): 211–30.
- "One Is Not Equal to Many (Oedipus Tyrannus 836)." *Reader* 24 (1990): 60–71.
- "Toby Olson's Life of Jesus." *Review of Contemporary Fiction* 11 (1991): 81–86.
- "The Apocryphal Acts of Peter: An Ideological Novel." *Arethusa* 25 (1992): 445–55.
- "The Self as Sufferer." *HTR* 85 (1992): 245–72.
- "The Acts of Peter as Intertext: A Response to Dennis MacDonald." Pages 627–33 in *Society of Biblical Literature 1993 Seminar Papers*. SBLSP 32. Atlanta: Scholars Press, 1993.
- "The Representation of Suffering in Early Greek Saints' Lives." Pages 255–74 in *Greek Fiction: The Greek Novel in Context*. Edited by John Morgan. London: Routledge, 1994.

+ "The Social World of the Acts of Peter." Pages 296–307 in *The Search for the Ancient Novel*. Edited by James Tatum. Baltimore: Johns Hopkins University Press, 1994.

+ "The Passion of Perpetua: A Narrative of Empowerment." *Latomus: Revue d'Etudes Latines* 53 (1994): 837–47.

+ *The Suffering Self: Pain and Narrative Representation in the Early Christian Era*. London: Routledge, 1995.

+ "Family Relations and Roman Religion." *Longman Latin Newsletter* (1995): 12–16.

+ "This World or Another? The Intertextuality of the Greek Romances, The Apocryphal Acts and Apuleius' *Metamorphoses*." *Semeia* 80 (1997): 247–60.

+ *Ancient Fiction and Early Christian Narrative*. Edited with Ronald F. Hock and J. Bradley Chance. Atlanta: Scholars Press, 1998.

+ "An Ancient Passing Novel: Heliodorus's *Aithiopika*." *Arethusa* 32 (1999): 197–214.

+ "*Family and Familia in Roman Law and Life* by Jane F. Gardner." *The Historian* 63 (2000): 191–92.

+ "Space, Place, Voice in the Acts of the Martyrs and the Greek Romance." Pages 117–37 in *Mimesis and Intertextuality in Early Christian Literature*. Edited by Dennis R. MacDonald. Harrisburg, PA: Trinity Press International, 2001.

+ "*Being Greek under Rome: Cultural Identity, the Second Sophistic, and the Development of Empire* by Simon Goldhill." *AJP* 123 (2002): 637–41.

+ "The Angel of History." *CW* 96 (2003): 421–26.

+ "Animal Voices." *R&T* 12 (2005): 385–96.

+ "Trimalchio: Naming Power." Pages 132–68 in *Metaphor and the Ancient Novel: Ancient Narrative, Supplementum 4*. Edited by Stephen Harrison, Michael Paschalis, and Stavros Frangoulidis. Groningen: Barkhuis, 2005.

+ "Fictional Narratives and Social Critique." Pages 46–69 in vol. 2 of *Late Ancient Christianity: A People's History of Christianity*. Edited by Virginia Burrus and Rebecca Lyman. Minneapolis: Fortress, 2005.

+ "Resurrection and Social Perspective in the Apocryphal *Acts of Peter* and *Acts of John*." Pages 217–38 in *Ancient Fiction: The Matrix of Jewish and Christian Narrative*. Edited by Jo-Ann A. Brant, Charles W. Hedrick, and Chris Shea. Atlanta: Society of Biblical Literature, 2005.

♦ "Fictive *Scheintod* and Christian Resurrection." *R&T* 13 (2006): 396–418.

♦ "The Rhetoric of the Maternal Body in the Passion of Perpetua." Pages 313–32 in *Mapping Gender in Ancient Religious Discourses*. Edited by Todd Penner and Caroline Vander Stichele. Atlanta: Society of Biblical Literature, 2007.

♦ *Roman Imperial Identities in the Early Christian Era*. RMCS. London: Routledge, 2009.

♦ "Early Christian and Judicial Bodies." Pages 237–55 in *Bodies and Boundaries in Graeco-Roman Antiquity*. Edited by Thorsten Fögen and Mireille M. Lee. Berlin: de Gruyter, 2009.

♦ "The Other Christs: Imitating Jesus in Ancient Christian Ideologies of Martyrdom by Candida Moss." *JECS* 19 (Summer 2011): 319–21.

♦ *Roman Literature, Gender, and Reception: Domina Illustris; Essays in Honor of Judith Peller Hallett*. Edited with Donald Lateiner and Barbara K. Gold. RMCS. London: Routledge, 2013.

♦ *The Ancient Novel and Early Christian and Jewish Narrative: Fictional Intersections*. Edited with Marília P. Futre Pinheiro and Richard I. Pervo. Ancient Narrative Supplementum 16. Groningen: Barkhuis, 2013.

♦ "Jesus Was No Sophist: Education in Christian Fiction." Pages 109–31 in *The Ancient Novel and Early Christian and Jewish Narrative: Fictional Intersections*. Edited by Marília P. Futre Pinheiro, Judith Perkins, and Richard I. Pervo. Ancient Narrative Supplementum 16. Groningen: Barkhuis, 2013.

♦ *Early Christian and Jewish Narrative: The Role of Religion in Shaping Narrative Forms*. Edited with Ilaria Ramelli. Tübingen: Mohr Siebeck, 2015.

♦ "Competing Voices in Imperial Fiction." Pages 275–302 in *Early Christian and Jewish Narrative: The Role of Religion in Shaping Narrative Forms*. Edited with Ilaria Ramelli. WUNT 348. Tübingen: Mohr Siebeck, 2015.

Index of Primary Sources

Index of Modern Authors

Subject Index